C-966

Career Examination Series

This Is Your

COURT OFFICER

PASSBOOK®

TEST PREPARATION STUDY GUIDE

QUESTIONS & ANSWERS

NLC

NATIONAL LEARNING CORPORATION

PASSBOOKS®
Preferred By
More Test Takers
•Up-To-Date
•Easy To Use
•All Tests •No Filler

PLASTIC BOUND-
LIES FLAT FOR
STUDY EASE!

C-966

ISBN 0-8373-0966-2

THE PASSBOOK® SERIES

PASSBOOKS®

FOR

CAREER OPPORTUNITIES

COURT OFFICER

National Learning Corporation

212 Michael Drive, Syosset, New York 11791

(516) 921-8888

Copyright © **1996** by

National Learning Corporation

212 Michael Drive, Syosset, New York 11791
(516) 921-8888

PRINTED IN THE UNITED STATES OF AMERICA

PASSBOOK®

NOTICE

This book is *SOLELY* intended for, is sold *ONLY* to, and its use is *RESTRICTED* to *individual,* bona fide applicants or candidates who qualify by virtue of having seriously filed applications for appropriate license, certificate, professional and/or promotional advancement, higher school matriculation, scholarship, or other legitimate requirements of educational and/or governmental authorities.

This book is *NOT* intended for use, class instruction, tutoring, training, duplication, copying, reprinting, excerption, or adaptation, etc., by:

(1) Other Publishers

(2) Proprietors and/or Instructors of "Coaching" and/or Preparatory Courses

(3) Personnel and/or Training Divisions of commercial, industrial, and governmental organizations

(4) Schools, colleges, or universities and/or their departments and staffs, including teachers and other personnel

(5) Testing Agencies or Bureaus

(6) Study groups which seek by the purchase of a single volume to copy and/or duplicate and/or adapt this material for use by the group as a whole without having purchased individual volumes for each of the members of the group

(7) Et al.

Such persons would be in violation of appropriate Federal and State statutes.

PROVISION OF LICENSING AGREEMENTS. — Recognized educational commercial, industrial, and governmental institutions and organizations, and others legitimately engaged in educational pursuits, including training, testing, and measurement activities, may address a request for a licensing agreement to the copyright owners, who will determine whether, and under what conditions, including fees and charges, the materials in this book may be used by them. In other words, a licensing facility *exists* for the legitimate use of the material in this book on other than an individual basis. However, it is asseverated and affirmed here that the materials in this book *CANNOT* be used without the receipt of the express permission of such a licensing agreement from the Publishers.

NATIONAL LEARNING CORPORATION
212 Michael Drive
Syosset, New York 11791

Inquiries re licensing agreements should be addressed to:
The President
National Learning Corporation
212 Michael Drive
Syosset, New York 11791

PASSBOOK SERIES®

THE *PASSBOOK SERIES®* has been created to prepare applicants and candidates for the ultimate academic battlefield—the examination room.

At some time in our lives, each and every one of us may be required to take an examination—for validation, matriculation, admission, qualification, registration, certification, or licensure.

Based on the assumption that every applicant or candidate has met the basic formal educational standards, has taken the required number of courses, and read the necessary texts, the *PASSBOOK SERIES®* furnishes the one special preparation which may assure passing with confidence, instead of failing with insecurity. Examination questions—together with answers—are furnished as the basic vehicle for study so that the mysteries of the examination and its compounding difficulties may be eliminated or diminished by a sure method.

This book is meant to help you pass your examination provided that you qualify and are serious in your objective.

The entire field is reviewed through the huge store of content information which is succinctly presented through a provocative and challenging approach—the question-and-answer method.

A climate of success is established by furnishing the correct answers at the end of each test.

You soon learn to recognize types of questions, forms of questions, and patterns of questioning. You may even begin to anticipate expected outcomes.

You perceive that many questions are repeated or adapted so that you gain acute insights, which may enable you to score many sure points.

You learn how to confront new questions, or types of questions, and to attack them confidently and work out the correct answers.

You note objectives and emphases, and recognize pitfalls and dangers, so that you may make positive educational adjustments.

Moreover, you are kept fully informed in relation to new concepts, methods, practices, and directions in the field.

You discover that you are actually taking the examination all the time: you are preparing for the examination by "taking" an examination, not by reading extraneous and/or supererogatory textbooks.

In short, this PASSBOOK®, used directedly, should be an important factor in helping you to pass your test.

CAREER OPPORTUNITIES IN THE NEW YORK STATE UNIFIED COURT SYSTEM

THE OFFICE OF COURT ADMINISTRATION ANNOUNCES AN OPEN-COMPETITIVE EXAMINATION

Title: Court Officer   Exam Number: 45-648

Starting Salary: Court Officer is graded at JG-16. The current hiring rate is $29,040. Appointees in New York City, Nassau, Suffolk, Rockland and Westchester Counties also receive $768 in annual location pay.

Application Fee: A **$20.00 NON-REFUNDABLE** application fee is being charged to file for this examination. Please refer to the General Information Statement at the end of this announcement for further information regarding fees.

Important Note Regarding Exam Administration: Due to the anticipated response to this announcement, this examination will be held on October 19 and November 2, 1996. Admission Notices will be mailed to all candidates around October 9, informing candidates as to where and when to report. Candidates who are available on only one of the two test dates must call (212) 417-5891 with their test date preference no later than Friday, September 6th. Further, with some exceptions, which are outlined in the <u>Alternate Test Date Policy</u> section at the end of this announcement, requests for alternate or make-up dates (i.e., a date other than October 19 or November 2) will NOT be considered.

Location of Positions: Currently, the Court Officer title exists in the Civil, Criminal, Family, and Surrogate's Courts in New York City, in District, Family and Surrogate's Courts in Nassau and Suffolk Counties, and in Family, Surrogate's, and City Courts in the 9th Judicial District (Dutchess, Orange, Putnam, Rockland, and Westchester Counties).

Distinguishing features of work: Court Officers are responsible for maintaining order and providing security in court facilities. They work under the direct supervision of security supervisors and court clerks. Court Officers are peace officers, required to wear uniforms, and may be authorized to carry firearms. They perform clerical duties while handling court documents and forms, may coordinate the activities of other court security personnel, and perform related duties.

Benefits: Court employees receive 20 days of paid vacation during the first year of service in addition to 12 paid holidays. They also accrue 13 days of paid sick leave annually. Participation in medical, dental, life insurance, and retirement plans is offered.

Written Examination is Scheduled To be Held **OCTOBER 19 & NOVEMBER 2, 1996**	**Applications Must Be Postmarked No Later Than** **JUNE 28, 1996**

Minimum Qualifications: At the time of appointment, a Court Officer candidate must be at least 18 years old and possess a High School diploma or its equivalent. Candidates must be legally eligible to carry firearms. A felon who has not received a Certificate of Relief from Disabilities is ineligible to carry firearms under federal law.

Citizenship: Candidates must be citizens of the United States.

Residency: Candidates must be residents of New York State at the time of appointment.

WRITTEN EXAMINATION

The written examination will be held in test centers throughout New York State. The examination will consist of multiple choice questions and will assess the following:

REMEMBERING FACTS AND INFORMATION

Candidates will be provided with a description of an event or incident. After a brief period of time to review and study it, the description will be removed from the candidates. Candidates will then be asked questions about the facts involved in the event or incident.

READING, UNDERSTANDING AND INTERPRETING WRITTEN MATERIAL

These questions are designed to measure how well candidates understand what they have read. The written examination will include two types of questions:

Format A - Candidates are provided with brief reading selections followed by questions regarding the selections. All of the information required to answer the questions is provided in the selections. Candidates are not required to have any special knowledge relating to the content area covered in the selections;

Format B - Candidates are provided with short written passages from which words have been removed. They are then required to select from four alternatives the word that best fits in each of the spaces.

APPLYING FACTS AND INFORMATION TO GIVEN SITUATIONS

These questions measure a candidate's ability to take information which they have read and apply it to a specific situation defined by a given set of facts. Each question contains a brief paragraph which describes a regulation, policy or procedure which must be applied to a particular situation. All of the information to answer the questions is contained in the paragraph and in the description of the situation.

CLERICAL CHECKING

These questions measure a candidate's ability to distinguish between sets of names, numbers, letters and/or codes which are almost exactly alike. Material usually is presented in three columns, and candidates are asked to compare the information in the three sets.

RECORD KEEPING

These questions measure a candidate's ability to read, combine, and manipulate written information organized from several sources. Candidates are presented with different types of tables which contain names, numbers, codes and other information, and must combine and reorganize the information to answer specific questions.

INFORMATION FOR OPEN-COMPETITIVE CANDIDATES-READ CAREFULLY

Application Fee: A **non-refundable** application fee of $20 is required to apply for this examination. Your application must be accompanied by a money order payable to **NYS Office of Court Administration** and mailed to: State of New York Unified Court System, Office of Court Administration, P.O. Box 1879, Albany, New York 12201. **DO NOT SEND CASH.** The following information should be written on the money order: Applicant's name, Social Security number, home address, title of the examination and the examination number.

An exception to the fee requirement is made for employees of the Unified Court System and individuals providing Foster Care, receiving Supplemental Social Security payments, public assistance (Home Relief or Aid to Dependent Children) from the New York City Department of Social Services or certified as eligible under The Job Training Partnership Act through a state or local social service agency. An exception also will be made for applicants who are unemployed and who are primarily responsible for the support of a household.

Individuals wishing to claim waiver of the fee on the basis of Supplemental Social Security, Home Relief or Aid to Dependent Children must certify on their application that they are receiving public assistance and indicate the type of assistance they are receiving, the agency providing the assistance and their case number. Persons claiming a waiver through the Foster Care or Job Training Partnership Act Certification must specify the program and name of their contact agency. Individuals claiming public assistance from the New York City Department of Social Services must submit a photocopy of a current Social Services Identification Card containing the applicant's picture, and a current medical identification card.

Failure to provide the required information will result in disapproval of the application. All claims are subject to later verification and, if not supported by appropriate documentation, are grounds for barring or rescinding an appointment.

Veterans: Veterans and disabled veterans who are eligible for extra credit will have 5 and 10 points, respectively, added to their scores, if they are otherwise successful in the examination. Eligible veterans must claim those credits when they file their application. Further information regarding instructions for filing and eligibility is contained in the application. If veterans credits are granted, eligibles will have an option to waive them anytime prior to appointment.

Verification of Qualifications: The Office of Court Administration may refuse to examine an applicant, or, after examination, to include a candidate on the eligible list, or may remove or restrict from the eligible list an applicant who is found to lack any of the established requirements for admission to the examination or for appointment from the resultant eligible list.

Examination Ratings: Examination final ratings are reported on a scale of 100 with the passing mark set at 70.

Special Testing Accommodations: Applicants requesting special accommodations relating to a disability MUST contact the Coordinator of Special Accommodations at (212) 417-2392 or TDD (telecommunications device for the deaf) at (212) 417-5794 **by the close of the filing period. Documentation regarding the nature and extent of the disability will be required.**

Alternate Test Date Policy: An alternate test date (i.e., a date **other** than October 19 or November 2) will be provided for candidates who can establish one of the following:

-Religious beliefs which preclude taking the examination on the announced date (Sabbath Observer).

-Hospital confinement or medical emergency or health problem which precludes participation on the test date, **if documented by attending physician.**

-A death in the immediate family or the household in which the candidate resides within the week immediately preceding the announced test date.

-Military duty.

-A conflict with a court ordered appearance.

-Emergency weather conditions, **verified by the local public safety agency,** which prevent a candidate from reaching the test center.

-Where appropriate, a situation in which **Special Testing Accommodations** must be offered (see above).

ASIDE FROM THE ABOVE EXCEPTIONS, REQUESTS FOR MAKE-UP DATES WILL NOT BE ACCEPTED.

Warning: Anyone found unlawfully possessing or disclosing questions and answers from civil service examinations, or giving or taking test information from another candidate during the examination, or anyone found taking a civil service examination for someone else or enlisting another person to take an examination for another will be subject to being disqualified from that examination and may be barred from taking any further examination with the Unified Court System and may be subject to other penalties as prescribed by law.

The Unified Court System is an Equal Opportunity Employer.

POST-WRITTEN EXAMINATION SCREENING PROCESS

Candidates who are successful on the written portion of the examination will be called, in order of their rank on the eligible list, to qualify on the medical, physical ability, and psychological examinations and undergo a background investigation. The Office of Court Administration reserves the right to modify any its post-written examination screening processes at any time during the life of the eligible list.

MEDICAL EXAMINATION

Each candidate is required to be free of any medical conditions which would impair his or her ability to effectively carry out the duties of the position.

Candidates are required to meet specific medical requirements both at the time of the medical examination and at the time of appointment.

PHYSICAL ABILITY EXAMINATION

Each candidate will be required to qualify on a series of physical ability tests designed to assess his or her ability to safely perform the physically demanding tasks required by the job.

BACKGROUND INVESTIGATION

Each candidate's background (e.g., employment history, educational qualifications, military servic record, arrest and conviction record, and other relevant factors) will be investigated to determine his or h fitness for serving in the Court Officer job.

PSYCHOLOGICAL EXAMINATION

Each candidate will be required to undergo a psychological assessment designed to test for emotional or psychological problems that might interfere with effectively carrying out the duties of the position.

FINGERPRINT FEE

A fingerprint fee, currently $50, will be charged to all candidates who are successful on the writte and medical portions of the examination and who are reached for further screening.

Probationary Period: All appointees will be required to successfully complete a one (1) year probationa period subsequent to their appointment. The first six (6) months will consist of training in defensive tacti academics, physical, field, and firearms training.

CANDIDATES SHOULD CONTACT THE OFFICE OF COURT ADMINISTRATION AT (212) 417-5891 THEY HAVE NOT RECEIVED THEIR ADMISSION NOTICE BY OCTOBER 16, 1996.

Issue Date: June 3, 1996

About the Court Officer Job

Security is the primary function of Court Officers. They provide a safe and secure environment for the fair and prompt resolution of all matters before the courts.

But the job is actually a blend of security work, public relations, law enforcement, prisoner management, and clerical duties. A strong sense of responsibility is necessary, as well as good judgment, patience and impartiality. Court Officers must not favor one party over another in a court proceeding. They protect and enhance the judicial process itself.

Court Officers may be assigned to the Civil, Criminal, Family and Surrogate's Courts in New York City; the Family, District and Surrogate's Courts in Nassau and Suffolk Counties; or the Family Court in Westchester County. They maintain order and decorum and provide security in courtrooms, waiting rooms, and other public areas on the court premises. In all aspects of their work, Court Officers must adhere to a strict, uniform set of rules and procedures like those of other law enforcement professionals. They work under the direct supervision of security supervisors and Senior Court Clerks.

The man or woman in uniform, the Court Officer, is usually the first person a visitor to court will approach for information. The officer's tone and demeanor can help set people at ease and establish confidence in the judicial process. In all their actions, Court Officers must reflect the impartiality, fairness and commitment to justice of the court system itself.

Some aspects of the work are similar to those of police officers or corrections officers. But the Court Officer job differs in significant ways. Court Officers are usually assigned to a security post in a defined, limited area, whereas police officers patrol large territories. And although Court Officers may escort prisoners, they do so in a different setting than corrections officers, who work in prisons or jails.

General Duties Court Officers are peace officers. They are required to wear uniforms on the job, are certified to carry firearms, and they can make arrests. They may be assigned to operate a metal detector, guard people accused or convicted of crimes of all kinds, deliver and retrieve court documents, administer first aid treatment, or respond to an emergency. They may have to control a crowd of people, or take steps to maintain order or to subdue an unruly person.

Typical assignments require a Court Officer to speak aloud in court when calling the calendar, guard a jury, or prepare written court records, among other tasks. Court Officers must learn proper court procedures and legal terminology. In some assignments they are required to annotate court calendars or make entries on other court documents. The work may entail standing or walking for long periods of time. Assignments can be in hectic environments or quiet security posts.

Typical Day The day usually begins at 9:00 am, when the Court Officer arrives at the courthouse, checks the assignment board, and then receives orders from the supervisory officer. Special equipment that might be needed for an assignment is picked up and the officer proceeds to the assigned post.

If it is a security post or an information desk, the officer must know the duties and conditions of the post, remain on post until relieved, and be alert and attentive. Answering questions, screening visitors, completing forms, and handling court documents can be a large part of the day's work.

Some Court Officers are assigned to a particular courtroom (called a court "part"). At the start of the day, the officer must conduct a security search of the courtroom and adjacent areas, post the calendar and admit the public at the appropriate time. Throughout the day, he or she assumes a post in the courtroom, and follows the orders of the presiding judge, clerk of the part, and supervising officer. Working as part of a courtroom team that includes the clerk, the court interpreter or court reporter, and other court employees, the officer helps maintain order and decorum in the courtroom.

The assignment may entail completing forms, or retrieving papers, files, and books as requested. Court officers assist in the swearing-in of witnesses and jurors, supervise juries, and handle evidence. Officers also announce recesses, and remain in the part during recess to safeguard equipment, evidence and documents. At all times the officer protects the judge, jurors, court employees, witnesses and spectators. This includes escorting the judge to and from chambers.

Court proceedings are quiet, orderly, and dignified. One of the primary functions of the Court Officer is to help maintain this atmosphere and to anticipate and prevent any disruption. If an incident should occur, be it a minor or a serious one, the Court Officer is trained to restore order by applying intelligent and controlled security techniques and proper judgment.

Unusual situations or circumstances must be reported to the supervising officer. In the course of a day, a Court Officer may also have to respond to emergency calls for assistance, provide first aid, and prepare incident reports.

At the end of the morning session and again at the end of the day, the Court Officer announces when the next court session will begin. When the morning session or the business of the day is completed, the officer clears and locks the courtroom. He or she informs the Captain's office of early adjournments, security problems, controversial cases and other information. The lunch recess is usually from 1:00 pm to 2:00 pm, and the workday usually ends at 5:00 pm.

The questions on the Court Officer examination will measure your abilities in the following four areas: (1) Read, Understand and Interpret Written Materials; (2) Remember Facts and Information; (3) Apply Facts and Information to Given Situations; and (4) Recognize and Size Up Written Information.

A description of each of these areas and sample questions follow. Not all questions may be in this exact form, but the samples should give you a good idea of what to expect. Go through each section carefully and make certain you understand the directions and know how to answer every question.

You can use these questions to assess your strengths and weaknesses. They may help you determine areas in which you need additional work. You may also be able to find similar questions and other general test-taking study materials at your public library. Ask your librarian to suggest what might be helpful.

If you feel more comfortable with the test material, you will be less anxious. And if you are less anxious, you will tend to do better on the exam.

Written Examination Test #1

Read, Understand, and Interpret Written Material

This section of the written exam measures your ability to read and understand written material. There are two ways or formats which may be used to measure your reading ability. The test may contain either or both of the formats. You need to familiarize yourself with both formats for Test #1 - Read, Understand, and Interpret Written Material. A complete description of each format and sample items are provided on the following pages.

Format A

Questions on this test measure how well you understand what you have read. Each question contains a brief reading selection. Following the selection is a question or questions pertaining to the information in the selection. All of the information required to answer the question(s) is provided, so even if the reading selection is on a topic you are not familiar with, you will be able to answer the questions by reading the selection carefully. Remember, answer the questions based only on the information you read in the selection.

Directions: After reading the selection below, choose the alternative which best answers the question following the selection.

"In order to handle a horse successfully, you must establish that you are the boss. This doesn't mean that you should beat a horse into submission. Some people are too rough and others are too easy on a horse. Both types are horse spoilers. To be a horse's true boss and not his tyrannical master, you have to use his language to assert yourself. Horses, like most creatures (including humans) have a pecking order. What you have to do is establish that you are one notch above every horse that you handle."

Read, Understand, and Interpret Written Material: Format A (cont'd)

1. Which one of the following best describes how to establish yourself as a horse's boss?

   A. Always use physical force to make the horse listen to you

   B. Reward the horse frequently and never punish the horse

   C. Talk to the horse

   D. Assert yourself by communicating in a manner that the horse can understand

Solution: Answer D. You don't need to know anything about horses to answer this question - just read the selection carefully. Answer A is not correct, because the selection says that you should not "beat a horse into submission." Answer B is not correct, because the selection says you should not be "too easy on a horse." Answer C is not correct, the selection says to "use his language to assert yourself," not to "talk to the horse." D is the answer because it correctly states that to be a horse's boss "you have to use his language to assert yourself."

Format B

Questions on this test measure how well you understand what you have read. Each part of this test contains a short, written passage from which some words have been omitted. You need to select one (1) word from the four (4) alternatives that best fits each blank space.

Directions: The passage below contains 5 numbered blanks. Read the passage once quickly to get the overall idea of the passage. Read it a second time, this time thinking of words that might fit in the blanks. Below the passage are listed sets of words numbered to match the blanks. Pick the word from each set which seems to make the most sense both in the sentence and the total paragraph.

"A security deposit is a sum of money which ___(1)___ tenant is asked to deposit with the owner of the apartment ___(2)___ the time that the apartment is first rented. This ___(3)___ is intended to cover the cost of any damages ___(4)___ alterations made to the apartment during the period in ___(5)___ a tenant occupies it."

1. A. that	2. A. in	3. A. rent	4. A. or	5. A. which
B. one	B. at	B. owner	B. nor	B. when
C. your	C. for	C. money	C. either	C. what
D. a	D. to	D. tenant	D. neither	D. where

Solution to 1: Answer D. Answer A is not correct because you would not normally say "**that tenant**" unless the paragraph indicated that you were talking about a specific person. Answer B is not correct because "**one tenant**" would also only be used if you were talking about a specific person. Answer "C" is not correct because you would not say "**your tenant**" when the

Written Examination Test #1 (cont'd)

Read, Understand, and Interpret Written Material : Format B (cont'd)

sentence goes on to say, more generally, "the owner of the apartment." Answer D is correct because "a tenant" fits the general paragraph as well as the specific sentence in which the blank appears.

Other Solutions: 2 - B, 3 - C, 4 - A, 5 - A

Written Examination Test #2

Remember Facts and Information

This section of the exam measures your ability to remember the details in written information after a brief period of time. A written description of an incident or event will be given to candidates who will have a short time to study it. The description will then be removed and candidates will later be asked questions regarding the facts and details presented in the written description.

Directions: Read the brief story below. Study it for five (5) minutes. Then, turn the story over and answer the five questions on the following page.

Memory Story

A large newspaper stand is located just north of the elevators on the ground floor of the Oneida Court House Annex. In addition to newspapers and magazines, the stand sells cigarettes, film, candy bars, soda, and assorted snacks. In the mornings between 8:00 and 10:00, coffee and donuts are also available. Employees of the Court and members of the public who have court business often purchase items there. People also stop to ask directions because the information desk is located at the main entrance to the Court House, which is on the other side of the building.

The stand is open daily from 8:00 AM to 2:00 PM. It is operated by Joe Richards, who is 50 years old, has gray hair, blue eyes, and a slight build. His sister, Louise Miller, is a semi-retired widow, helps out part-time.

On the morning of Tuesday, February 5, 1991 at about 8:30 A.M., Court Officer Marion Mueller stopped at the stand to purchase a cup of coffee. While he was getting his coffee, a young woman came up and asked how to get to the Chief Clerk's office. He told her to take the elevator to the third floor and then turn left at the double doors. While he was giving the directions, he noticed that Ms. Miller was attempting to open a box of Hersey Almond candy bars with a pair of long scissors.

At that moment, the scissors slipped and cut a gash about 3 inches long in her left forearm. First aide was administered by the Court Officer, and she was rushed to St. Mark's Hospital which is nearby. She received six stitches and a tetanus shot. Ms. Miller was not able to return to work at the magazine stand for two weeks.

Questions About the Memory Story

1. Who administered the first aid?

   A.   Joe Richards

   B.   Louise Miller

   C.   Jim Matthews

   D.   Marion Muller

2. On what day of the week did the incident occur?

   A.   Monday

   B.   Tuesday

   C.   Wednesday

   D.   Friday

3. The name of the hospital was:

   A.   St. Peter's

   B.   St. Matthew's

   C.   St. Mark's

   D.   St. Anne's

4. The Chief Clerk's office was:

   A.   on the 2nd floor

   B.   on the 3rd floor

   C.   on the 4th floor

   D.   on the 5th floor

5. What hours is the newspaper stand open:

   A.   8:00 AM to 2:00 PM

   B.   8:00 AM to 5:00 PM

   C.   8:00 AM to 10:00 AM

   D.   8:00 AM to 4:00 PM

Solution: Answers can be found in the Memory Story.

1 - D; 2 - B; 3 - C; 4 - B; 5 - A

Apply Facts and Information to Given Situations

This section of the written exam measures your ability to take information which you have read and apply it to a specific situation defined by a given set of facts. Each question contains a brief paragraph which describes a regulation, procedure or law. The selection is followed by a description of a specific situation. Then, a question is asked which requires you to apply the law, regulation, or procedure described in the paragraph to the specific situation. Remember, all of the information you need to answer the question is contained in the paragraph and in the description of the situation. You need to read and understand both before you attempt to answer the question.

Directions: Use the information proceeding each question to answer the question. Only that information should be used in answering the questions. Do not use any prior knowledge you may have on the subject. Choose the alternative that best answers the question.

Procedure: "Absentee sick calls must be made between 9:00 and 9:30 a.m. on the first day of illness. If illness extends into the third day, a doctor's certificate must be presented stating the nature of the illness and the approximate date of return to duty. The Officer or a member of his/her family should keep the Associate regularly informed of his/her condition."

Situation: Officer Susan Jenner becomes sick on the evening of May 2 while at home. At 9:15 on the morning of May 3, Jenner calls in to say she is sick and will not be in. On May 5, Jenner submits a doctor's report describing her illness and stating that she will return to work on May 20th. On May 18, Mr. Jenner calls to let the Associate know of his wife's condition.

1. Based on the above procedure and the incident, which one of the following statements regarding Jenner's actions is correct?

    A. Jenner should have submitted the doctor's report on May 4, not May 5.

    B. Jenner should not have had her doctor include the nature of her illness on her report.

    C. Jenner should have had her husband call the Associate to let him know the situation before May 18.

    D. Jenner should have called in sick as soon as she knew other officers would be on duty, which is 8:00 in the morning.

Solution: Answer C. According to the procedure, "the Officer or a member of his/her family should keep the Associate regularly informed of his/her condition." Since the last contact with the Court was on May 5th, and Jenner was expected back on May 20th, Jenner should have contacted her office before May 18th. Answer A is wrong because the doctor's report was due by the third day of absence or May 5th. Answer B is wrong because the doctor's certificate needs to include the nature of her illness. Answer D is wrong because "absentee sick calls must be made between 9:00 and 9:30 a.m. on the first day of illness."

Written Examination Test #4

Recognize and Size Up Written Information

This section of the written exam measures your ability to work with written materials, specifically, performing checking and recordkeeping tasks. The two parts to this section of the test will be given to you separately from the rest of the test. You will have a specified period of time to answer the questions on this section of the written exam before the exam booklet is collected. The two parts of the "Recognize and Size Up Written Information" test together count 25% of your total score.

Description of the two parts of the "Recognize and Size Up Written Information" test follow.

Format A - Clerical Checking

Format A measures your ability to determine whether different sets of words, numbers, names and codes are similar. Clerical Checking items may be in three possible forms. An example of each form is provided below. No matter what the form of the item, the candidate is required to do the same thing: scan the sets of information, identify where the sets differ, and use the directions to determine the correct answer.

Directions: Questions 1 & 2

The following two questions, numbered 1 and 2, consist of three sets of information.

Compare the information in the three sets presented in each question. On your answer sheet mark:

Choice A:	if all **three** sets are exactly alike
Choice B:	if only the **first** and **third** sets are exactly alike
Choice C:	if only the **first** and **second** sets are exactly alike
Choice D:	if **none** of the sets are exactly alike.

1. (In this format the information is on the same line in each set)

ISBNO652319127	ISBNO652319127	ISBNO652319127
Hayt, Emanuel	Hayt, Emanuel	Hayt, Emanuel
Law of hospital and patient	Law of hospital & patient	Law of hospital and patient
Physician's Record Co.	Physician's Record Co.	Physician's Record Co.
KF3821.H391972	KF3821.H391972	KF3821.H391972

Solution: Answer B. The "and" in the third line of the second set was typed "&" but the first and third sets contain exactly the same information; therefore the correct answer is B.

2. (In this format the information is not on the same line in each set)

Deming, Richard	KF387.D39	Civil law at work
Civil law at work	Deming, Richard	New York: Hawthorn Books
New York: Hawthorn Books	Civil law at work	KF387.D39
KF387.D39	New York: Hawthorn Books	Deming, Richard

Solution: Answer A. The information in each of these sets is the same, even though the order of the information is on different lines in each set.

Recognize and Size Up Written Information: Format A - Clerical Checking (cont'd)

Directions: Question 3

The following question, number 3, consists of four sets of information and a model. Compare the information in the four sets with the model and on your answer sheet mark:

Choice A:	if **none** of the sets match the model
Choice B:	if any **two** sets match the model
Choice C:	if any **three** sets match the model
Choice D:	if **all** of the sets match the model

3. (In this form you must compare each set of information to the model)

Model: Total Justice
        Friedman, Lawrence Meir
        Russell Sage Foundation
        KF384.F751985

Total Justice
Friedman, Laurence Meir
Russell Sage Foundation
KF384.F751985

Total Justice
Friedman, Lawrence Meir
Russell Sage Foundation
KF384.F751985

Total Justice
Friedman, Lawrence Meir
Russell Sage Foundation
KF384.F751985

Total Justice
Friedman, Lawrence Meir
Russell Sage Foundation
KF384.F751895

Solution: Answer B. "Laurence" in the second line of the first set and "KF384.F75<u>1895</u>" in the fourth line of the fourth set do not match the model. As two sets match, "B" is the correct answer.

Written Examination Test #4 (cont'd)

Recognize and Size Up Written Information

Format B - Recordkeeping

Format B - measures your ability to read, combine, and manipulate information organized onto different types of tables.

The following example is a simplified version of the type of recordkeeping exercise that will be included in the written examination. The Recordkeeping test on the written examination that you will take will have different types of tables and information. The purpose of this example is to show you how a Recordkeeping test might look so that you can be better prepared to answer the questions in this section of the written examination.

Directions: Answer the four (4) questions based on the information contained in the following tables. Remember, all of the information needed to answer the questions correctly can be found in the tables. (Hint: Complete the "Daily Breakdown of Cases" and "Summary of Cases" tables before you attempt to answer any of the questions.)

DAILY LOG OF CASES			
Thursday			
Judge	Date Filed	Status	Money Award
Abrams	11/6/85	Adjourned	X
Kotter	11/30/85	Adjourned	X
Roth	2/10/86	Dismissed	X
Ethan	6/28/86	Dismissed	X
Roth	8/23/86	Dismissed	X

DAILY LOG OF CASES			
Friday			
Judge	Date Filed	Status	Money Award
D'Amico	7/14/85	Settled	$ 1,595
Ethan	7/9/86	Settled	$11,400
Roth	7/15/86	Dismissed	X
Abrams	6/30/86	Dismissed	X
Ethan	10/1/85	Defaulted	X
D'Amico	6/9/85	Adjourned	X
Abrams	7/17/86	Settled	$760.
Roth	9/23/86	Settled	$6,500

Format B - Recordkeeping (cont'd)

DAILY BREAKDOWN OF CASES Thursday and Friday	Thurs.	Fri.	Total Cases
CASE STATUS			
Dismissed	3	2	5
Adjourned			
Defaulted			
Settled-No Money Award			
Settled-Money Award			
Total Cases			
CASES FILED BY YEAR			
1984	0	0	0
1985			
1986			
Total Cases			

SUMMARY OF CASES

Thursday and Friday

Judge	Status			Settled No Money Award	Settled Money Award	Total Cases
	Dismissed	Adjourned	Defaulted			
Abrams						
D'Amico						
Ethan						
Kotter						
Roth						

Format B - Recordkeeping (cont'd)

1. What was the total number of adjourned cases on Thursday?
   A.   2
   B.   3
   C.   5
   D.   8

Solution: Answer A. You could have answered this question by counting up all the cases in Thursday's "Daily Log of Cases" that said "Adjourned" in the "Status" column. Alternatively, you could have looked in your completed "Daily Breakdown of Cases" table under "Thursday" and across from "Adjourned."

2. What were the number of cases on Friday that were filed during 1985?
   A.   0
   B.   3
   C.   5
   D.   8

Solution: Answer B. Same strategy as above - you could count the 1985 cases in the Friday's "Daily Log of Cases". Alternatively, you could have looked in your completed "Daily Breakdown of Cases" table under "Fri." and across from "1985."

3. How many settled cases on Thursday and Friday had money awards of less than $2000?
   A.   0
   B.   1
   C.   2
   D.   3

Solution: Answer C. To answer this question you need to refer directly to Friday's "Daily Log of Cases." Since money awards are only made for settled cases, you need to look only in the "Money Award" column and count the number of times an award of less than $2000 appears.

4. How many cases before Judge Roth on Thursday and Friday were dismissed?
   A.   0
   B.   1
   C.   2
   D.   3

Solution: Answer D. The easiest way to answer this question is to refer to your completed "Summary of Cases" table which includes cases from Thursday and Friday. Look across the name from "Roth" and down the column marked "Dismissed."

HOW TO TAKE A TEST

I. YOU MUST PASS AN EXAMINATION

A. *WHAT EVERY CANDIDATE SHOULD KNOW*

Examination applicants often ask us for help in preparing for the written test. What can I study in advance? What kinds of questions will be asked? How will the test be given? How will the papers be graded?

As an applicant for a civil service examination, you may be wondering about some of these things. Our purpose here is to suggest effective methods of advance study and to describe civil service examinations.

Your chances for success on this examination can be increased if you know how to prepare. Those "pre-examination jitters" can be reduced if you know what to expect. You can even experience an adventure in good citizenship if you know why civil service examinations are given.

B. *WHY ARE CIVIL SERVICE EXAMINATIONS GIVEN?*

Civil service examinations are important to you in two ways. As a citizen, you want public jobs filled by employees who know how to do their work. As a job-seeker, you want a fair chance to compete for that job on an equal footing with other candidates. The best known means of accomplishing this two-fold goal is the competitive examination.

Examinations are widely publicized throughout the nation. They may be administered for jobs in federal, state, city, municipal, town, or village governments or agencies.

Any citizen may apply, with some limitations, such as the age or residence of applicants. Your experience and education may be reviewed to see whether you meet the requirements for the particular examination. When these requirements exist, they are reasonable and are applied consistently to all applicants. Thus, a competitive examination may cause you some uneasiness now, but it is your privilege and safeguard.

C. *HOW ARE CIVIL SERVICE EXAMINATIONS DEVELOPED?*

Examinations are carefully written by trained technicians who are specialists in the field known as "psychological measurement," in consultation with recognized authorities in the field of work that the test will cover. These experts recommend the subject matter areas or skills to be tested; only those knowledges or skills important to your success on the job are included. The most reliable books and source materials available are used as references. Together, the experts and technicians judge the difficulty level of the questions.

Test technicians know how to phrase questions so that the problem is clearly stated. Their ethics do not permit "trick" or "catch" questions. Questions may have been tried out on sample groups, or subjected to statistical analysis, to determine their usefulness.

Written tests are often used in combination with performance tests, ratings of training and experience, and oral interviews. All of these measures combine to form the best known means of finding the right man for the right job.

II. HOW TO PASS THE WRITTEN TEST

A. *NATURE OF THE EXAMINATION*

To prepare intelligently for civil service examinations, you should know how they differ from school examinations you have taken. In school you were assigned certain definite pages to read or subjects to cover. The examination questions were quite detailed and usually emphasized memory. Civil service examinations, on the other hand, try to discover your present ability to perform the duties of a position, plus your potentiality to learn these duties. In other words, a civil service examination attempts to predict how successful you will be. Questions cover such a broad area that they cannot be as minute and detailed as school examination questions.

In the public service similar kinds of work, or positions, are grouped together in one "class." This process is known as "position-classification." All the positions in a class are paid according to the salary range for that class. One class title covers all these positions, and they are all tested by the same examination.

B. *FOUR BASIC STEPS*

1. Study the Announcement.--How, then, can you know what subjects to study? Our best answer is: "Learn as much as possible about the class of positions for which you have applied." The examination will test the knowledge, skills, and abilities needed to do the work.

Your most valuable source of information about the position you want is the official announcement of the examination. This announcement lists the training and experience qualifications. Check these standards and apply only if you come reasonably close to meeting them.

The brief description of the position in the examination announcement offers some clues to the subjects which will be tested. Think about the job itself. Review the duties in your mind. Can you perform them, or are there some in which you are rusty? Fill in the blank spots in your preparation.

Many jurisdictions preview the written test in the examination announcement by including a section called "Knowledge and Abilities Required," "Scope of Examination," or some similar heading. Here you will find out specifically what fields will be tested.

2. Review Your Own Background.-- Once you learn in general what the position is all about, and what you need to know to do the work, ask yourself which subjects you already know fairly well and which need improvement. You may wonder whether to concentrate on improving your strong areas or on building some background in your fields of weakness. When the announcement has specified "some knowledge" or "considerable knowledge," or has used adjectives such as "beginning principles of ...." or "advanced .....methods," you can get a clue as to the number and difficulty of questions to be asked in any given field. More questions, and hence broader coverage, would be included for those subjects which are more important in the work. Now weigh your strengths and weaknesses against the job requirements and prepare accordingly.

3. Determine the Level of the Position.-- Another way to tell how intensively you should prepare is to understand the level of the job for which you are applying. Is it the entering level? In other words, is this the position in which beginners in a field of work are hired? Or is it an intermediate or advanced level? Sometimes this is indicated by such words as "Junior" or "Senior" in the class title.Other jurisdictions use Roman numerals to designate the level: Clerk I,

Clerk II, for example. The word "Supervisor" sometimes appears in the title. If the level is not indicated by the title, check the description of duties. Will you be working under very close supervision, or will you have responsibility for independent decisions in this work?

4. Choose Appropriate Study Materials.-- Now that you know the subjects to be examined and the relative amount of each subject to be covered, you can choose suitable study materials. For beginning level jobs, or even advanced ones, if you have a pronounced weakness in some aspect of your training, read a modern, standard textbook in that field. Be sure it is up-to-date and has general coverage. Such books are normally available at your library, and the librarian will be glad to help you locate one. For entry level positions, questions of appropriate difficulty are chosen -- neither highly advanced questions, nor those too simple. Such questions require careful thought but not advanced training.

If the position for which you are applying is technical or advanced, you will read more advanced, specialized material. If you are already familiar with the basic principles of your field, elementary textbooks would waste your time. Concentrate on advanced textbooks and technical periodicals. Think through the concepts and review difficult problems in your field.

These are all general sources. You can get more ideas on your own initiative, following these leads. For example, training manuals and publications of the government agency which employs workers in your field can be useful, particularly for technical and professional positions. A letter or visit to the government department involved may result in more specific study suggestions, and certainly will provide you with a more definite idea of the exact nature of the position you are seeking.

II. KINDS OF TESTS

Tests are used for purposes other than measuring knowledge and ability to perform specified duties. For some positions, it is equally important to test ability to make adjustments to new situations or to profit from training. In others, basic mental abilities not dependent upon information are essential. Questions which test these things may not appear as pertinent to the duties of the position as those which test for knowledge and information. Yet they are often highly important parts of a fair examination. For very general questions, it is almost impossible to help you direct your study efforts. What we can do is to point out some of the more common of these general abilities needed in public service positions and describe some typical questions.

1. General Information

Broad, general information has been found useful for predicting job success in some kinds of work. This is tested in a variety of ways, from vocabulary lists to questions about current events. Basic background in some field of work, such as sociology or economics, may be sampled in a group of questions. Often these are principles which have become familiar to most persons through "exposure" rather than through formal training. It is difficult to advise you how to study for these questions; being alert to the world around you is our best suggestion.

2. Verbal Ability

An example of an ability needed in many positions is verbal or language ability. Verbal ability is, in brief, the ability to use and understand words. Vocabulary and grammar tests are typical measures of this ability. "Reading comprehension" or "paragraph interpretation" questions are common in many kinds of civil service tests. You are given a paragraph of written material and asked to find its central meaning.

3. Numerical Ability

Number skills can be tested by the familiar arithmetic problem, by checking paired lists of numbers to see which are alike and which are different, or by interpreting charts and graphs. In the latter test, a graph may be printed in the test booklet which you are asked to use as the basis for answering questions.

4. Observation

A popular test for law-enforcement positions is the observation test. A picture is shown to you for several minutes, then taken away. Questions about the picture test your ability to observe both details and larger elements.

5. Following Directions

In many positions in the public service, the employee must be able to carry out written instructions dependably and accurately. You may be given a chart with several columns, each column listing a variety of information. The questions require you to carry out directions involving the information given in the chart.

6. Skills and Aptitudes

Performance tests effectively measure some manual skills and aptitudes. When the skill is one in which you are trained, such as typing or shorthand, you can practice. These tests are often very much like those given in business school or high school courses. For many of the other skills and aptitudes, however, no short-time preparation can be made. Skills and abilities natural to you or that you have developed throughout your lifetime are being tested.

Many of the general questions just described provide all the data needed to answer the questions and ask you to use your reasoning ability to find the answers. Your best preparation for these tests, as well as for tests of facts and ideas, is to be at your physical and mental best. You, no doubt, have your own methods of getting into an exam-taking mood and keeping "in shape." The next section lists some ideas on this subject.

IV. KINDS OF QUESTIONS

Only rarely is the "essay" question, which you answer in narrative form, used in civil service tests. Civil service tests are usually of the short-answer type. Full instructions for answering these questions will be given to you at the examination. But in case this is your first experience with short-answer questions and separate answer sheets, here is what you need to know.

1. Multiple-Choice Questions

Most popular of the short-answer questions is the "multiple-choice" or "best-answer" question. It can be used, for example, to test for factual knowledge, ability to solve problems, or judgment in meeting situations found at work.

A multiple-choice question is normally one of three types:

(1) It can begin with an incomplete statement followed by several possible endings. You are to find the one ending which *best* completes the statement, although some of the others may not be entirely wrong.

(2) It can also be a complete statement in the form of a question which is answered by choosing one of the statements listed.

(3) It can be in the form of a problem -- again you select the best answer.

Here is an example of a multiple-choice question with a discussion which should give you some clues as to the method for choosing the right answer.

SAMPLE QUESTION:

When an employee has a complaint about his assignment, the action which will *best* help him overcome his difficulty is

  (A) to discuss his difficulty with his co-workers
  (B) to take the problem to the head of the organization
  (C) to take the problem to the person who gave him the assignment
  (D) to say nothing to anyone about his complaint

In answering this question you should study each of the choices to find which is best. Consider choice (A). Certainly an employee may discuss his complaint with fellow employees, but no change or improvement can result, and the complaint remains unsolved. Choice (B) is a poor choice since the head of the organization probably does not know what assignment you have been given, and taking your problem to him is known as "going over the head" of the supervisor. The supervisor, or person who made the assignment, is the person who can clarify it or correct any injustice. Choice (C) is, therefore, correct. To say nothing, as in choice (D), is unwise. Supervisors have an interest in knowing the problems employees are facing, and the employee is seeking a solution to his problem.

2. True-False Questions

The "true-false" or "right-wrong" form of question is sometimes used. Here a complete statement is given. Your problem is to decide whether the statement is right or wrong.

SAMPLE QUESTION:

A person-to-person long distance telephone call costs less than a station-to-station call to the same city.

This question is wrong, or "false," since person-to-person calls are more expensive.

This is not a complete list of all possible question forms, although most of the others are variations of these common types. You will always get complete directions for answering questions. Be sure you understand *how* to mark your answers -- ask questions until you do.

V. RECORDING YOUR ANSWERS

For an examination with very few applicants, you may be told to record your answers in the test booklet itself. Separate answer sheets are much more common. If this separate answer sheet is to be scored by machine -- and this is often the case -- it is highly important that you mark your answers correctly in order to get credit.

An electric test-scoring machine is often used in civil service offices because of the speed with which papers can be scored. Machine-scored answer sheets must be marked with a special pencil, which will be given to you. This pencil has a high graphite content which responds to the electrical scoring machine. As a matter of fact, stray dots may register as answers, so do not let your pencil rest on the answer sheet while you are pondering the correct answer. Also, if your pencil lead breaks or is otherwise defective, ask for another.

Since the answer sheet will be dropped in a slot in the scoring machine, be careful not to bend the corners or get the paper crumpled.

The answer sheet normally has five vertical columns of numbers, with 30 numbers to a column. These numbers correspond to the question numbers in your test booklet. After each number, going across the page, are four or five pairs of dotted lines. These short dotted lines have small letters or numbers above them. The first two pairs may also have a "T" and "F" above the letters. This indicates that the first two pairs only are to be used if the questions are of the true-false type. If the questions are multiple-choice, disregard this "T" and "F" completely, and pay attention only to the small number or letters.

Answer your questions in the manner of the sample that follows. Proceed in the sequential steps outlined below.

Assume that you are answering question 32, which is:

    32. The largest city in the United States is:

        A. Washington, D.C.   B. New York City   C. Chicago
        D. Detroit   E. San Francisco

1. Choose the answer you think is best.

    New York City is the largest, so choice B is correct.

2. Find the row of dotted lines numbered the same as the question you are answering.

    This is question number 32, so find row number 32.

3. Find the pair of dotted lines corresponding to the answer you have chosen.

    You have chosen answer B, so find the pair of dotted lines marked "B".

4. Make a solid black mark between the dotted lines.

    Go up and down two or three times with your pencil so plenty of graphite rubs off, but do not let the mark get outside or above the dots.

VI. BEFORE THE TEST

Common sense will help you find procedures to follow to get ready for an examination. Too many of us, however, overlook these sensible measures. Indeed, nervousness and fatigue have been found to be the most serious reasons why applicants fail to do their best on civil service tests. Here is a list of reminders.

1. Begin Your Preparation Early

Don't wait until the last minute to go scurrying around for books and materials or to find out what the position is all about.

2. Prepare Continuously

An hour a night for a week is better than an all-night cram session. This has been definitely established. What is more, a night a week for a month will return better dividends than crowding your study into a shorter period of time.

3. Locate the Place of the Examination

You have been sent a notice telling you when and where to report for the examination. If the location is in a different town or otherwise unfamiliar to you, it would be well to inquire the best route and learn something about the building.

4. Relax the Night Before the Test

Allow your mind to rest. Do not study at all that night. Plan some mild recreation or diversion; then go to bed early and get a good night's sleep.

5. Get Up Early Enough to Make a Leisurely Trip to the Place for the Test

Then unforeseen events, traffic snarls, unfamiliar buildings, will not upset you.

6. Dress Comfortably

A written test is not a fashion show. You will be known by number and not by name, so wear something comfortable.

7. Leave Excess Paraphernalia at Home

Shopping bags and odd bundles will get in your way. You need bring only the items mentioned in the official notice sent to you; usually everything you need is provided. Do not bring reference books to the examination. They will only confuse those last minutes and be taken away from you when in the test room.

8. Arrive Somewhat Ahead of Time

If because of transportation schedules you must get there very early, bring a newspaper or magazine to take your mind off yourself while waiting.

9. Locate the Examination Room

When you have found the proper room, you will be directed to the seat or part of the room where you will sit. Sometimes you are given a sheet of instructions to read while you are waiting. Do not fill out any forms until you are told to do so; just read them and be ready.

10. Relax and Prepare to Listen to the Instructions

11. If you have **any physical problem** that may keep you from doing your best, be sure to tell the test administrator. If you are sick, or in poor health, **you really cannot** do your best on the test. You can come back and take the test some other time.

II. AT THE TEST

The day of the test is here and you have the test booklet in your hand. The temptation to get going is very strong. Caution! There is more to success than knowing the right answers. You must know how to identify your **papers and under**stand variations in the type of short-answer **question used in this** particular examination. Follow these suggestions for maximum results from your efforts:

1. Cooperate with the Monitor

The test administrator has a duty to create a situation in which you can be as much at ease as possible. He will give instructions, tell you when to begin, check to see that you are marking your answer sheet correctly. He is not there to guard you, although he will see that your competitors do not take unfair advantage. He wants to help you do your best.

2. Listen to All Instructions

Don't jump the gun! Wait until you understand all directions. In most civil service tests you get more time than you need to answer the questions. So don't get in a hurry. Read each word of instructions until you clearly understand the meaning. Study the examples. Listen to all announcements. Follow directions. Ask questions if you do not understand what to do.

3. Identify Your Papers

Civil service examinations are usually identified by number only. You will be assigned a number; you must not put your name on your test papers. Be sure to copy your number correctly. Since more than one examination may be given, copy your exact examination title.

4. Plan Your Time

Unless you are told that a test is a "speed" or "rate-of-work" test, speed itself is not usually important. Time enough to answer all the questions will be provided. But this does not mean that you have all day. An overall time limit has been set. Divide the total time (in minutes) by the number of questions to get the approximate time you have for each question.

5. Do Not Linger Over Difficult Questions

If you come across a difficult question, mark it with a paper clip (useful to have along) and come back to it when you have been through the booklet. One caution if you do this -- be sure to skip a number on your answer sheet too. Check often to be sure that you have not lost your place and that you are marking in the row numbered the same as the question you are answering.

6. Read the Questions

Be sure you know what the question asks! Many capable people are unsuccessful because they failed to *read* the questions correctly.

7. Answer All Questions

Unless you have been instructed that a penalty will be deducted for incorrect answers, it is better to guess than to omit a question.

8. Speed Tests

It is often better *not* to guess on speed tests. It has been found that on timed tests people are tempted to spend the last few seconds before time is called in marking answers at random -- without even reading them -- in the hope of picking up a few extra points. To discourage this practice, the instructions may warn you that your score will be "corrected" for guessing. That is, a penalty will be applied. The incorrect answers will be deducted from the correct ones, or some other penalty formula will be used.

9. Review Your Answers

If you finish before time is called, go back to the questions you guessed or omitted to give further thought to them. Review other answers if you have time.

10. Return Your Test Materials

If you are ready to leave before others have finished or time is called, take *all* your materials to the monitor and leave quietly. Never take any test material with you. The monitor can discover whose papers are not complete, and taking a test booklet may be grounds for disqualification.

VIII. EXAMINATION TECHNIQUES

1. Read the *general* instructions carefully. These are usually printed on the first page of the examination booklet. As a rule, these instructions refer to the timing of the examination; the fact that you should not start work until the signal and must stop work at a signal, etc. If there are any *special* instructions, such as a choice of questions to be answered, make sure that you note this instruction carefully.

2. When you are ready to start work on the examination, that is as soon as the signal has been given, read the instructions to each question booklet, underline any key words or phrases, such as *least, best, outline, describe,* and the like. In this way you will tend to answer as requested rather than discover on reviewing your paper that you *listed without describing,* that you selected the *worst* choice rather than the *best* choice, etc.

3. If the examination is of the objective or so-called multiple-choice type, that is, each question will also give a series of possible answers: A, B, C, or D, and you are called upon to select the best answer and write the letter next to that answer on your answer paper, it is advisable to start answering each question in turn. There may be anywhere from 50 to 100 such questions in the three or four hours allotted and you can see how much time would be taken if you read through all the questions before beginning to answer any. Furthermore, if you come across a question or a group of questions which you know would be difficult to answer, it would undoubtedly affect your handling of all the other questions.

4. If the examination is of the esssay-type and contains but a few questions, it is a moot point as to whether you should read all the questions before starting to answer any one. Of course if you are given a choice, say five out of seven and the like, then it is essential to read all the questions so you can eliminate the two which are most difficult. If, however, you are asked to answer all the questions, there may be danger in trying to answer the easiest one first because you may find that you will spend too much time on it. The best technique is to answer the first question, then proceed to the second, etc.

5. Time your answers. Before the examination begins, write down the time it started, then add the time allowed for the examination and write down the time it must be completed, then divide the time available somewhat as follows:

(a) If 3½ hours are allowed, that would be 210 minutes. If you have 80 objective-type questions, that would be an average of 2½ minutes per question. Allow yourself no more than 2 minutes per question, or a total of 160 minutes, which will permit about 50 minutes to review.

(b) If for the time allotment of 210 minutes, there are 7 essay questions to answer, that would average about 30 minutes a question. Give yourself only 25 minutes per question so that you have about 35 minutes to review.

6. The most important instruction is *to read each question* and make sure you know what is wanted. The second most important instruction is to *time yourself properly* so that you answer every question. The third most important instruction is to *answer every question*. Guess if you have to but include something for each question. Remember that you will receive no credit for a blank and will probably receive some credit if you write something in answer to an essay question. If you guess a letter, say "B" for a multiple-choice question, you may have guessed right. If you leave a blank as the answer to a multiple-choice question, the examiners may respect your feelings but it will not add a point to your score.

7. Suggestions

   a. <u>Objective-Type Questions</u>

     (1) Examine the question booklet for proper sequence of pages and questions.

     (2) Read all instructions carefully.

     (3) Skip any question which seems too difficult; return to it after all other questions have been answered.

     (4) Apportion your time properly; do not spend too much time on any single question or group of questions.

     (5) Note and underline key words -- *all, most, fewest, least, best, worst, same, opposite*.

     (6) Pay particular attention to negatives.

     (7) Note unusual option, e.g., unduly long, short, complex, different or similar in content to the body of the question.

     (8) Observe the use of "hedging" words -- *probably, may, most likely, etc.*

     (9) Make sure that your answer is put next to the same number as the question.

    (10) Do not second-guess unless you have good reason to believe the second answer is definitely more correct.

    (11) Cross out original answer if you decide another answer is more accurate; do not erase.

    (12) Answer all questions; guess unless instructed otherwise.

    (13) Leave time for review.

   b. <u>Essay-Type Questions</u>

     (1) Read each question carefully.

     (2) Determine exactly what is wanted. Underline key words or phrases.

     (3) Decide on outline or paragraph answer.

     (4) Include many different points and elements unless asked to develop any one or two points or elements.

     (5) Show impartiality by giving pros and cons unless directed to select one side only.

     (6) Make and write down any assumptions you find necessary to answer the question.

     (7) Watch your English, grammar, punctuation, choice of words.

     (8) Time your answers; don't crowd material.

8. Answering the Essay Question

   Most essay questions can be answered by framing the specific response around several key words or ideas. Here are a few such key words or ideas:

M's: manpower, materials, methods, money, management;
P's: purpose, program, policy, plan, procedure, practice, problems, pitfalls, personnel, public relations.

a. <u>Six Basic Steps in Handling Problems</u>:
   (1) Preliminary plan and background development
   (2) Collect information, data and facts
   (3) Analyze and interpret information, data and facts
   (4) Analyze and develop solutions as well as make recommendations
   (5) Prepare report and sell recommendations
   (6) Install recommendations and follow up effectiveness

b. <u>Pitfalls to Avoid</u>
   (1) *Taking things for granted*
       A statement of the situation does not necessarily imply that each of the elements is necessarily true; for example, a complaint may be invalid and biased so that all that can be taken for granted is that a complaint has been registered.
   (2) *Considering only one side of a situation*
       Wherever possible, indicate several alternatives and then point out the reasons you selected the best one.
   (3) *Failing to indicate follow-up*
       Whenever your answer indicates action on your part, make certain that you will take proper follow-up action to see how successful your recommendations, procedures, or actions turn out to be.
   (4) *Taking too long in answering any single question*
       Remember to time your answers properly.

IX. AFTER THE TEST

Scoring procedures differ in detail among civil service jurisdictions although the general principles are the same. Whether the papers are hand-scored or graded by the electric scoring machine we have described, they are nearly always graded by number. That is, the person who marks the paper knows only the number -- never the name -- of the applicant. Not until all the papers have been graded will they be matched with names. If other tests, such as training and experience or oral interview ratings have been given, scores will be combined. Different parts of the examination usually have different weights. For example, the written test might count 60 percent of the final grade, and a rating of training and experience 40 percent. In many jurisdictions, veterans will have a certain number of points added to their grades.

After the final grade has been determined, the names are placed in grade order and an eligible list is established. There are various methods for resolving ties between those who get the same final grade: probably the most common is to place first the name of the person whose application was received first. Job offers are made from the eligible list in the order the names appear on it.

You will be notified of your grade and your rank order as soon as all these computations have been made. This will be done as rapidly as possible.

People who are found to meet the requirements in the announcement are called "eligibles." Their names are put on a list of eligibles. An eligible's chances of getting a job depend on how high he stands on this list and how fast agencies are filling jobs from the list.

When a job is to be filled from a list of eligibles, the agency asks for the names of people on the list of eligibles for that job.

When the civil service commission receives this request, it sends to the agency the names of the three people highest on the list. Or, if the job to be filled has specialized requirements, the office sends the agency, from the general list, the names of the top three persons who meet those requirements.

The appointing officer makes a choice from among the three people whose names were sent to him. If the selected person accepts the appointment, the names of the others are put back on the list to be considered for future openings.

That is the rule in hiring from all kinds of eligible lists, whether they are for typist, carpenter, chemist, or something else. For every vacancy, the appointing officer has his choice of any one of the top three eligibles on the list. This explains why the person whose name is on top of the list sometimes does not get an appointment when some of the persons lower on the list do. If the appointing officer chooses the No. 2 or No. 3 eligible, the No. 1 eligible does not get a job at once, but stays on the list until he is appointed or the list is terminated.

X. HOW TO PASS THE INTERVIEW TEST

The examination for which you applied requires an oral interview test. You have already taken the written test and you are now being called for the interview test -- the final part of the formal examination.

You may think that it is not possible to prepare for an interview test and that there are no procedures to follow during an interview.

Our purpose is to point out some things you can do in advance that will help you and some good rules to follow and pitfalls to avoid while you are being interviewed.

A. WHAT IS AN INTERVIEW SUPPOSED TO TEST?

The written examination is designed to test the technical knowledge and competence of the candidate; the oral is designed to evaluate intangible qualities, not readily measured otherwise, and to establish a list showing the relative fitness of each candidate, *as measured against his competitors*, for the position sought. Scoring is not on the basis of "right" or "wrong," but on a sliding scale of values ranging from "not passable" to "outstanding." As a matter of fact, it is possible to achieve a relatively low score without a single "incorrect" answer because of evident weakness in the qualities being measured,

Occasionally, an examination may consist entirely of an oral test -- either an individual or a group oral. In such cases, information is sought concerning the technical knowledges and abilities of the candidate, since there has been no written examination for this purpose. More commonly, however, an oral test is used to supplement a written examination.

B. WHO CONDUCTS INTERVIEWS?

The composition of oral boards varies among different jurisdictions. In nearly all, a representative of the personnel department serves as chairman. One of the members of the board may be a representative of the department in which the candidate would work. In some cases, "outside experts" are used, and frequently a business man or some other representative of the general public is asked to serve. Labor and management or other special groups may be represented. The aim is to secure the services of experts in the appropriate field.

However the board is composed, it is a good idea (and not at all improper or unethical) to ascertain in advance of the interview who the members are and what groups they represent. When you are introduced to them, you will have some idea of their backgrounds and interests, and at least you will not stutter and stammer over their names.

C. WHAT TO DO BEFORE THE INTERVIEW

While knowledge about the board members is useful and takes some of the surprise element out of the interview, there is other preparation which is more substantive. It *is* possible to prepare for an oral -- in several ways:

1. Keep a Copy of Your Application and Review it Carefully Before the Interview

   This may be the only document before the oral board, and the starting point of the interview. Know what experience and education you have listed there, and the sequence and dates of it. Sometimes the board will ask *you* to review the highlights of your experience for them; you should not have to hem and haw doing it.

2. Study the Class Specification and the Examination Announcement

   Usually, the oral board has one or both of these to guide them. The qualities, characteristics, or knowledges required by the position sought are stated in these documents. They offer valuable clues as to the nature of the oral interview. For example, if the job involves supervisory responsibilities, the announcement will usually indicate that knowledge of modern supervisory methods and the qualifications of the candidate as a supervisor will be tested. If so, you can expect such questions, frequently in the form of a hypothetical situation which you are expected to solve. *Never* go into an oral without knowledge of the duties and responsibilities of the job you seek.

3. Think Through Each Qualification Required

   Try to visualize the kind of questions *you* would ask if you were a board member. How well could you answer them? Try especially to appraise your own knowledge and background in each area, *measured against the job sought,* and identify any areas in which you are weak. Be critical and realistic -- do not flatter yourself.

4. Do Some General Reading in Areas in Which You Feel You May be Weak

   For example, if the job involves supervision and your past experience has *not,* some general reading in supervisory methods and practices, particularly in the field of human relations, might be useful. *Do not* study agency procedures or detailed manuals. The oral board will be testing your understanding and capacity, *not* your memory.

5. Get a Good Night's Sleep and Watch Your General Health and Mental Attitude

   You will want a clear head at the interview. Take care of a cold or other minor ailment, and, of course, *no hangovers.*

D. WHAT TO DO THE DAY OF THE INTERVIEW

Now comes the day of the interview itself. Give yourself plenty of time to get there. Plan to arrive somewhat ahead of the scheduled time, particularly if your appointment is in the fore part of the day. If a previous candidate fails to appear, the board might be ready for you a bit early. By early afternoon an oral board is almost invariably behind schedule if there are many candidates, and you may have to wait. Take along a book or magazine to read, or your application to review. But leave any extraneous material in the waiting room when you go in for your interview. In any event, relax and compose yourself.

The matter of dress is important. The board is forming impressions about you -- from your experience, your manners, your attitudes, and from your appearance. Give your personal appearance careful attention. Dress your *best*, but not your flashiest. Choose conservative, appropriate clothing, and be sure it and you are immaculate. This is a business interview, and your appearance should indicate that you regard it as such. Besides, being well-groomed and properly dressed will help boost your confidence.

Sooner or later, someone will call your name and escort you into the interview room. *This is it.* From here on you are on your own. It is too late for any more preparation. But, remember, you asked for this opportunity to prove your fitness, and you are here because your request was granted.

E. WHAT HAPPENS WHEN YOU GO IN?

The usual sequence of events will be as follows: The clerk (who is often the board stenographer) will introduce you to the chairman of the oral board, who will introduce you to each other member of the board. Acknowledge the introductions before you sit down. Do not be surprised if you find a microphone facing you or a stenotypist sitting by. Oral interviews are usually recorded, in the event of an appeal or other review.

Usually the chairman of the board will open the interview by reviewing the highlights of your education and work experience from your application -- primarily for the benefit of the other members of the board, as well as to get the material into the record. Do not interrupt or comment unless there is an error or significant misinterpretation; if so, do not hesitate. But do not quibble about insignificant matters. Usually, also, he will ask you some question about your education, your experience, or your present job -- partly to get you started talking, to establish the interviewing "rapport." He may start the actual questioning, or turn it over to one of the other members. Frequently each member undertakes the questioning on a particular area, one in which he is perhaps most competent. So you can expect each member to participate in the examination. And because the time is limited, you may expect some rather abrupt switches in the direction the questioning takes. Do not be upset by it. Normally, a board member will not pursue a single line of questioning unless he discovers a particular strength or weakness.

After each member has participated, the chairman will usually ask whether any member has any further questions, then will ask you if you have anything you wish to add. Unless you are expecting this question, it may floor you. Or worse, it may start you off on an extended, extemporaneous speech. The board is not usually seeking more information. The question is principally to offer you a last opportunity to present further qualifications or to indicate that you have nothing to add. So, if you feel that a significant qualification or characteristic has been overlooked, it is proper to point it out in a sentence or so. Do not compliment the board on the thoroughness of their examination -- they have been sketchy, and you know it. If you wish, merely say, "No thank you, I have nothing further to add." This is a point where you can "talk yourself out" of a good impression or fail to present an important bit of information. *Remember, you close the interview yourself.*

The chairman will then say,"That is all,Mr.Smith,thank you." Do not be startled; the interview is over, and quicker than you think. Say,"Thank you and good morning," gather up your belongings and take your leave. Save your sigh of relief for the other side of the door.

F. *HOW TO PUT YOUR BEST FOOT FORWARD*

Throughout all this process, you may feel that the board individually and collectively is trying to pierce your defenses, to seek out your hidden weaknesses, and to embarrass and confuse you. Actually, this is not true. They are obliged to make an appraisal of your qualifications for the job you are seeking, and they *want to see you in your best light*. Remember, they must interview all candidates and a noncooperative candidate may become a failure in spite of their best efforts to bring out his qualifications. Here are fifteen(15) suggestions that will help you:

1. Be Natural. Keep Your Attitude Confident,But Not Cocky

If *you* are not confident that you can do the job, do not ex-expect the *board* to be. Do not apologize for your weaknesses, try to bring out your strong points. The board is interested in a positive, not a negative presentation. Cockiness will antagonize any board member, and make him wonder if you are covering up a weakness by a false show of strength.

2. Get Comfortable, But Don't Lounge or Sprawl

Sit erectly but not stiffly. A careless posture may lead the board to conclude you are careless in other things, or at least that you are not impressed by the importance of the occasion to you.Either conclusion is natural, even if incorrect. Do not fuss with your clothing, or with a pencil or an ashtray. Your hands may occasionally be useful to emphasize a point; do not let them become a point of distraction.

3. Do Not Wisecrack or Make Small Talk

This is a serious situation, and your attitude should show that you consider it as such. Further, the time of the board is limited; they do not want to waste it, and neither should you.

4. Do Not Exaggerate Your Experience or Abilities

In the first place, from information in the application,from other interviews and other sources, the board may know more about you than you think; in the second place, you probably will not get away with it in the first place. An experienced board is rather adept at spotting such a situation. Do not take the chance.

5. If You Know a Member of the Board, Do Not Make a Point of It, Yet Do Not Hide It.

Certainly you are not fooling him, and probably not the other members of the board. Do not try to take advantage of your acquaintanceship -- it will probably do you little good.

6. Do Not Dominate the Interview

Let the board do that. They will give you the clues -- do not assume that you have to do all the talking. Realize that the board has a number of questions to ask you, and do not try to take up all the interview time by showing off your extensive knowledge of the answer to the first one.

7. Be Attentive

You only have twenty minutes or so, and you should keep your attention at its sharpest throughout. When a member is addressing a problem or a question to you, give him your undivided attention. Address your reply principally to him, but do not exclude the other members of the board.

8. Do Not Interrupt

A board member may be stating a problem for you to analyze. He will ask you a question when the time comes. Let him state the problem, and wait for the question.

9. Make Sure You Understand the Question

Do not try to answer until you are sure what the question is. If it is not clear, restate it in your own words or ask the board member to clarify it for you. But do not haggle about minor elements.

10. Reply Promptly But Not Hastily

A common entry on oral board rating sheets is "candidate responded readily," or "candidate hesitated in replies." Respond as promptly and quickly as you can, but do not jump to a hasty, ill-considered answer.

11. Do Not Be Peremptory in Your Answers

A brief answer is proper -- but do not fire your answer back. That is a losing game from your point of view. The board member can probably ask questions much faster than you can answer them.

12. Do Not Try To Create the Answer You Think the Board Member Wants

He is interested in what kind of mind you have and how it works -- not in playing games. Furthermore, he can usually spot this practice and will usually grade you down on it.

13. Do Not Switch Sides in Your Reply Merely to Agree With a Board Member

Frequently, a member will take a contrary position merely to draw you out and to see if you are willing and able to defend your point of view. Do not start a debate, yet do not surrender a good position. If a position is worth taking, it is worth defending.

14. Do Not Be Afraid to Admit an Error in Judgment if You Are Shown to Be Wrong

The board knows that you are forced to reply without any opportunity for careful consideration. Your answer may be demonstrably wrong. If so, admit it and get on with the interview.

15. Do Not Dwell at Length on Your Present Job

The opening question may relate to your present assignment. Answer the question but do not go into an extended discussion. You are being examined for a *new* job, not your present one. As a matter of fact, try to phrase *all* your answers in terms of the job for which you are being examined.

G. BASIS OF RATING

Probably you will forget most of these "do's" and "don'ts" when you walk into the oral interview room. Even remembering them all will not insure you a passing grade. Perhaps you did not have the qualifications in the first place. But remembering them *will* help you to put your best foot forward, without treading on the toes of the board members.

Rumor and popular opinion to the contrary notwithstanding, an oral board wants you to make the best appearance possible. They know you are under pressure -- but they also want to see how you respond to it as a guide to what your reaction would be under the pressures of the job you seek. They will be influenced by the degree of poise you display, the personal traits you show, and the manner in which you respond.

EXAMINATION SECTION

EXAMINATION SECTION

DIRECTIONS: Each question or incomplete statement is followed by several suggested answers or completions. Select the one that BEST answers the question or completes the statement. *PRINT THE LETTER OF THE CORRECT ANSWER IN THE SPACE AT THE RIGHT.*

1. Physical and mental health are essential to the officer.   1.___
   According to this statement, the officer MUST be
      A. as wise as he is strong
      B. smarter than most people
      C. sound in mind and body
      D. stronger than the average criminal

2. Teamwork is the basis of successful law enforcement.   2.___
   The factor stressed by this statement is
      A. cooperation   B. determination
      C. initiative   D. pride

3. Legal procedure is a means, not an end. Its function is   3.___
   merely to accomplish the enforcement of legal rights.
   A litigant has no vested interest in the observance of
   the rules of procedure as such. All that he should be
   entitled to demand is that he be given an opportunity for
   a fair and impartial trial of his case. He should not be
   permitted to invoke the aid of technical rules merely to
   embarrass his adversary.
   According to this paragraph, it is MOST correct to state
   that
      A. observance of the rules of procedure guarantees a
         fair trial
      B. embarrassment of an adversary through technical rules
         does not make a fair trial
      C. a litigant is not interested in the observance of
         rules of procedure
      D. technical rules must not be used in a trial

4. One theory states that all criminal behavior is taught by   4.___
   a process of communication within small intimate groups.
   An individual engages in criminal behavior if the number
   of criminal patterns which he has acquired exceed the
   number of non-criminal patterns.
   This statement indicates that criminal behavior is
      A. learned   B. instinctive
      C. hereditary   D. reprehensible

5. The law enforcement staff of today requires training and   5.___
   mental qualities of a high order. The poorly or partially
   prepared staff member lowers the standard of work, retards
   his own earning power, and fails in a career meant to
   provide a livelihood and social improvement.

According to this statement,
   A. an inefficient member of a law enforcement staff will still earn a good livelihood
   B. law enforcement officers move in good social circles
   C. many people fail in law enforcement careers
   D. persons of training and ability are essential to a law enforcement staff

6. In any state, no crime can occur unless there is a written law forbidding the act or the omission in question; and even though an act may not be exactly in harmony with public policy, such act is not a crime unless it is expressly forbidden by legislative statement.
   According to the above statement,
   A. a crime is committed with reference to a particular law
   B. acts not in harmony with public policy should be forbidden by law
   C. non-criminal activity will promote public welfare
   D. legislative enactments frequently forbid actions in harmony with public policy

6.___

7. The unrestricted sale of firearms is one of the main causes of our shameful crime record.
   According to this statement, one of the causes of our crime record is
   A. development of firepower
   B. ease of securing weapons
   C. increased skill in using guns
   D. scientific perfection of firearms

7.___

8. Every person must be informed of the reason for his arrest unless he is arrested in the actual commission of a crime. Sufficient force to effect the arrest may be used, but the courts frown on brutal methods.
   According to this statement, a person does not have to be informed of the reason for his arrest if
   A. brutal force was not used in effecting it
   B. the courts will later turn the defendant loose
   C. the person arrested knows force will be used if necessary
   D. the reason for it is clearly evident from the circumstances

8.___

9. An important duty of an officer is to keep order in the court.
   On the basis of this statement, it is PROBABLY true that
   A. it is more important for an officer to be strong than it is for him to be smart
   B. people involved in court trials are noisy if not kept in check
   C. not every duty of an officer is important
   D. the maintenance of order is important for the proper conduct of court business

9.___

10. Ideally, a correctional system should include several   10.___
    types of institutions to provide different degrees of
    custody.
    On the basis of this statement, one could MOST reasonably
    say that
        A. as the number of institutions in a correctional system
           increases, the efficiency of the system increases
        B. the difference in degree of custody for the inmate
           depends on the types of institutions in a correctional
           system
        C. the greater the variety of institutions, the stricter
           the degree of custody that can be maintained
        D. the same type of correctional institution is not
           desirable for the custody of all prisoners

11. The enforced idleness of a large percentage of adult men   11.___
    and women in our prisons is one of the direct causes of
    the tensions which burst forth in riot and disorder.
    On the basis of this statement, a GOOD reason why inmates
    should perform daily work of some kind is that
        A. better morale and discipline can be maintained when
           inmates are kept busy
        B. daily work is an effective way of punishing inmates
           for the crimes they have committed
        C. law-abiding citizens must work, therefore labor
           should also be required of inmates
         D. products of inmates' labor will in part pay the cost
           of their maintenance

12. With industry invading rural areas, the use of the auto-   12.___
    mobile, and the speed of modern communications and trans-
    portation, the problems of neglect and delinquency are no
    longer peculiar to cities but an established feature of
    everyday life.
    This statement implies MOST directly that
        A. delinquents are moving from cities to rural areas
        B. delinquency and neglect are found in rural areas
        C. delinquency is not as much of a problem in rural
           areas as in cities
        D. rural areas now surpass cities in industry

13. Young men from minority groups, if unable to find employ-   13.___
    ment, become discouraged and hopeless because of their
    economic position and may finally resort to any means of
    supplying their wants.
    The MOST reasonable of the following conclusions that may
    be drawn from this statement only is that
        A. discouragement sometimes leads to crime
        B. in general, young men from minority groups are
           criminals
        C. unemployment turns young men from crime
        D. young men from minority groups are seldom employed

14. To prevent crime, we must deal with the possible criminal   14.____
    long before he reaches the prison. Our aim should be not
    merely to reform the law breakers but to strike at the
    roots of crime: neglectful parents, bad companions,
    unsatisfactory homes, selfishness, disregard for the
    rights of others, and bad social conditions.
    The above statement recommends
       A. abolition of prisons   B. better reformatories
       C. compulsory education   D. general social reform

15. There is evidence which shows that comic books which   15.____
    glorify the criminal and criminal acts have a distinct
    influence in producing young criminals.
    According to this statement,
       A. comic books affect the development of criminal careers
       B. comic books specialize in reporting criminal acts
       C. young criminals read comic books exclusively
       D. young criminals should not be permitted to read
          comic books

16. Suppose a study shows that juvenile delinquents are equal   16.____
    in intelligence but three school grades behind juvenile
    non-delinquents.
    On the basis of this information only, it is MOST reasonable
    to say that
       A. a delinquent usually progresses to the educational
          limit set by his intelligence
       B. educational achievement depends on intelligence only
       C. educational achievement is closely associated with
          delinquency
       D. lack of intelligence is closely associated with
          delinquency

17. There is no proof today that the experience of a prison   17.____
    sentence makes a better citizen of an adult. On the
    contrary, there seems some evidence that the experience
    is an unwholesome one that frequently confirms the
    criminality of the inmate.
    From the above paragraph only, it may be BEST concluded
    that
       A. prison sentences tend to punish rather than rehabili-
          tate
       B. all criminals should be given prison sentences
       C. we should abandon our penal institutions
       D. penal institutions are effective in rehabilitating
          criminals

18. Some courts are referred to as *criminal* courts while   18.____
    others are known as *civil* courts.
    This distinction in name is MOST probably based on the
       A. historical origin of the court
       B. link between the court and the police
       C. manner in which the judges are chosen
       D. type of cases tried there

19. Many children who are exposed to contacts and experiences   19.___
of a delinquent nature become educated and trained in
crime in the course of participating in the daily life of
the neighborhood.
From this statement only, we may reasonably conclude that
    A. delinquency passes from parent to child
    B. neighborhood influences are usually bad
    C. schools are training grounds for delinquents
    D. none of the above conclusions is reasonable

20. Old age insurance, for whose benefits a quarter of a   20.___
million city employees may elect to become eligible, is
one feature of the Social Security Act that is wholly
administered by the Federal government.
On the basis of this paragraph only, it may MOST reasonably
be inferred that
    A. a quarter of a million city employees are drawing old
       age insurance
    B. a quarter of a million city employees have elected
       to become eligible for old age insurance
    C. the city has no part in administering Social Security
       old age insurance
    D. only the Federal government administers the Social
       Security Act

21. An officer's revolver is a defensive, and not offensive,   21.___
weapon.
On the basis of this statement only, an officer should
BEST draw his revolver to
    A. fire at an unarmed burglar
    B. force a suspect to confess
    C. frighten a juvenile delinquent
    D. protect his own life

22. Prevention of crime is of greater value to the community   22.___
than the punishment of crime.
If this statement is accepted as true, GREATEST emphasis
should be placed on
    A. malingering   B. medication
    C. imprisonment   D. rehabilitation

23. The criminal is rarely or never reformed.   23.___
Acceptance of this statement as true would mean that
GREATEST emphasis should be placed on
    A. imprisonment   B. parole
    C. probation   D. malingering

24. The MOST accurate of the following statements about   24.___
persons convicted of crimes is that
    A. their criminal behavior is almost invariably the
       result of low intelligence
    B. they are almost invariably legally insane
    C. they are more likely to come from underprivileged
       groups than from other groups
    D. they have certain facial characteristics which
       distinguish them from non-criminals

25. Suppose a study shows that the I.Q. (Intelligence Quotient) 25.___
    of prison inmates is 95 as opposed to an I.Q. of 100 for
    a numerically equivalent civilian group.
    A claim, on the basis of this study, that criminals have
    a lower I.Q. than non-criminals would be
    A. *improper*; prison inmates are criminals who have been
       caught
    B. *proper*; the study was numerically well done
    C. *improper*; the sample was inadequate
    D. *proper*; even misdemeanors are sometimes penalized by
       prison sentences

Questions 26-45.

DIRECTIONS: Select the number of the word or expression that MOST
            NEARLY expresses the meaning of the capitalized word
            in the group.

26. ABDUCT   26.___
    A. lead   B. kidnap   C. sudden   D. worthless

27. BIAS   27.___
    A. ability   B. envy   C. prejudice   D. privilege

28. COERCE   28.___
    A. cancel   B. force   C. rescind   D. rugged

29. CONDONE   29.___
    A. combine   B. pardon   C. revive   D. spice

30. CONSISTENCY   30.___
    A. bravery   B. readiness
    C. strain   D. uniformity

31. CREDENCE   31.___
    A. belief   B. devotion
    C. resemblance   D. tempo

32. CURRENT   32.___
    A. backward   B. brave
    C. prevailing   D. wary

33. CUSTODY   33.___
    A. advisement   B. belligerence
    C. guardianship   D. suspicion

34. DEBILITY   34.___
    A. deceitfulness   B. decency
    C. strength   D. weakness

35. DEPLETE   35.___
    A. beg   B. empty   C. excuse   D. fold

36. ENUMERATE   36.___
    A. name one by one   B. disappear
    C. get rid of   D. pretend

37. FEIGN   37.___
    A. allow   B. incur   C. pretend   D. weaken

38. INSTIGATE   38.___
    A. analyze   B. coordinate
    C. oppose   D. provoke

39. LIABLE   39.___
    A. careless   B. growing
    C. mistaken   D. responsible

40. PONDER   40.___
    A. attack   B. heavy   C. meditate   D. solicit

41. PUGILIST   41.___
    A. farmer   B. politician
    C. prize fighter   D. stage actor

42. QUELL   42.___
    A. explode   B. inform   C. shake   D. suppress

43. RECIPROCAL   43.___
    A. mutual   B. organized
    C. redundant   D. thoughtful

44. RUSE   44.___
    A. burn   B. impolite   C. rot   D. trick

45. STEALTHY   45.___
    A. crazed   B. flowing   C. sly   D. wicked

Questions 46-50.

DIRECTIONS: Each of the sentences in Questions 46 through 50 may
              be classified under one of the following four categories:
                A. faulty because of incorrect grammar
                B. faulty because of incorrect punctuation
                C. faulty because of incorrect capitalization or
                   incorrect spelling
                D. correct
              Examine each sentence carefully to determine under which
              of the above four options it is best classified. Then,
              in the space at the right, print the capital letter
              preceding the option which is the BEST of the four
              suggested above. Each faulty sentence contains but one
              type of error. Consider a sentence to be correct if it
              contains none of the types of errors mentioned, even
              though there may be other correct ways of expressing the
              same thought.

46. They told both he and I that the prisoner had escaped.   46.___

47. Any superior officer, who, disregards the just complaints   47.___
of his subordinates, is remiss in the performance of his
duty.

48. Only those members of the national organization who   48.___
resided in the Middle west attended the conference in
Chicago.

49. We told him to give the investigation assignment to   49.___
whoever was available.

50. Please do not disappoint and embarass us by not appearing   50.___
in court.

51. Suppose a man falls from a two-story high scaffold and is   51.___
unconscious.
You should
    A. call for medical assistance and avoid moving the man
    B. get someone to help you move him indoors to a bed
    C. have someone help you walk him around until he revives
    D. hold his head up and pour a stimulant down his throat

52. For proper first aid treatment, a person who has fainted   52.___
should be
    A. doused with cold water and then warmly covered
    B. given artificial respiration until he is revived
    C. laid down with his head lower than the rest of his
       body
    D. slapped on the face until he is revived

53. If you are called on to give first aid to a person who   53.___
is suffering from shock, you should
    A. apply cold towels   B. give him a stimulant
    C. keep him awake   D. wrap him warmly

54. Artificial respiration would NOT be proper first aid for   54.___
a person suffering from
    A. drowning   B. electric shock
    C. external bleeding   D. suffocation

55. Suppose you are called on to give first aid to several   55.___
victims of an accident.
First attention should be given to the one who is
    A. bleeding severely   B. groaning loudly
    C. unconscious   D. vomiting

56. If an officer's weekly salary is increased from $480 to   56.___
$540, then the percent of increase is _____ percent.
    A. 10   B. 11 1/9   C. 12½   D. 20

57. Suppose that one-half the officers in a department have   57.___
served for more than ten years and one-third have served
for more than 15 years.
Then, the fraction of officers who have served between
ten and fifteen years is
    A. 1/3   B. 1/5   C. 1/6   D. 1/12

58. In a city prison there are four floors on which prisoners   58.___
    are housed. The top floor houses one-quarter of the
    inmates, the bottom floor houses one-sixth of the inmates,
    one-third are housed on the second floor. The rest of the
    inmates are housed on the third floor.
    If there are 90 inmates housed on the third floor, the
    TOTAL number of inmates housed on all four floors together
    is
        A. 270   B. 360   C. 450   D. 540

59. Suppose that ten percent of those who commit serious   59.___
    crimes are convicted and that fifteen percent of those
    convicted are sentenced for more than 3 years.
    The percentage of those committing serious crimes who
    are sentenced for more than 3 years is _____ percent.
        A. 15   B. 1.5   C. .15   D. .015

60. Assume that there are 1,100 employees in a city agency.   60.___
    Of these, 15 percent are officers, 80 percent of whom are
    attorneys; of the attorneys, two-fifths have been with
    the agency over five years.
    Then, the number of officers who are attorneys and have
    over five years experience with the agency is MOST NEARLY
        A. 45   B. 53   C. 132   D. 165

61. An employee who has 500 cartons of supplies to pack can   61.___
    pack them at the rate of 50 an hour. After this employee
    has worked for ½ hour, he is joined by another employee
    who can pack 45 cartons an hour.
    Assuming that both employees can maintain their respective
    rates of speed, then the TOTAL number of hours required
    to pack all the cartons is
        A. 4½   B. 5   C. 5½   D. 6½

62. Thirty-six officers can complete an assignment in 22 days.   62.___
    Assuming that all officers work at the same rate of speed,
    the number of officers that would be needed to complete
    this assignment in 12 days is
        A. 42   B. 54   C. 66   D. 72

Questions 63-65.

DIRECTIONS: Questions 63 through 65 are to be answered on the basis
              of the table below. Data for certain categories have
              been omitted from the table. You are to calculate the
              missing numbers if needed to answer the questions.

	1987	1988	Numerical Increase
Correction Officers	1,226	1,347	121
Court Officers	495	529	34
Deputy Sheriffs	38	40	2
Supervisors	421	498	77
	2,180	2,414	234

63. The number in the *Supervisors* group in 1987 was MOST NEARLY   63.____

    A. 500   B. 475   C. 450   D. 425

64. The LARGEST percentage increase from 1987 to 1988 was in the group of   64.____

    A. Correction Officers   B. Court Officers
    C. Deputy Sheriffs   D. Supervisors

65. In 1988, the ratio of the number of Correction Officers to the total of the other three categories of employees was MOST NEARLY   65.____

    A. 1:1   B. 2:1   C. 3:1   D. 4:1

66. A directed verdict is made by a court when   66.____
    A. the facts are not disputed
    B. the defendant's motion for a directed verdict has been denied
    C. there is no question of law involved
    D. neither party has moved for a directed verdict

67. Papers on appeal of a criminal case do NOT include one of the following: 67.____
    A. Summons
    B. Minutes of trial
    C. Complaint
    D. Intermediate motion papers

68. A pleading titled *Smith vs. Jones, et al* indicates   68.____
    A. two plaintiffs   B. two defendants
    C. more than two defendants   D. unknown defendants

69. A District Attorney makes a *prima facie* case when   69.____
    A. there is proof of guilt beyond a reasonable doubt
    B. the evidence is sufficient to convict in the absence of rebutting evidence
    C. the prosecution presents more evidence than the defense
    D. the defendant fails to take the stand

70. A person is NOT qualified to act as a trial juror in a criminal action if he or she   70.____
    A. has been convicted previously of a misdemeanor
    B. is under 18 years of age
    C. has scruples against the death penalty
    D. does not own property of a value at least $500

71. A court clerk who falsifies a court record commits a(n)   71.____
    A. misdemeanor
    B. offense
    C. felony
    D. no crime, but automatically forfeits his tenure

72. Insolent and contemptuous behavior to a judge during a court of record proceeding is punishable as   72.____
    A. civil contempt   B. criminal contempt
    C. disorderly conduct   D. a disorderly person

73. Offering a bribe to a court clerk would not constitute a crime UNLESS the
    A. court clerk accepted the bribe
    B. bribe consisted of money
    C. bribe was given with intent to influence the court clerk in his official functions
    D. court was actually in session

73.___

74. A defendant comes to trial in the same court in which he had previously been defendant in a similar case.
The court officer should
    A. tell him, *Knew we'd be seeing you again*
    B. tell newspaper reporters what he knows of the previous action
    C. treat him the same as he would any other defendant
    D. warn the judge that the man had previously been a defendant

74.___

75. Suppose in conversation with you, an attorney strongly criticizes a ruling of the judge and you believe the attorney to be correct.
You should
    A. assure him you feel the same way
    B. tell him the judge knows the law
    C. tell him to ask for an exception
    D. refuse to discuss the matter

75.___

76. Assume that you are a court officer. A woman sees you in the hall and attempts to register a complaint that her husband raped her two hours earlier.
Which one of the following is the MOST appropriate action for you to take FIRST in this case?
    A. Refer her to Family Court.
    B. Advise her that her husband has not committed any crime.
    C. Ask her for additional information about the circumstances surrounding her allegation so that you may refer her to the proper office or agency.
    D. Have her sign a criminal information in the court.

76.___

77. Which one of the following is the BEST example of a privileged communication which is NOT admissible as evidence in a court of law without the consent of the communicator?
    A. Client to his accountant
    B. Informant to a law enforcement officer
    C. Parent to his child
    D. Defendant to his spouse

77.___

78. A court officer has many contacts with the public.
In these contacts, it is MOST important that he
    A. be brief and complete in his answers
    B. be courteous and helpful
    C. go along with what they ask
    D. know the law

78.___

79. Suppose a witness becomes engaged in a very heated
argument with an attorney who is cross-examining him.
The court officer should
    A. ask the attorney to avoid exciting the witness
    B. ask the judge if he wishes any action to be taken
    C. await the judge's order before interceding
    D. caution the witness to be more respectful

79.____

80. Suppose that you are a court officer stationed at the
door of the courtroom to prevent anyone from entering
while the judge is charging the jury. A man whom you
recognize as a City Councilman, accompanied by a woman,
attempts to enter the courtroom.
The BEST action for you to take is to
    A. apologize and explain why they cannot be permitted
       to enter
    B. permit the man to enter since he is a Councilman
       but exclude the woman
    C. permit them to enter since the judge would surely
       make an exception for them
    D. send a note in to the judge to find if they may be
       permitted to enter

80.____

81. It is desirable that a court officer acquire a knowledge
of the procedures of the court to which he is assigned
MAINLY because such knowledge will help him
    A. become familiar with anti-social behavior
    B. discharge his duties properly
    C. gain insight into causes of crime
    D. in any personal legal proceeding

81.____

82. Since he is a city employee, a court officer who refuses
to waive immunity from prosecution when called on to
testify in court automatically terminates his employment.
From this statement ONLY, it may be BEST inferred that
    A. a court officer is a city employee
    B. all city employees are court officers
    C. city employees may be fired only for malfeasance
    D. court attendants who waive immunity may not be
       prosecuted

82.____

83. Referees of the Civil Court are former judges of this
court who have served at least ten years and whose term
of office terminated at the age of 55 or over, or any
judge who has served in a court of record and has
retired.
According to this statement, a person can be a referee
of the Civil Court ONLY if he
    A. has been a judge
    B. has retired
    C. has served at least 10 years in the court
    D. meets certain age requirements

83.____

84. Assume that you are assigned to a jury room where you   84.___
    are to guard the jury until 4 P.M. Your relief does not
    arrive and the jury is still deliberating.
    Of the following, the BEST action for you to take is to
      A. ask the foreman of the jury to assume responsibility
         until your relief arrives
      B. find out what the jurors may need, get it, and then
         lock them in for the night
      C. inform your supervisor but remain on duty until you
         are relieved
      D. wait until 5 P.M., your usual closing time, and then
         leave if the relief has not arrived by then

85. When, at a trial, a piece of evidence is tagged as   85.___
    Exhibit A, the CHIEF purpose is to
      A. assure its return to the owner
      B. make it possible to examine it for fingerprints
         without chance of error
      C. make it possible to identify and refer to it easily
      D. prevent the defendant from denying he had it

86. In one case, a mistrial was declared because the indict-   86.___
    ment used the pronoun he instead of she.
    The MOST useful information a court attendant can derive
    from this statement is that
      A. accuracy is important
      B. mistrial is a legal term
      C. one must always use good grammar
      D. to misrepresent is criminal

87. Suppose a newspaper reporter asks you for information   87.___
    about what happened at a trial where the judge had ordered
    the courtroom cleared of reporters and spectators.
    You should
      A. give him the information he wants
      B. refer him to the judge for information
      C. refuse to talk to him unless reporters from other
         papers are present
      D. give him misleading information

88. Assume that you are the court officer on duty outside the   88.___
    judge's chambers in the court house. One day, one of the
    judges informs you that he will be too busy that day to
    see any visitors, and he tells you to refer them to his
    secretary for new appointments. Later in the day, an
    important visitor comes in and asks to see the judge about
    urgent business.
    Of the following, the BEST course of action for you to
    take in this situation is to
      A. ask the visitor to come back another day when the
         judge may be able to see him
      B. call the judge on the phone and tell him that the
         visitor has urgent business to discuss with him
      C. refer the visitor to one of the other judges who
         may be present in chambers
      D. tell the visitor that the judge is not available, but
         his secretary may be able to help him or make a new
         appointment

89. To gain a verdict against X in a trial, it was necessary   89.___
    to show that he could have been at Y Street at 5 P.M.
    It was proven that he was seen at Z Street at 4:45 P.M.
    The question that MUST be answered to show whether the
    verdict should be against X is:
    A. How long does it take to get from Z Street to
       Y Street?
    B. In what sort of neighborhood is Y Street located?
    C. Was X acting suspiciously on the day in question?
    D. Who was with X when he was seen at Z Street at
       4:45 P.M.?

90. If, at the instructions of the judge, a court officer   90.___
    calls the name of a defendant in a lawsuit and the person
    does not answer, the court officer should FIRST
    A. ask the judge if he called the person's name correctly
    B. call the person's name again
    C. look outside the doors of the courtroom for the
       defendant
    D. tell the judge the person doesn't answer

91. When X is accused of having cheated Y of a sum of money   91.___
    and Y is proven to have been deprived of the money, there
    is an additional requirement for a verdict against X.
    The additional requirement is to prove that
    A. the money was stolen from Y
    B. X had the money after Y had it
    C. X had the money before Y had it
    D. X cheated Y of the money

92. Assume that you are on duty in a courtroom and during   92.___
    the judge's absence one of the witnesses for a pending
    case becomes very angry about the delay.
    Of the following, the BEST action for you to take is to
    A. listen to him until he calms down and then explain
       the reason for the delay
    B. tell him your court is no different from any other
       court
    C. walk away from him so that you will not get involved
       in a dispute
    D. warn him that the judge may be back at any minute and
       will hold him in contempt

93. Assume that you are assigned to the post outside judge's   93.___
    chambers in the court house. A visitor tells you he has
    an appointment with Judge Jones who is expected to arrive
    shortly. He asks for permission to wait in the judge's
    office which is unoccupied at the present time.
    For you to permit him to wait there would be
    A. *wise*; the judge would no doubt wish to speak to the
       man privately
    B. *wise*; it would keep the anteroom where you are
       stationed clear, allowing other employees to work
       without any disturbance

C. *unwise*; it is rude to allow a visitor to sit alone in an office

D. *unwise*; there may be confidential material on the judge's desk or bookcases

94. A court officer shall not receive a gift from any defendant or other person on the defendant's behalf.
The BEST explanation for this rule is that
   A. acceptance of a gift has no significance
   B. defendants cannot usually afford gifts
   C. favors may be expected in return
   D. gifts are only an expression of good will

94.___

95. When a jury is selected, the attorney for each side has a right to refuse to accept a certain number of prospective jurors without giving any reason therefor.
The reason for this is MAINLY that
   A. attorneys can exclude persons likely to be biased even though no prejudice is admitted
   B. persons who will suffer economically by being summoned for jury duty can be excused forthwith
   C. relatives of the litigants can be excused thus insuring a fair trial for each side
   D. there will be a greater number of people from which the jury can be selected

95.___

96. Where the defendant in a criminal case is too poor to afford counsel, the court will assign one and he will be paid by the government.
The principle BEST established by this statement is that
   A. it is improper for the government to provide both prosecuting and defending counsel in a trial
   B. laws are usually violated because of poverty and defendants are too poor to employ counsel
   C. only wealthy law violators may hope to be represented by competent counsel
   D. the government is obligated to shield the innocent as well as punish the guilty

96.___

97. If a visitor to the court asks foolish questions, the BEST action for the court officer to take is to
   A. answer in a brusque manner to discourage further foolish questions
   B. refer the questioner to his supervisor
   C. answer them the same way as he would any other questions
   D. ignore them since the person doesn't really expect an answer

97.___

98. A man plus a uniform makes a good court officer.
This statement is FALSE because
   A. a court officer is also required to wear a badge
   B. a good court officer is not made merely by putting on a uniform
   C. it makes no mention of the fact that the uniform must be neat
   D. patrolmen as well as court officers wear uniforms

98.___

99. It is a frequent misconception that court officers can be   99.___
recruited from those registers established for the recruit-
ment of city police or firemen. While it is true that
many common qualifications are found in all of these,
specific standards for court work are indicated, varying
with the size, geographical location, and policies of the
court.
According to this paragraph ONLY, it may BEST be inferred
that
   A. a successful court officer must have some qualifica-
      tions not required of a policeman or fireman
   B. qualifications which make a successful patrolman will
      also make a successful fireman
   C. the same qualifications are required of a court
      officer regardless of the court to which he is
      assigned
   D. the successful court officer is required to be both
      more intelligent and stronger than a fireman

100. One of the duties of a court officer is to assist the   100.___
public with their problems.
A PROPER exercise of this duty by a court officer would
be for the officer to
   A. advise members of the public to settle their differ-
      ences out of court
   B. advise a member of the public how to fill out forms
      required by the court
   C. lend money to a member of the public to pay the
      required court fees
   D. recommend a lawyer to a member of the public who does
      not have one

KEY (CORRECT ANSWERS)

1. C	21. D	41. C	61. C	81. B
2. A	22. D	42. D	62. C	82. A
3. B	23. A	43. A	63. D	83. A
4. A	24. C	44. D	64. D	84. C
5. D	25. A	45. C	65. A	85. C
6. A	26. B	46. A	66. A	86. A
7. B	27. C	47. B	67. D	87. B
8. D	28. B	48. C	68. C	88. D
9. D	29. B	49. D	69. B	89. A
10. D	30. D	50. C	70. B	90. B
11. A	31. A	51. A	71. C	91. D
12. B	32. C	52. C	72. B	92. A
13. A	33. C	53. D	73. C	93. D
14. D	34. D	54. C	74. C	94. C
15. A	35. B	55. A	75. D	95. A
16. C	36. A	56. C	76. C	96. D
17. A	37. C	57. C	77. D	97. C
18. D	38. D	58. B	78. B	98. B
19. D	39. D	59. B	79. C	99. A
20. C	40. C	60. B	80. A	100. B

EXAMINATION SECTION

TEST 1

DIRECTIONS: Each question or incomplete statement is followed by several suggested answers or completions. Select the one that BEST answers the question or completes the statement. *PRINT THE LETTER OF THE CORRECT ANSWER IN THE SPACE AT THE RIGHT.*

1. Of the following, the MOST important single factor in any building security program is
   A. a fool-proof employee identification system
   B. an effective control of entrances and exits
   C. bright illumination of all outside areas
   D. clearly marking public and non-public areas

   1.___

2. There is general agreement that the BEST criterion of what is a good physical security system in a large public building is
   A. the number of uniformed officers needed to patrol sensitive areas
   B. how successfully the system prevents rather than detects violations
   C. the number of persons caught in the act of committing criminal offenses
   D. how successfully the system succeeds in maintaining good public relations

   2.___

3. Which one of the following statements MOST correctly expresses the chief reason why women were made eligible for appointment to the position of officer?
   A. Certain tasks in security protection can be performed best by assigning women.
   B. More women than men are available to fill many vacancies in this position.
   C. The government wants more women in law enforcement because of their better attendance records.
   D. Women can no longer be barred from any government jobs because of sex.

   3.___

4. The MOST BASIC purpose of patrol by officers is to
   A. eliminate as much as possible the opportunity for successful misconduct
   B. investigate criminal complaints and accident cases
   C. give prompt assistance to employees and citizens in distress or requesting their help
   D. take persons into custody who commit criminal offenses against persons and property

   4.___

5. The highest quality of patrol service is MOST generally obtained by
   A. frequently changing the post assignments of each officer
   B. assigning officers to posts of equal size
   C. assigning problem officers to the least desirable posts
   D. assigning the same officers to the same posts

   5.___

6. The one of the following requirements which is MOST   6.___
   essential to the successful performance of patrol duty
   by individual officers is their
   A. ability to communicate effectively with higher-level
      officers
   B. prompt signalling according to a prescribed schedule
      to insure post coverages at all times
   C. knowledge of post conditions and post hazards
   D. willingness to cover large areas during periods of
      critical manpower shortages

7. Officers on patrol are constantly warned to be on the alert   7.___
   for suspicious persons, actions, and circumstances.
   With this in mind, a senior officer should emphasize the
   need for them to
   A. be cautious and suspicious when dealing officially
      with any civilian regardless of the latter's overt
      actions or the circumstances surrounding his dealings
      with the police
   B. keep looking for the unusual persons, actions, and
      circumstances on their posts and pay less attention
      to the usual
   C. take aggressive police action immediately against any
      unusual person or condition detected on their posts,
      regardless of any other circumstances
   D. become thoroughly familiar with the usual on their
      posts so as to be better able to detect the unusual

8. Of primary importance in the safeguarding of property   8.___
   from theft is a good central lock and key issuance and
   control system.
   Which one of the following recommendations about main-
   taining such a control system would be LEAST acceptable?
   A. In selecting locks to be used for the various gates,
      building, and storage areas, consideration should be
      given to the amount of security desired.
   B. Master keys should have no markings that will identify
      them as such and the list of holders of these keys
      should be frequently reviewed to determine the
      continuing necessity for the individuals having them.
   C. Whenever keys for outside doors or gates or for other
      doors which permit access to important buildings and
      areas are misplaced, the locks should be immediately
      changed or replaced pending an investigation.
   D. Whenever an employee fails to return a borrowed key
      at the time specified, a prompt investigation should
      be made by the security force.

9. In a crowded building, a fire develops in the basement,   9.___
   and smoke enters the crowded rooms on the first floor.
   Of the following, the BEST action for an officer to take
   after an alarm is turned in is to
   A. call out a warning that the building is on fire and
      that everyone should evacuate because of the immediate
      danger
   B. call all of the officers together for an emergency
      meeting and discuss a plan of action

    C. immediately call for assistance from the local police
       station to help in evacuating the crowd
    D. tell everyone that there is a fire in the building
       next door and that they should move out onto the
       streets through available exits

10. Which of the following is in a key position to carry out   10.___
    successfully a safety program of an agency? The
    A. building engineer   B. bureau chiefs
    C. immediate supervisors   D. public relations director

11. It is GENERALLY considered that a daily roll call inspec-   11.___
    tion, which checks to see that the officers and their
    equipment are in good order, is
    A. *desirable*, chiefly because it informs the superior
       officer what men will have to purchase new uniforms
       within a month
    B. *desirable*, chiefly because the public forms their
       impressions of the organization from the appearance
       of the officers
    C. *undesirable*, chiefly because this kind of daily
       inspection unnecessarily delays officers in getting
       to their assigned patrol posts
    D. *undesirable*, chiefly because roll call inspection
       usually misses individuals reporting to work late

12. A supervising officer in giving instructions to a group   12.___
    of officers on the principles of accident investigation
    remarked, "A conclusion that appears reasonable will often
    be changed by exploring a factor of apparently little
    importance".
    Which one of the following precautions does this statement
    emphasize as MOST important in any accident investigation?
    A. Every accident clue should be fully investigated.
    B. Accidents should not be too promptly investigated.
    C. Only specially trained officers should investigate
       accidents.
    D. Conclusions about accident causes are highly
       unreliable.

13. On a rainy day, a senior officer found that 9 of his 50   13.___
    officers reported to work.
    What percentage of his officers was ABSENT?
    A. 18%   B. 80%   C. 82%   D. 90%

14. Officer A and Officer B work at the same post on the same   14.___
    days, but their hours are different. Officer A comes to
    work at 9:00 A.M. and leaves at 5:00 P.M., with a lunch
    period between 12:15 P.M. and 1:15 P.M. Officer B comes
    to work at 10:50 A.M. and works until 6:50 P.M., and he
    takes an hour for lunch between 3:00 P.M. and 4:00 P.M.
    What is the total amount of time between 9:00 A.M. and
    6:50 P.M. that only ONE officer will be on duty?
    A. 4 hours   B. 4 hours and 40 minutes
    C. 5 hours   D. 5 hours and 40 minutes

15. An officer's log recorded the following attendance of   15.___
    30 officers:

Monday	20 present;	10 absent
Tuesday	28 present;	2 absent
Wednesday	30 present;	0 absent
Thursday	21 present;	9 absent
Friday	16 present;	14 absent
Saturday	11 present;	19 absent
Sunday	14 present;	16 absent

On the average, how many men were present on the weekdays
(Monday - Friday)?
    A. 21   B. 23   C. 25   D. 27

16. An angry woman is being questioned by an officer when she   16.___
    begins shouting abuses at him.
    The BEST of the following procedures for the officer to
    follow is to
        A. leave the room until she has cooled off
        B. politely ignore anything she says
        C. place her under arrest by handcuffing her to a fixed
           object
        D. warn her that he will have to use force to restrain
           her making remarks

17. Of the following, which is NOT a recommended practice for   17.___
    an officer placing a woman offender under arrest?
        A. Assume that the offender is an innocent and virtuous
           person and treat her accordingly.
        B. Protect himself from attack by the woman.
        C. Refrain from using excessive physical force on the
           offender.
        D. Make the public aware that he is not abusing the
           woman.

Questions 18-21.

DIRECTIONS: Questions 18 through 21 are to be answered SOLELY on
              the basis of the following passage.

*Specific measures for prevention of pilferage will be based on
careful analysis of the conditions at each agency. The most practical and effective method to control casual pilferage is the
establishment of psychological deterrents.*

*One of the most common means of discouraging casual pilferage
is to search individuals leaving the agency at unannounced times
and places. These spot searches may occasionally detect attempts
at theft but greater value is realized by bringing to the attention
of individuals the fact that they may be apprehended if they do
attempt the illegal removal of property.*

*An aggressive security education program is an effective means
of convincing employees that they have much more to lose than they
do to gain by engaging in acts of theft. It is important for all
employees to realize that pilferage is morally wrong no matter how
insignificant the value of the item which is taken. In establishing*

any deterrent to casual pilferage, security officers must not lose sight of the fact that most employees are honest and disapprove of thievery. Mutual respect between security personnel and other employees of the agency must be maintained if the facility is to be protected from other more dangerous forms of human hazards. Any security measure which infringes on the human rights or dignity of others will jeopardize, rather than enhance, the overall protection of the agency.

18. The $100,000 yearly inventory of an agency revealed that $50 worth of goods had been stolen; the only individuals with access to the stolen materials were the employees. Of the following measures, which would the author of the preceding paragraph MOST likely recommend to a security officer?
    A. Conduct an intensive investigation of all employees to find the culprit.
    B. Make a record of the theft, but take no investigative or disciplinary action against any employee.
    C. Place a tight security check on all future movements of personnel.
    D. Remove the remainder of the material to an area with much greater security.

19. What does the passage imply is the percentage of employees whom a security officer should expect to be honest?
    A. No employee can be expected to be honest all of the time
    B. Just 50%
    C. Less than 50%
    D. More than 50%

20. According to the passage, the security officer would use which of the following methods to minimize theft in buildings with many exits when his staff is very small?
    A. Conduct an inventory of all material and place a guard near that which is most likely to be pilfered.
    B. Inform employees of the consequences of legal prosecution for pilfering.
    C. Close off the unimportant exits and have all his men concentrate on a few exits.
    D. Place a guard at each exit and conduct a casual search of individuals leaving the premises.

21. Of the following, the title BEST suited for this passage is:
    A. Control Measures for Casual Pilfering
    B. Detecting the Potential Pilferer
    C. Financial losses Resulting from Pilfering
    D. The Use of Moral Persuasion in Physical Security

22. Of the following first aid procedures, which will cause the GREATEST harm in treating a fracture?
    A. Control hemorrhages by applying direct pressure
    B. Keep the broken portion from moving about
    C. Reset a protruding bone by pressing it back into place
    D. Treat the suffering person for shock

23. During a snowstorm, a man comes to you complaining of   23.___
    frostbitten hands.
    PROPER first aid treatment in this case is to
    A. place the hands under hot running water
    B. place the hands in lukewarm water
    C. call a hospital and wait for medical aid
    D. rub the hands in melting snow

24. While on duty, an officer sees a woman apparently in a   24.___
    state of shock.
    Of the following, which one is NOT a symptom of shock?
    A. Eyes lacking luster
    B. A cold, moist forehead
    C. A shallow, irregular breathing
    D. A strong, throbbing pulse

25. You notice a man entering your building who begins   25.___
    coughing violently, has shortness of breath, and complains
    of severe chest pains.
    These symptoms are GENERALLY indicative of
    A. a heart attack   B. a stroke
    C. internal bleeding   D. an epileptic seizure

26. When an officer is required to record the rolled finger-   26.___
    print impressions of a prisoner on the standard fingerprint
    form, the technique recommended by the F.B.I. as MOST
    likely to result in obtaining clear impressions is to roll
    A. all fingers away from the center of the prisoner's body
    B. all fingers toward the center of the prisoner's body
    C. the thumbs away from and the other fingers toward the
       center of the prisoner's body
    D. the thumbs toward and the other fingers away from the
       center of the prisoner's body

27. The principle which underlies the operation and use of a   27.___
    lie detector machine is that
    A. a person who is not telling the truth will be able
       to give a consistent story
    B. a guilty mind will unconsciously associate ideas in
       a very indicative manner
    C. the presence of emotional stress in a person will
       result in certain abnormal physical reactions .
    D. many individuals are not afraid to lie

Questions 28-32.

DIRECTIONS: Questions 28 through 32 are based SOLELY on the
             following diagram and the paragraph preceding this
             group of questions. The paragraph will be divided
             into two statements. Statement one (1) consists of
             information given to the senior officer by an agency
             director; *this information will detail the specific
             security objectives the senior officer has to meet.*
             Statement two (2) gives the resources available to
             the senior officer.

NOTE: The questions are correctly answered only when all of the agency's objectives have been met and when the officer has used all his resources efficiently (i.e., to their maximum effectiveness) in meeting these objectives. All X's in the diagram indicate possible locations of officers' posts. Each X has a corresponding number which is to be used when referring to that location.

DIAGRAM

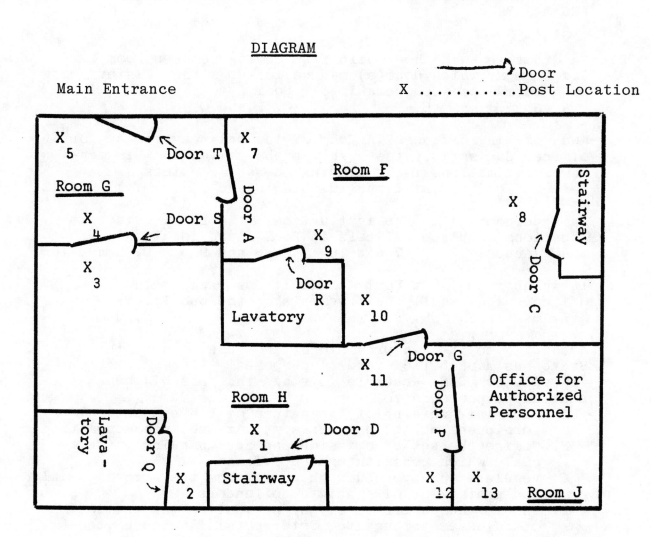

PARAGRAPH

STATEMENT 1: Room G will be the public intake room from which persons will be directed to Room F or Room H; under no circumstances are they to enter the wrong room, and they are not to move from Room F to Room H or vice-versa. A minimum of two officers must be in each room frequented by the public at all times, and they are to keep unauthorized individuals from going to the second floor or into restricted areas. All usable entrances or exits must be covered.

STATEMENT 2: The senior officer can lock any door except the main entrance and stairway doors. He has a staff of five officers to carry out these operations.

NOTE: The senior officer is available for guard duty. Room J is an active office.

28. According to the instructions, how many officers should be assigned inside the office for authorized personnel (Room J)?
    A. 0   B. 1   C. 2   D. 3

28.___

29. In order to keep the public from moving between Room F and Room H, which door(s) can be locked without interfering with normal office operations? Door
    A. G   B. P   C. R and Q   D. S

29.___

30. When placing officers in Room H, the only way the senior officer can satisfy the agency's objectives and his man-power limitations is by placing men at locations
    A. 1 and 3   B. 1 and 12   C. 3 and 11   D. 11 and 12

30.___

31. In accordance with the instructions, the LEAST effective locations to place officers in Room F are locations
    A. 7 and 9   B. 7 and 10   C. 8 and 9   D. 9 and 10

31.___

32. In which room is it MOST difficult for each of the officers to see all the movements of the public? Room
    A. G   B. F   C. H   D. J

32.___

33. According to its own provisions, the Penal Law of the State has a number of general purposes.
It would be LEAST accurate to state that one of these general purposes is to
    A. give fair warning of the nature of the conduct forbidden and the penalties authorized upon conviction
    B. define the act or omission and accompanying mental state which constitute each offense
    C. regulate the procedure which governs the arrest, trial, and punishment of convicted offenders
    D. insure the public safety by preventing the commission of offenses through the deterrent influence of the sentences authorized upon conviction

33.___

34. Officers must be well-informed about the meaning of certain terms in connection with their enforcement duties. Which one of the following statements about such terms would be MOST accurate according to the Penal Law of the State? A(n)
    A. offense is always a crime
    B. offense is always a violation
    C. violation is never a crime
    D. felony is never an offense

34.___

35. According to the Penal Law of the State, the one of the following elements which must ALWAYS be present in order to justify the arrest of a person for criminal assault is
    A. the infliction of an actual physical injury
    B. an intent to cause an injury
    C. a threat to inflict a physical injury
    D. the use of some kind of weapon

35.___

36. A recent law of the State defines who are police officers and who are peace officers.
    The official title of this law is: The
    A. Criminal Code of Procedure
    B. Law of Criminal Procedure
    C. Criminal Procedure Law
    D. Code of Criminal Procedure

36.___

37. If you are required to appear in court to testify as the complainant in a criminal action, it would be MOST important for you to
    A. confine your answers to the questions asked when you are testifying
    B. help the prosecutor even if some exaggeration in your testimony may be necessary
    C. be as fair as possible to the defendant even if some details have to be omitted from your testimony
    D. avoid contradicting other witnesses testifying against the defendant

37.___

38. A senior officer is asked by the television news media to explain to the public what happened on his post during an important incident.
    When speaking with departmental permission in front of the tape recorders and cameras, the senior officer can give the MOST favorable impression of himself and his department by
    A. refusing to answer any questions but remaining calm in front of the cameras
    B. giving a detailed report of the wrong decisions made by his agency for handling the particular incident
    C. presenting the appropriate factual information in a competent way
    D. telling what should have been done during the incident and how such incidents will be handled in the future

38.___

39. Of the following suggested guidelines for officers, the one which is LEAST likely to be effective in promoting good manners and courtesy in their daily contacts with the public is:
    A. Treat inquiries by telephone in the same manner as those made in person
    B. Never look into the face of the person to whom you are speaking
    C. Never give misinformation in answer to any inquiry on a matter on which you are uncertain of the facts
    D. Show respect and consideration in both trivial and important contacts with the public

39.___

40. Assume you are an officer who has had a record of submit-   40.___
    ting late weekly reports and that you are given an order
    by your supervisor which is addressed to all line officers.
    The order states that weekly reports will be replaced by
    twice-weekly reports.
    The MOST logical conclusion for you to make, of the
    following, is:
    A. Fully detailed information was missing from your past
       reports
    B. Most officers have submitted late reports
    C. The supervisor needs more timely information
    D. The supervisor is attempting to punish you for your
       past late reports

41. A young man with long hair and "mod" clothing makes a   41.___
    complaint to an officer about the rudeness of another
    officer.
    If the senior officer is not on the premises, the officer
    receiving the complaint should
    A. consult with the officer who is being accused to see
       if the youth's story is true
    B. refer the young man to central headquarters
    C. record the complaint made against his fellow officer
       and ask the youth to wait until he can locate the
       senior officer
    D. search for the senior officer and bring him back to
       the site of the complainant

42. During a demonstration, which area should ALWAYS be kept   42.___
    clear of demonstrators?
    A. Water fountains   B. Seating areas
    C. Doorways   D. Restrooms

43. During demonstrations, an officer's MOST important duty   43.___
    is to
    A. aid the agency's employees to perform their duties
    B. promptly arrest those who might cause incidents
    C. promptly disperse the crowds of demonstrators
    D. keep the demonstrators from disrupting order

44. Of the following, what is the FIRST action a senior   44.___
    officer should take if a demonstration develops in his
    area without advance warning?
    A. Call for additional assistance from the police
       department
    B. Find the leaders of the demonstrators and discuss
       their demands
    C. See if the demonstrators intend to break the law
    D. Inform his superiors of the event taking place

45. If a senior officer is informed in the morning that a   45.___
    demonstration will take place during the afternoon at his
    assigned location, he should assemble his officers to
    discuss the nature and aspects of this demonstration.
    Of the following, the subject which it is LEAST important
    to discuss during this meeting is

A. making a good impression if an officer is called before the television cameras for a personal interview
B. the known facts and causes of the demonstration
C. the attitude and expected behavior of the demonstrators
D. the individual responsibilities of the officers during the demonstration

46. A male officer has probable reason to believe that a group   46.___
of women occupying the ladies' toilet are using illicit
drugs.
The BEST action, of the following, for the officer to take
is to
    A. call for assistance and, with the aid of such assistance, enter the toilet and escort the occupants outside
    B. ignore the situation but recommend that the ladies' toilet be closed temporarily
    C. immediately rush into the ladies' toilet and search the occupants therein
    D. knock on the door of the ladies' toilet and ask their permission to enter so that he will not be accused of trying to molest them

47. Assume that you know that a group of demonstrators will   47.___
not cooperate with your request to throw handbills in a
waste basket instead of on the sidewalk. You ask one of
the leaders of the group, who agrees with you, to speak
to the demonstrators and ask for their cooperation in this
matter.
Your request of the group leader is
    A. *desirable*, chiefly because an officer needs civilians to control the public since the officer is usually unfriendly to the views of public groups
    B. *undesirable*, chiefly because an officer should never request a civilian to perform his duties
    C. *desirable*, chiefly because the appeal of an acknowledged leader helps in gaining group cooperation
    D. *undesirable*, chiefly because an institutional leader is motivated to maneuver a situation to gain his own personal advantage

48. A vague letter received from a female employee in the   48.___
agency accuses an officer of improper conduct.
The initial investigative interview by the senior officer
assigned to check the accusation should GENERALLY be with
the
    A. accused officer
    B. female employee
    C. highest superior about disciplinary action against the officer
    D. immediate supervisor of the female employee

Questions 49-50.

DIRECTIONS: Questions 49 and 50 are to be answered SOLELY on the
              basis of the information in the following paragraph.

*The personal conduct of each member of the Department is the
primary factor in promoting desirable police-community relations.
Tact, patience, and courtesy shall be strictly observed under all
circumstances. A favorable public attitude toward the police must
be earned; it is influenced by the personal conduct and attitude
of each member of the force, by his personal integrity and courteous
manner, by his respect for due process of law, by his devotion to
the principles of justice, fairness, and impartiality.*

49. According to the preceding paragraph, what is the BEST   49.____
    action an officer can take in dealing with people in a
    neighborhood?
      A. Assist neighborhood residents by doing favors for
         them.
      B. Give special attention to the community leaders in
         order to be able to control them effectively.
      C. Behave in an appropriate manner and give all community
         members the same just treatment.
      D. Prepare a plan detailing what he, the officer, wants
         to do for the community and submit it for approval.

50. As used in the paragraph, the word *impartiality* means   50.____
    most nearly
      A. observant   B. unbiased
      C. righteousness   D. honesty

KEY (CORRECT ANSWERS)

1. B	11. B	21. A	31. D	41. C
2. B	12. A	22. C	32. C	42. C
3. A	13. C	23. B	33. C	43. D
4. A	14. D	24. D	34. C	44. D
5. D	15. B	25. A	35. A	45. A
6. C	16. B	26. D	36. C	46. A
7. D	17. A	27. C	37. A	47. C
8. C	18. B	28. A	38. C	48. B
9. D	19. D	29. A	39. B	49. C
10. C	20. B	30. B	40. C	50. B

TEST 2

DIRECTIONS: Each question or incomplete statement is followed by several suggested answers or completions. Select the one that BEST answers the question or completes the statement. *PRINT THE LETTER OF THE CORRECT ANSWER IN THE SPACE AT THE RIGHT.*

Questions 1-5.

DIRECTIONS: Questions 1 through 5 consist of short paragraphs. Each paragraph contains one word which is INCORRECTLY used because it is NOT in keeping with the meaning of the paragraph. Find the word in each paragraph which is INCORRECTLY used, and then select as the answer the suggested word which should be substituted for the incorrectly used word.

SAMPLE QUESTION

In determining who is to do the work in your unit, you will have to decide just who does what from day to day. One of your lowest responsibilities is to assign work so that everybody gets a fair share and that everyone can do his part well.
    A. new   B. old   C. important   D. performance

EXPLANATION

The word which is NOT in keeping with the meaning of the paragraph is "lowest". This is the INCORRECTLY used word. The suggested word "important" would be in keeping with the meaning of the paragraph and should be substituted for "lowest". Therefore, the CORRECT answer is Choice C.

1. If really good practice in the elimination of preventable injuries is to be achieved and held in any establishment, top management must refuse full and definite responsibility and must apply a good share of its attention to the task.   1.___
    A. accept   B. avoidable   C. duties   D. problem

2. Recording the human face for identification is by no means the only service performed by the camera in the field of investigation. When the trial of any issue takes place, a word picture is sought to be distorted to the court of incidents, occurrences, or events which are in dispute.   2.___
    A. appeals   B. description
    C. portrayed   D. deranged

3. In the collection of physical evidence, it cannot be emphasized too strongly that a haphazard systematic search at the scene of the crime is vital. Nothing must be overlooked. Often the only leads in a case will come from the results of this search.   3.___

A. important   B. investigation
C. proof ·   D. thorough

4. If an investigator has reason to suspect that the witness   4.___
   is mentally stable or a habitual drunkard, he should leave
   no stone unturned in his investigation to determine if the
   witness was under the influence of liquor or drugs, or was
   mentally unbalanced either at the time of the occurrence
   to which he testified or at the time of the trial.
       A. accused   B. clue   C. deranged   D. question

5. The use of records is a valuable step in crime investiga-   5.___
   tion and is the main reason every department should maintain
   accurate reports. Crimes are not committed through the
   use of departmental records alone but from the use of all
   records, of almost every type, wherever they may be found
   and whenever they give any incidental information regarding
   the criminal.
       A. accidental   B. necessary   C. reported   D. solved

Questions 6-8.

DIRECTIONS: Questions 6 through 8 are to be answered SOLELY on
               the basis of the following passage.

*The mass media are an integral part of the daily life of virtually
every American. Among these media, the youngest, television, is the
most persuasive. Ninety-five percent of American homes have at least
one television set, and on the average that set is in use for about 40
hours each week. The central place of television in American life
makes this medium the focal point of a growing national concern over
the effects of media portrayals of violence on the values, attitudes,
and behavior of an ever increasing audience.*

*In our concern about violence and its causes, it is easy to make
television a scapegoat. But we emphasize the fact that there is no
simple answer to the problem of violence -- no single explanation of
its causes, and no single prescription for its control. It should
be remembered that America also experienced high levels of crime and
violence in periods before the advent of television.*

*The problem of balance, taste, and artistic merit in entertaining
programs on television are complex. We cannot <u>countenance</u> government
censorship of television. Nor would we seek to impose arbitrary
limitations on programming which might jeopardize television's ability
to deal in dramatic presentations with controversial social issues.
Nonetheless, we are deeply troubled by television's constant portrayal
of violence, not in any genuine attempt to focus artistic expression
on the human condition, but rather in pandering to a public preoccupa-
tion with violence that television itself has helped to generate.*

6. According to the passage, television uses violence MAINLY   6.___
       A. to highlight the reality of everyday existence
       B. to satisfy the audience's hunger for destructive action
       C. to shape the values and attitudes of the public
       D. when it films documentaries concerning human conflict

7. Which one of the following statements is BEST supported   7.___
   by this passage?
   A. Early American history reveals a crime pattern which
      is not related to television.
   B. Programs should give presentations of social issues
      and never portray violent acts.
   C. Television has proven that entertainment programs can
      easily make the balance between taste and artistic
      merit a simple matter.
   D. Values and behavior should be regulated by governmental
      censorship.

8. Of the following, which word has the same meaning as   8.___
   countenance, as it is used in the above passage?
   A. approve   B. exhibit   C. oppose   D. reject

Questions 9-12.

DIRECTIONS: Questions 9 through 12 are to be answered SOLELY on
              the basis of the following graph relating to the
              burglary rate in the city, 1973 to 1978, inclusive.

BURGLARY RATE - 1973-1978

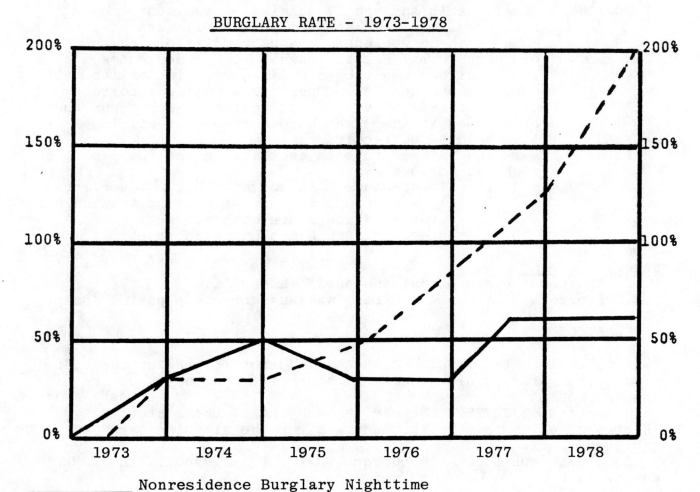

_____ Nonresidence Burglary Nighttime

------------ Nonresidence Burglary Daytime

1973-1978

9. At the beginning of what year was the percentage increase   9.___
   in daytime and nighttime burglaries the SAME?
   A. 1974   B. 1975   C. 1976   D. 1978

10. In what year did the percentage of nighttime burglaries   10.___
    DECREASE?
    A. 1973   B. 1975   C. 1976   D. 1978

11. In what year was there the MOST rapid increase in the   11.___
    percentage of daytime non-residence burglaries?
    A. 1974   B. 1976   C. 1977   D. 1978

12. At the end of 1977, the actual number of nighttime   12.___
    burglaries committed
    A. was about 20%
    B. was 40%
    C. was 400
    D. cannot be determined from the information given

Questions 13-17.

DIRECTIONS: Questions 13 through 17 consist of two sentences
                 numbered 1 and 2 taken from police officers' reports.
                 Some of these sentences are correct according to
                 ordinary formal English usage. Other sentences are
                 incorrect because they contain errors in English
                 usage or punctuation. Consider a sentence correct
                 if it contains no errors in English usage or punctu-
                 ation even if there may be other ways of writing
                 the sentence correctly.
                 Mark your answer to each question in the space at the
                 right as follows:
                 A. If only sentence 1 is correct, but not sentence 2
                 B. If only sentence 2 is correct, but not sentence 1
                 C. If sentences 1 and 2 are both correct
                 D. If sentences 1 and 2 are both incorrect

SAMPLE QUESTION
   1. The woman claimed that the purse was her's.
   2. Everyone of the new officers was assigned to a patrol post.

EXPLANATION

   Sentence 1 is INCORRECT because of an error in punctuation. The
possessive words, "ours, yours, hers, theirs," do not have the
apostrophe (').
   Sentence 2 is CORRECT because the subject of the sentence is
"Everyone" which is singular and requires the singular verb "was
assigned".
   Since only sentence 2 is correct, but not sentence 1, the CORRECT
answer is B.

13.   1. Either the patrolman or his sergeant are always ready   13.___
         to help the public.
      2. The sergeant asked the patrolman when he would finish
         the report.

14. 1. The injured man could not hardly talk.   14.___
     2. Every officer had ought to hand in their reports on time.

15. 1. Approaching the victim of the assault, two large   15.___
        bruises were noticed by me.
     2. The prisoner was arrested for assault, resisting
        arrest, and use of a deadly weapon.

16. 1. A copy of the orders, which had been prepared by the   16.___
        captain, was given to each patrolman.
     2. It's always necessary to inform an arrested person of
        his constitutional rights before asking him any questions.

17. 1. To prevent further bleeding, I applied a tourniquet to   17.___
        the wound.
     2. John Rano a senior officer was on duty at the time of
        the accident.

Questions 18-25.

DIRECTIONS: Answer each of Questions 18 through 25 SOLELY on the
              basis of the statement preceding the questions.

18. The criminal is one whose habits have been erroneously   18.___
     developed or, we should say, developed in anti-social
     patterns, and therefore the task of dealing with him is
     not one of punishment, but of treatment.
     The basic principle expressed in this statement is BEST
     illustrated by the
         A. emphasis upon rehabilitation in penal institutions
         B. prevalence of capital punishment for murder
         C. practice of imposing heavy fines for minor violations
         D. legal provision for trial by jury in criminal cases

19. The writ of habeas corpus is one of the great guarantees   19.___
     of personal liberty.
     Of the following, the BEST justification for this statement
     is that the writ of habeas corpus is frequently used to
         A. compel the appearance in court of witnesses who are
            outside the state
         B. obtain the production of books and records at a
            criminal trial
         C. secure the release of a person improperly held in
            custody
         D. prevent the use of deception in obtaining testimony
            of reluctant witnesses

20. Fifteen persons suffered effects of carbon dioxide   20.___
     asphyxiation shortly before noon recently in a seventh-
     floor pressing shop. The accident occurred in a closed
     room where six steam presses were in operation. Four men
     and one woman were overcome.
     Of the following, the MOST probable reason for the fact
     that so many people were affected simultaneously is that
         A. women evidently show more resistance to the effects
            of carbon dioxide than men
         B. carbon dioxide is an odorless and colorless gas

C. carbon dioxide is lighter than air
D. carbon dioxide works more quickly at higher altitudes

21. Lay the patient on his stomach, one arm extended directly   21.___
    overhead, the other arm bent at the elbow, and with the
    face turned outward and resting on hand or forearm.
    To the officer who is skilled at administering first aid,
    these instructions should IMMEDIATELY suggest
        A. application of artificial respiration
        B. treatment for third degree burns of the arm
        C. setting a dislocated shoulder
        D. control of capillary bleeding in the stomach

22. The soda and acid fire extinguisher is the hand extinguish- 22.___
    er most commonly used by officers. The main body of the
    cylinder is filled with a mixture of water and bicarbonate
    of soda. In a separate interior compartment, at the top,
    is a small bottle of sulphuric acid. When the extinguisher
    is inverted, the acid spills into the solution below and
    starts a chemical reaction. The carbon dioxide thereby
    generated forces the solution from the extinguisher.
    The officer who understands the operation of this fire
    extinguisher should know that it is LEAST likely to operate
    properly
        A. in basements or cellars
        B. in extremely cold weather
        C. when the reaction is of a chemical nature
        D. when the bicarbonate of soda is in solution

23. Suppose that, at a training lecture, you are told that   23.___
    many of the men in our penal institutions today are
    second and third offenders.
    Of the following, the MOST valid inference you can make
    SOLELY on the basis of this statement is that
        A. second offenders are not easily apprehended
        B. patterns of human behavior are not easily changed
        C. modern laws are not sufficiently flexible
        D. laws do not breed crimes

24. In all societies of our level of culture, acts are   24.___
    committed which arouse censure severe enough to take the
    form of punishment by the government. Such acts are crimes,
    not because of their inherent nature, but because of their
    ability to arouse resentment and to stimulate repressive
    measures.
    Of the following, the MOST valid inference which can be
    drawn from this statement is that
        A. society unjustly punishes acts which are inherently
           criminal
        B. many acts are not crimes but are punished by society
           because such acts threaten the lives of innocent people
        C. only modern society has a level of culture
        D. societies sometimes disagree as to what acts are crimes

25. Crime cannot be measured directly. Its amount must be   25.___
    inferred .from the frequency of some occurrence connected
    with it; for example, crimes brought to the attention of
    the police, persons arrested, prosecutions, convictions,
    and other dispositions, such as probation or commitment.
    Each of these may be used as an index of the amount of
    crime. SOLELY on the basis of the foregoing statement, it
    is MOST correct to state that
    A. the incidence of crime cannot be estimated with any
       accuracy
    B. the number of commitments is usually greater than the
       number of probationary sentences
    C. the amount of crime is ordinarily directly correlated
       with the number of persons arrested
    D. a joint consideration of crimes brought to the
       attention of the police and the number of prosecutions
       undertaken gives little indication of the amount of
       crime in a locality

_____

KEY (CORRECT ANSWERS)

1.	B	11.	D
2.	C	12.	D
3.	D	13.	D
4.	C	14.	D
5.	D	15.	B
6.	B	16.	C
7.	A	17.	A
8.	A	18.	A
9.	A	19.	C
10.	B	20.	B

21.	A
22.	B
23.	B
24.	D
25.	C

_____

EXAMINATION SECTION

TEST 1

DIRECTIONS: Each question or incomplete statement is followed by
several suggested answers or completions. Select the
one that BEST answers the question or completes the
statement. *PRINT THE LETTER OF THE CORRECT ANSWER IN
THE SPACE AT THE RIGHT.*

Questions 1-4.

DIRECTIONS: Questions 1 through 4 are to be answered on the basis
of the following passage.

Those engaged in the exercise of First Amendment rights by
pickets, marches, parades, and open-air assemblies are not exempted
from obeying valid local traffic ordinances. In a recent pronounce-
ment, Mr. Justice Baxter, speaking for the Supreme Court, wrote:

*The rights of free speech and assembly, while fundamental to
our democratic society, still do not mean that everyone with
opinions or beliefs to express may address a group at any
public place and at any time. The constitutional guarantee
of liberty implies the existence of an organized society
maintaining public order, without which liberty itself would
be lost in the excesses of anarchy. The control of travel
on the streets is a clear example of governmental responsibility to insure this necessary order. A restriction in that
relation, designed to promote the public convenience in the
interest of all, and not susceptible to abuses of discriminatory application, cannot be disregarded by the attempted
exercise of some civil rights which, in other circumstances,
would be entitled to protection. One would not be justified
in ignoring the familiar red light because this was thought
to be a means of social protest. Governmental authorities
have the duty and responsibility to keep their streets open
and available for movement. A group of demonstrators could
not insist upon the right to cordon off a street, or entrance
to a public or private building, and allow no one to pass
who did not agree to listen to their exhortations.*

1. Which of the following statements BEST reflects Mr.   1.___
Justice Baxter's view of the relationship between liberty
and public order?
    A. Public order cannot exist without liberty.
    B. Liberty cannot exist without public order.
    C. The existence of liberty undermines the existence of
       public order.
    D. The maintenance of public order insures the existence
       of liberty.

2. According to the above passage, local traffic ordinances
   result from   2.___
   A. governmental limitations on individual liberty
   B. governmental responsibility to insure public order
   C. majority rule as determined by democratic procedures
   D. restrictions on expression of dissent

3. The foregoing passage suggests that government would be   3.___
   acting IMPROPERLY if a local traffic ordinance
   A. was enforced in a discriminatory manner
   B. resulted in public inconvenience
   C. violated the right of free speech and assembly
   D. was not essential to public order

4. Of the following, the MOST appropriate title for the above 4.___
   passage is:
   A. THE RIGHTS OF FREE SPEECH AND ASSEMBLY
   B. ENFORCEMENT OF LOCAL TRAFFIC ORDINANCES
   C. FIRST AMENDMENT RIGHTS AND LOCAL TRAFFIC ORDINANCES
   D. LIBERTY AND ANARCHY

Questions 5-8.

DIRECTIONS: Questions 5 through 8 are to be answered on the basis
of the following passage.

On November 8, 1976, the Supreme Court refused to block the payment of Medicaid funds for elective abortions. The Court's action means that a new Federal statute that bars the use of Federal funds for abortions unless abortion is necessary to save the life of the mother will not go into effect for many months, if at all.

A Federal District Court in Brooklyn ruled the following month that the statute was unconstitutional and ordered that Federal reimbursement for the costs of abortions continue on the same basis as reimbursements for the costs of pregnancy and childbirth-related services.

Technically, what the Court did today was to deny a request by Senator Howard Ramsdell and others for a stay blocking enforcement of the District Court order pending appeal. The Court's action was a victory for New York City. The City's Health and Hospitals Corporation initiated one of the two lawsuits challenging the new statute that led to the District Court's decision. The Corporation also opposed the request for a Supreme Court stay of that decision, telling the Court in a memorandum that a stay would subject the Corporation to a "grave and irreparable injury."

5. According to the above passage, it would be CORRECT to   5.___
   state that the Health and Hospitals Corporation
   A. joined Senator Ramsdell in his request for a stay
   B. opposed the statute which limited reimbursement for
   the cost of abortions

       C. claimed that it would experience a loss if the
          District Court order was enforced
       D. appealed the District Court decision

6. The above passage indicates that the Supreme Court acted   6.___
   in DIRECT response to
       A. a lawsuit initiated by the Health and Hospitals
          Corporation
       B. a ruling by a Federal District Court
       C. a request for a stay
       D. the passage of a new Federal statute

7. According to the above passage, it would be CORRECT to   7.___
   state that the Supreme Court
       A. blocked enforcement of the District Court order
       B. refused a request for a stay to block enforcement of
          the Federal statute
       C. ruled that the new Federal statute was unconstitutional
       D. permitted payment of Federal funds for abortion to
          continue

8. Following are three statements concerning abortion that   8.___
   might be correct:
      I. Abortion costs are no longer to be Federally reimbursed
        on the same basis as those for pregnancy and child-
        birth
     II. Federal funds have not been available for abortions
        except to save the life of the mother
   III. Medicaid has paid for elective abortions in the past

   According to the passage given above, which of the following CORRECTLY classifies the above statements into those
   that are true and those that are not true?
       A. I is true, but II and III are not.
       B. I and III are true, but II is not.
       C. I and II are true, but III is not.
       D. III is true, but I and II are not.

9. A legal memorandum will often include the following six   9.___
   sections:
      I. Conclusions   II. Issues
    III. Analysis   IV. Facts
      V. Unknowns   VI. Counter-analysis

   Which of the following choices lists these sections in
   the sequence that is generally MOST appropriate for a
   legal memorandum?
      A. III, VI, IV, V, II, I   B. IV, II, III, VI, I, V
      C. V, II, IV, III, VI, I   D. II, IV, V, III, I, VI

Questions 10-13.

DIRECTIONS: Questions 10 through 13 consist of two sentences each. The sentences deal with the use of court opinions and cases in the writing of legal memoranda.
Select answer
 A. if only sentence I is correct
 B. if only sentence II is correct
 C. if both sentences are correct
 D. if neither sentence is correct

10. I. State the issues in the case as narrowly and precisely as possible. 10._____
 II. Quote frequently and at great length from the court opinions.

11. I. Describe briefly the issues in the case that are not related to your problem. 11._____
 II. Do not mention discrepancies between the facts of the case and the facts of your problem.

12. I. Do not refer to the holding or ruling in the case if it is harmful to your client. 12._____
 II. If the holding or ruling in the case is beneficial to your client, try to show that the facts of your problem are analogous to the facts of the case.

13. I. After stating your position concerning the issues and facts, present the opposite viewpoint as effectively as you can. 13._____
 II. Avoid stating your own opinions or conclusions concerning the applicability of the case.

14. Column V lists four publications in the legal field. Column W contains descriptions of basic subject matter of legal publications. 14._____
Select the one of the following choices which BEST matches the publications in Column V with the subject matter in Column W.

Column V	Column W
I. Harvard Law Review	1. Law
II. Supreme Court Reporter	2. Commentary on law
III. McKinney's Consolidated Laws of New York	3. Combination of law and commentary
IV. The Criminal Law Reporter	

A. I-3; II-1; III-2; IV-3 B. I-2; II-3; III-2; IV-3
C. I-2; II-1; III-3; IV-3 D. I-2; II-3; III-3; IV-1

15. Tickler systems are used in many legal offices for   15.___
    scheduling and calendar control.
    Of the following, the LEAST common use of a tickler system
    is to
    A. keep papers filed in such a way that they may easily
       be retrieved
    B. arrange for the appearance of witnesses when they
       will be needed
    C. remind lawyers when certain papers are due
    D. arrange for the gathering of certain types of evidence

---

KEY (CORRECT ANSWERS)

1. B	6. C	11. D
2. B	7. D	12. B
3. A	8. D	13. A
4. C	9. B	14. C
5. B	10. A	15. A

TEST 2

DIRECTIONS: Each question or incomplete statement is followed by several suggested answers or completions. Select the one that BEST answers the question or completes the statement. *PRINT THE LETTER OF THE CORRECT ANSWER IN THE SPACE AT THE RIGHT.*

1. Studying the legislative history of a statute by reading the transcript of the hearings that were held on that subject is useful to the legal researcher PRIMARILY because it
   A. is informative of the manner in which laws are enacted
   B. helps him to understand the intent of the statute
   C. provides leads to statutes on the same subject
   D. clarifies the meaning of other statutes

1.___

2. Following are three statements concerning legal research that might be correct:
   I. The researcher may begin with a particular premise and, in researching it, may discover an entirely new approach to the problem
   II. When the researcher has located a relevant statute, it is not necessary to read court opinions interpreting or applying this statute
   III. A statute which is related to, but not the same as, the point being researched may have notes which will refer the researcher to more relevant cases

   Which of the following ACCURATELY classifies the above statements into those which are correct and those which are not?
   A. II and III are correct, but I is not.
   B. I and III are correct, but II is not.
   C. I and II are correct, but III is not.
   D. I, II, and III are all correct.

2.___

3. Of the following, the FIRST action a legal researcher should take in order to locate the laws relevant to a case is to
   A. search the index of a law book
   B. read statutes on similar subjects to discover pertinent annotations
   C. read a legal digest to become familiar with the law on the subject
   D. prepare a list of descriptive words applicable to the facts of the case

3.___

4. Which of the following is the BEST source for a legal researcher to consult in order to find historical data, cross-references, and case excerpts on cases, statutes, and regulations?
   A. Annotations   B. Digests
   C. Hornbooks   D. Casebooks

4.___

Questions 5-8.

DIRECTIONS: Each of Questions 5 through 8 contains two sentences concerning criminal law. Some of the sentences contain errors in English grammar or usage. A sentence does not contain an error simply because it could be written in a different manner.
For each question, choose answer
    A. if only sentence I is correct
    B. if only sentence II is correct
    C. if both sentences are correct
    D. if neither sentence is correct

5.   I. Limiting the term *property* to tangible property, in the criminal mischief setting, accords with prior case law holding that only tangible property came within the purview of the offense of malicious mischief.
   II. Thus, a person who intentionally destroys the property of another, but under an honest belief that he has title to such property, cannot be convicted of criminal mischief under the Revised Penal Law.

5.___

6.   I. Very early in its history, New York enacted statutes from time to time punishing, either as a felony or as a misdemeanor, malicious injuries to various kinds of property: piers, booms, dams, bridges, etc.
   II. The application of the statute is necessarily restricted to trespassory takings with larcenous intent: namely with intent permanently or virtually permanently to *appropriate* property or *deprive* the owner of its use.

6.___

7.   I. Since the former Penal Law did not define the instruments of forgery in a general fashion, its crime of forgery was held to be narrower than the common law offense in this respect and to embrace only those instruments explicitly specified in the substantive provisions.
   II. After entering the barn through an open door for the purpose of stealing, it was closed by the defendants.

7.___

8.   I. The use of fire or explosives to destroy tangible property is proscribed by the criminal mischief provisions of the Revised Penal Law.
   II. The defendant's taking of a taxicab for the immediate purpose of affecting his escape did not constitute grand larceny

8.___

Questions 9-13:

DIRECTIONS: Questions 9 through 13 are to be answered SOLELY on the basis of the following passage.

The law is quite clear that evidence obtained in violation of Section 605 of the Federal Communications Act is not admissible in federal court.   However, the law as to the admissibility of evidence in state court is far from clear.   Had the Supreme Court of the United States made the wiretap exclusionary rule applicable to the states, such confusion would not exist.

In the case of Alton v. Texas, the Supreme Court was called upon to determine whether wiretapping by state and local officers came within the proscription of the federal statute and, if so, whether Section 605 required the same remedies for its vindication in state courts.   In answer to the first question, Mr. Justice Minton, speaking for the court, flatly stated that Section 605 made it a federal crime for anyone to intercept telephone messages and divulge what he learned.   The court went on to say that a state officer who testified in state court concerning the existence, contents, substance, purport, effect or meaning of an intercepted conversation violated the federal law and committed a criminal act. In regard to the second question, however, the Supreme Court felt constrained by due regard for federal-state relations to answer in the negative.   Mr. Justice Minton stated that the court would not presume, in the absence of a clear manifestation of congressional intent, that Congress intended to supersede state rules of evidence.

Because the Supreme Court refused to apply the exclusionary rule to wiretap evidence that was being used in state courts, the states respectively made this decision for themselves.   According to hearings held before a congressional committee in 1975, six states authorize wiretapping by statute, 33 states impose total bans on wiretapping, and 11 states have no definite statute on the subject.   For examples of extremes, a statute in Pennsylvania will be compared with a statute in New York.

The Pennsylvania statute provides that no communications by telephone or telegraph can be intercepted without permission of both parties.   It also specifically prohibits such interception by public officials and provides that evidence obtained cannot be used in court.

The lawmakers in New York, recognizing the need for legal wiretapping, authorized wiretapping by statute.   A New York law authorizes the issuance of an ex parte order upon oath or affirmation for limited wiretapping.   The aim of the New York law is to allow court-ordered wiretapping and to encourage the testimony of state officers concerning such wiretapping in court.   The New York law was found to be constitutional by the New York State Supreme Court in 1975.   Other states, including Oregon, Maryland, Nevada, and Massachusetts, enacted similar laws which authorize court-ordered wiretapping.

To add to this legal disarray, the vast majority of the states, including New Jersey and New York, permit wiretapping evidence to be received in court even though obtained in violation of the state laws and of Section 605 of the Federal act. However, some states such as Rhode Island have enacted statutory exclusionary rules which provide that illegally procured wiretap evidence is incompetent in civil as well as criminal actions.

9. According to the above passage, a state officer who testifies in New York State court concerning the contents of a conversation he overheard through a court-ordered wiretap is in violation of _____ law.
    A. state law but not federal
    B. federal law but not state
    C. federal law and state
    D. neither federal nor state

9.___

10. According to the above passage, which of the following statements concerning states statutes on wiretapping is CORRECT?
    A. The number of states that impose total bans on wiretapping is three times as great as the number of states with no definite statute on wiretapping.
    B. The number of states having no definite statute on wiretapping is more than twice the number of states authorizing wiretapping.
    C. The number of states which authorize wiretapping by statute and the number of states having no definite statute on wiretapping exceed the number of states imposing total bans on wiretapping.
    D. More states authorize wiretapping by statute than impose total bans on wiretapping.

10.___

11. Following are three statements concerning wiretapping that might be valid:
    I. In Pennsylvania, only public officials may legally intercept telephone communications
    II. In Rhode Island, evidence obtained through an illegal wiretap is incompetent in criminal, but not civil, actions
    III. Neither Massachusetts nor Pennsylvania authorizes wiretapping by public officials

    According to the above passage, which of the following CORRECTLY classifies these statements into those that are valid and those that are not?
    A. I is valid, but II and III are not.
    B. II is valid, but I and III are not.
    C. II and III are valid, but I is not.
    D. None of the statements is valid.

11.___

12. According to the foregoing passage, evidence obtained in   12.___
    violation of Section 605 of the Federal Communications
    Act is inadmissible in
    A. federal court but not in any state courts
    B. federal court and all state courts
    C. all state courts but not in federal court
    D. federal court and some state courts

13. In regard to state rules of evidence, Mr. Justice Minton   13.___
    expressed the Court's opinion that Congress
    A. intended to supersede state rules of evidence, as
       manifested by Section 605 of the Federal Communica-
       tions Act
    B. assumed that federal statutes would govern state
       rules of evidence in all wiretap cases
    C. left unclear whether it intended to supersede state
       rules of evidence
    D. precluded itself from superseding state rules of
       evidence through its regard for federal-state rela-
       tions

14. You begin to ask follow-up questions of a witness who has   14.___
    given a statement. The witness starts to digress before
    answering an important question satisfactorily.
    In this situation, the BEST of the following steps is to
    A. guide the interview by suggesting answers to questions
       as they are asked
    B. ask questions which can be answered only with a simple
       yes or *no*
    C. construct questions as precisely as possible
    D. tell the witness to keep his answers brief

15. During an interview with a client, you have occasion to   15.___
    refer to a matter which is described in the legal pro-
    fession by a technical term.
    Of the following, it would generally be MOST appropriate
    for you to
    A. discuss the underlying legal concept in detail
    B. avoid the subject since it is too complicated
    C. ask the client if he is familiar with the technical
       term
    D. describe the matter in everyday language

KEY (CORRECT ANSWERS)

1. B	6. B	11. D
2. B	7. A	12. D
3. D	8. A	13. C
4. A	9. B	14. C
5. C	10. A	15. D

EXAMINATION SECTION

DIRECTIONS: Each question or incomplete statement is followed by several suggested answers or completions. Select the one that BEST answers the question or completes the statement. *PRINT THE LETTER OF THE CORRECT ANSWER IN THE SPACE AT THE RIGHT.*

Questions 1-8.

DIRECTIONS: Each of Questions 1 through 8 consists of a statement which contains a word (one of those underlined) that is either incorrectly used because it is not in keeping with the meaning the quotation is evidently intended to convey or is misspelled. There is only one INCORRECT word in each quotation. Of the four underlined words, determine if the first one should be replaced by the word lettered A, the second replaced by the word lettered B, the third replaced by the word lettered C, or the fourth replaced by the word lettered D. Print the letter of the replacement word you have selected in the space at the right.

1. Whether one depends on fluorescent or artificial light or   1.____
   both, adequate standards should be maintained by means of
   systematic tests.
       A. natural   B. safeguards
       C. established   D. routine

2. A policeman has to be prepared to assume his knowledge as   2.____
   a social scientist in the community.
       A. forced   B. role
       C. philosopher   D. street

3. It is practically impossible to indicate whether a sen-   3.____
   tence is too long simply by measuring its length.
       A. almost   B. tell   C. very   D. guessing

4. Strong leaders are required to organize a community for   4.____
   delinquency prevention and for dissemination of organized
   crime and drug addiction.
       A. tactics   B. important C. control   D. meetings

5. The demonstrators, who were taken to the Criminal Courts   5.____
   building in Manhattan (because it was large enough to
   accommodate them), contended that the arrests were
   unwarrented.
       A. exhibitors   B. legirons
       C. adjudicate   D. unwarranted

6. They were <u>guaranteed</u> a calm <u>atmosphere</u>, free from <u>harrass-</u>   6.____
   <u>ment</u>, which would be conducive to quiet consideration of
   the <u>indictments</u>.
      A. guarenteed   B. atmospher
      C. harassment   D. inditements

7. The <u>alleged</u> killer was <u>occasionally</u> <u>permitted</u> to <u>excercise</u>   7.____
   in the corridor.
      A. alledged   B. ocasionally
      C. permited   D. exercise

8. Defense <u>counsel</u> stated, in <u>affect</u>, that <u>their</u> conduct was   8.____
   <u>permissible</u> under the First Amendment.
      A. council   B. effect
      C. there   D. permissable

Questions 9-12.

DIRECTIONS: Each of the two sentences in Questions 9 through 12 may
                 be correct or may contain errors in punctuation, capi-
                 talization, or grammar.
                 If there is an error only in sentence I, mark your
                 answer A.
                 If there is an error only in sentence II, mark your
                 answer B.
                 If there is an error in both sentence I and sentence II,
                 mark your answer C.
                 If both sentence I and sentence II are correct, mark
                 your answer D.

9.   I. It is very annoying to have a pencil sharpener,   9.____
         which is not in working order.
    II. Patrolman Blake checked the door of Joe's Restaurant
         and found that the lock has been jammed.

10.   I. When you are studying a good textbook is important.   10.____
     II. He said he would divide the money equally between
         you and me.

11.   I. Since he went on the city council a year ago, one of   11.____
        his primary concerns has been safety in the streets.
     II. After waiting in the doorway for about 15 minutes,
        a black sedan appeared.

12.   I. The question is, "What is the difference between a   12.____
        lawful and an unlawful demonstration?"
     II. The captain assigned two detectives, John and I, to
        the investigation.

Questions 13-14.

DIRECTIONS: In each of Questions 13 and 14, the four sentences are
from a paragraph in a report. They are not in the
right order. Which of the following arrangements is
the BEST one?

13.   I. Most organizations favor one of the types but always   13.___
     include the others to a lesser degree.
  II. However, we can detect a definite trend toward greater
     use of symbolic control.
 III. We suggest that our local police agencies are today
     primarily utilizing material control.
  IV. Control can be classified into three types: physical,
     material, and symbolic

    The CORRECT answer is:
     A. IV, II, III, I   B. II, I, IV, III
     C. III, IV, II, I   D. IV, I, III, II

14.   I. They can and do take advantage of ancient political   14.___
     and geographical boundaries, which often give them
     sanctuary from effective police activity.
  II. This country is essentially a country of small police
     forces, each operating independently within the limits
     of its jurisdiction.
 III. The boundaries that define and limit police operations
     do not hinder the movement of criminals, of course.
  IV. The machinery of law enforcement in America is frag-
     mented, complicated, and frequently overlapping.

    The CORRECT answer is:
     A. III, I, II, IV   B. II, IV, I, III
     C. IV, II, III, I   D. IV, III, II, I

15. Generally, the frequency with which reports are to be   15.___
submitted or the length of the interval which they cover
should depend MAINLY on the
    A. amount of time needed to prepare the reports
    B. degree of comprehensiveness required in the reports
    C. availability of the data to be included in the
      reports
    D. extent of the variations in the data with the passage
      of time

16. Suppose you have to write a report on a serious infraction   16.___
of rules by one of the Police Administrative Aides you
supervise. The circumstances in which the infraction
occurred are quite complicated.
The BEST way to organize this report would be to
    A. give all points equal emphasis throughout the report
    B. include more than one point in a paragraph only if
      necessary to equalize the size of paragraphs

C. place the least important points before the most
   important points
D. present each significant point in a separate paragraph

17. Suppose that police expenses in the city in a certain year   17.___
    amounted to 7.5% of total expenses.
    In indicating this percentage on a *pie* or circular chart,
    which is 360°, the size of the angle between the two
    radiuses would be MOST NEARLY
      A. 3.7°   B. 7.5°   C. 27°   D. 54°

18. Suppose that in police precinct A, where there are 4180   18.___
    children, 627 children entered a contest sponsored by
    the Police Community Relations Bureau. In precinct B,
    where there were 7840 children, 1960 children entered the
    contest.
    The total percentage of all children in both precincts
    who entered the contest amounted to MOST NEARLY
      A. 19.5%   B. 20%   C. 21.5%   D. 22.5%

19. If Circle A represents Police   19.___
    Administrative Aides (PAA's) who
    scored above 85 on a PAA test and
    Circle B represents PAA's who
    scored above 85 on a Senior PAA
    test, then the diagram at the
    right means that

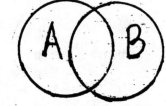

    A. no PAA who scored above 85 on a
       PAA test scored above 85 on the
       Senior PAA test
    B. the majority of PAA's who scored above 85 on a PAA
       test scored above 85 on the Senior PAA test
    C. there were some PAA's who did not take the Senior
       PAA test
    D. some PAA's who scored above 85 on a PAA test scored
       above 85 on the Senior PAA test

20. Suppose that in 1844 the city had a population of 550,000   20.___
    and a police force of 200, and that in 1982 the city had
    a population of 8,000,000 and a police force of 32,000.
    If the ratio of police to population in 1982 is compared
    with the same ratio in 1844, what is the resulting relation-
    ship of the 1982 ratio to the 1844 ratio?
      A. 160:11   B. 160:1   C. 16:1   D. 11:1

Questions 21-24.

DIRECTIONS: Questions 21 through 24 are to be answered SOLELY on
the basis of the information contained in the following
passage.

Of those arrested in the city in 1983 for felonies or misdemeanors, only 32% were found guilty of any charge. Fifty-six percent of such arrestees were acquitted or had their cases dismissed, 11% failed to appear for trial, and 1% received other dispositions. Of those found guilty, only 7.4% received any sentences of over one year in jail. Only 50% of those found guilty were sentenced to any further time in jail. When considered with the low probability of arrests for most crimes, these figures make it clear that the crime control system in the city poses little threat to the average criminal. Delay compounds the problem. The average case took four appearances for disposition after arraignment. Twenty percent of all cases took eight or more appearances to reach a disposition. Forty-four percent of all cases took more than one year to disposition.

21.   According to the above passage, crime statistics for 1983   21.___
      indicate that
      A. there is a low probability of arrests for all crimes
         in the city
      B. the average criminal has much to fear from the law in
         the city
      C. over 10% of arrestees in the city charged with felonies
         or misdemeanors did not show up for trial
      D. criminals in the city are less likely to be caught
         than criminals in the rest of the country

22.   The percentage of those arrested in 1983 who received   22.___
      sentences of over one year in jail amounted MOST NEARLY to
         A. .237   B. 2.4   C. 23.7   D. 24.0

23.   According to the above passage, the percentage of   23.___
      arrestees in 1983 who were found guilty was
      A. 20% of those arrested for misdemeanors
      B. 11% of those arrested for felonies
      C. 50% of those sentenced to further time in jail
      D. 32% of those arrested for felonies or misdemeanors

24.   According to the above paragraph, the number of appear-   24.___
      ances after arraignment and before disposition amounted to
      A. an average of four
      B. eight or more in 44% of the cases
      C. over four for cases which took more than a year
      D. between four and eight for most cases

Questions 25-27.

DIRECTIONS: Questions 25 through 27 are to be answered SOLELY on
the basis of the information contained in the following
paragraph.

*The traditional characteristics of a police organization, which
do not foster group-centered leadership, are being changed daily by
progressive police administrators. These characteristics are
authoritarian and result in a leader-centered style with all determination of policy and procedure made by the leader. In the group-
centered style, policies and procedures are a matter for group discussion and decision. The supposedly modern view is that the group-
centered style is the most conducive to improving organizational
effectiveness. By contrast, the traditional view regards the group-
centered style as an idealistic notion of psychologists. It is
questionable, however, that the situation determines the appropriate
leadership style. In some circumstances, it will be leader-centered;
in others, group-centered. Nevertheless, police supervisors will
see more situations calling for a leadership style that, while
flexible, is primarily group-centered. Thus, the supervisor in a
police department must have a capacity not just to issue orders but
to engage in behavior involving organizational leadership which
primarily emphasizes goals and work facilitation.*

25.   According to the above passage, there is reason to believe   25.___
that with regard to the effectiveness of different types
of leadership, the
   A. leader-centered type is better than the individual-
      centered type or the group-centered type
   B. leader-centered type is best in some situations and
      the group-centered type best in other situations
   C. group-centered type is better than the leader-
      centered type in all situations
   D. authoritarian type is least effective in democratic
      countries

26.   According to the above passage, police administrators   26.___
today are
   A. more likely than in the past to favor making decisions
      on the basis of discussions with subordinates
   B. likely in general to favor traditional patterns of
      leadership in their organizations
   C. more likely to be progressive than conservative
   D. practical and individualistic rather than idealistic
      in their approach to police problems

27.   According to the above passage, the role of the police   27.___
department is changing in such a way that its supervisors
must
   A. give greater consideration to the needs of individual
      subordinates
   B. be more flexible·in dealing with infractions of
      department rules

C. provide leadership which stresses the goals of the department and helps the staff to reach them
D. refrain from issuing orders and allow subordinates to decide how to carry out their assignments

Questions 28-31.

DIRECTIONS: Questions 28 through 31 are to be answered SOLELY on the basis of the information contained in the following paragraph.

Under the provisions of the Bank Protection Act of 1968, enacted July 8, 1968, each Federal banking supervisory agency, as of January 7, 1969, had to issue rules establishing minimum standards with which financial institutions under their control must comply with respect to the installation, maintenance, and operation of security devices and procedures, reasonable in cost, to discourage robberies, burglaries, and larcenies, and to assist in the identification and apprehension of persons who commit such acts. The rules set the time limits within which the affected banks and savings and loan associations must comply with the standards, and the rules require the submission of periodic reports on the steps taken. A violator of a rule under this Act is subject to a civil penalty not to exceed $100 for each day of the violation. The enforcement of these regulations rests with the responsible banking supervisory agencies.

28. The Bank Protection Act of 1968 was designed to   28.___
    A. provide Federal police protection for banks covered by the Act
    B. have organizations covered by the Act take precautions against criminals
    C. set up a system for reporting all bank robberies to the FBI
    D. insure institutions covered by the Act from financial loss due to robberies, burglaries, and larcenies

29. Under the provisions of the Bank Protection Act of 1968,   29.___
    each Federal banking supervisory agency was required to set up rules for financial institutions covered by the Act governing the
    A. hiring of personnel
    B. punishment of burglars
    C. taking of protective measures
    D. penalties for violations

30. Financial institutions covered by the Bank Protection   30.___
    Act of 1968 were required to
    A. file reports at regular intervals on what they had done to prevent theft
    B. identify and apprehend persons who commit robberies, burglaries, and larcenies
    C. draw up a code of ethics for their employees
    D. have fingerprints of their employees filed with the FBI

31. Under the provisions of the Bank Protection Act of 1968,   31.___
    a bank which is subject to the rules established under
    the Act and which violates a rule is liable to a penalty
    of NOT _____ than $100 for each _____.
       A. more; violation   B. less; day of violation
       C. less; violation   D. more; day of violation

Questions 32-36.

DIRECTIONS: Questions 32 through 36 are to be answered SOLELY on
             the basis of the information contained in the following
             paragraph.

*A statement which is offered in an attempt to prove the truth of
the matters therein stated, but which is not made by the author as a
witness before the court at the particular trial in which it is so
offered, is hearsay. This is so whether the statement consists of
words (oral or written), of symbols used as a substitute for words,
or of signs or other conduct offered as the equivalent of a statement. Subject to some well-established exceptions, hearsay is not
generally acceptable as evidence, and it does not become competent
evidence just because it is received by the court without objection.
One basis for this rule is simply that a fact cannot be proved by
showing that somebody stated it was a fact. Another basis for the
rule is the fundamental principle that in a criminal prosecution
the testimony of the witness shall be taken before the court, so
that at the time he gives the testimony offered in evidence he will
be sworn and subject to cross-examination, the scrutiny of the
court, and confrontation by the accused.*

32. Which of the following is hearsay?   32.___
    A(n)
       A. written statement by a person not present at the
          court hearing where the statement is submitted as
          proof of an occurrence
       B. oral statement in court by a witness of what he saw
       C. written statement of what he saw by a witness present
          in court
       D. re-enactment by a witness in court of what he saw

33. In a criminal case, a statement by a person not present   33.___
    in court is
       A. *acceptable* evidence if not objected to by the prose-
          cutor
       B. *acceptable* evidence if not objected to by the defense
          lawyer
       C. *not acceptable* evidence except in certain well-
          settled circumstances
       D. *not acceptable* evidence under any circumstances

34. The rule on hearsay is founded on the belief that
    A. proving someone said an act occurred is not proof that the act did occur
    B. a person who has knowledge about a case should be willing to appear in court
    C. persons not present in court are likely to be unreliable witnesses
    D. permitting persons to testify without appearing in court will lead to a disrespect for law

34.___

35. One reason for the general rule that a witness in a criminal case must give his testimony in court is that
    A. a witness may be influenced by threats to make untrue statements
    B. the opposite side is then permitted to question him
    C. the court provides protection for a witness against unfair questioning
    D. the adversary system is designed to prevent a miscarriage of justice

35.___

36. Of the following, the MOST appropriate title for the above passage would be
    A. WHAT IS HEARSAY?   B. RIGHTS OF DEFENDANTS
    C. TRIAL PROCEDURES   D. TESTIMONY OF WITNESSES

36.___

Questions 37-40.

DIRECTIONS: Questions 37 through 40 are to be answered SOLELY on the basis of the following graphs.

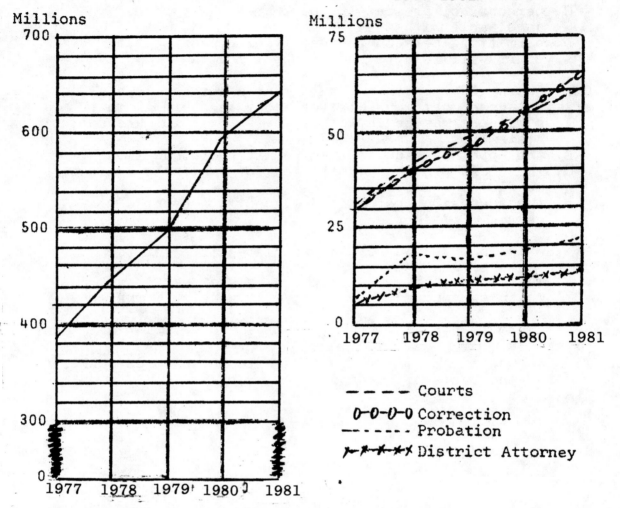

BUDGETS FOR POLICE
IN MILLIONS OF DOLLARS
(ACTUAL DOLLARS)
1977-1981

BUDGETS FOR OTHER
CRIMINAL JUSTICE EXPENDITURES
IN MILLIONS OF DOLLARS
(ACTUAL DOLLARS)
1977-1981

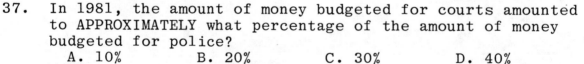

- - - - Courts
0-0-0-0 Correction
-·-·-·- Probation
x-x-x-x District Attorney

37. In 1981, the amount of money budgeted for courts amounted
    to APPROXIMATELY what percentage of the amount of money
    budgeted for police?
    A. 10%   B. 20%   C. 30%   D. 40%   37.___

38. In 1980, the police budget exceeded the sum of amounts
    budgeted for the four other criminal justice expenditures
    MOST NEARLY by
    A. $410,000,000   B. $459,000,000   38.___
    C. $475,000,000   D. $487,000,000

39. Between which of the following years did the amount of
    money budgeted for one category of criminal justice
    decrease by about one million dollars?
    A. 1977-1978   B. 1978-1979   39.___
    C. 1979-1980   D. 1980-1981

40. If the 1978 dollar was worth 96% of the 1977 dollar and   40.___
   the 1979 dollar was worth 90% of the 1977 dollar, the
   increase in the budget for Correction from 1978 to 1979,
   in terms of the 1977 dollar, amounted to
   A. $2,100,000   B. $4,200,000
   C. $4,320,000   D. $4,700,000

KEY (CORRECT ANSWERS)

1. A	11. C	21. C	31. D
2. B	12. B	22. B	32. A
3. B	13. D	23. D	33. C
4. C	14. C	24. A	34. A
5. D	15. D	25. B	35. B
6. C	16. D	26. A	36. A
7. D	17. C	27. C	37. A
8. B	18. C	28. B	38. B
9. C	19. D	29. C	39. B
10. A	20. D	30. A	40. A

EXAMINATION SECTION

TEST 1

DIRECTIONS: Each question or incomplete statement is followed by several suggested answers or completions. Select the one that BEST answers the question or completes the statement. *PRINT THE LETTER OF THE CORRECT ANSWER IN THE SPACE AT THE RIGHT.*

Questions 1-6.

DIRECTIONS: Questions 1 through 6 are to be answered SOLELY on the basis of the numbered boxes on the Arrest Report and paragraph below.

ARREST REPORT

1. Arrest Number	2. Precinct of Arrest		3. Date/Time of Arrest		4. Defendant's Name		5. Defendant's Address
6. Defendant's Date of Birth	7. Sex	8. Race	9. Height	10. Weight	11. Location of Arrest		12. Date and Time of Occurrence
13. Location of Occurrence	14. Complaint Number		15. Victim's Name	16. Victim's Address		17. Victim's Date of Birth	
18. Precinct of Complaint	19. Arresting Officer's Name		20. Shield Number	21. Assigned Unit Precinct		22. Date of Complaint	

On Friday, December 13, at 11:45 P.M., while leaving a store at 235 Spring Street, Grace O'Connell, a white female, 5'2", 130 lbs., was approached by a white male, 5'11", 200 lbs., who demanded her money and jewelry. As the man ran and turned down River Street, Police Officer William James, Shield Number 31724, assigned to the 14th Precinct, gave chase and apprehended him in front of 523 River Street. The prisoner, Gerald Grande, who resides at 17 Water Street, was arrested at 12:05 A.M., was charged with robbery, and taken to the 13th Precinct, where he was assigned Arrest Number 53048. Miss O'Connell, who resides at 275 Spring St., was given Complaint Number 82460.

1. On the basis of the Arrest Report and paragraph above,   1.___
   the CORRECT entry for Box Number 3 should be
        A. 11:45 P.M., 12/13   B. 11:45 P.M., 12/14
        C. 12:05 A.M., 12/13   D. 12:05 A.M., 12/14

2. On the basis of the Arrest Report and paragraph above,   2.___
   the CORRECT entry for Box Number 21 should be
        A. 13th Precinct   B. 14th Precinct
        C. Mounted Unit   D. 32nd Precinct

3. On the basis of the Arrest Report and paragraph above,   3.___
   the CORRECT entry for Box Number 11 should be
        A. 235 Spring St.   B. 523 River St.
        C. 275 Spring St.   D. 17 Water St.

4. On the basis of the Arrest Report and paragraph above,   4.___
   the CORRECT entry for Box Number 2 should be
        A. 13th Precinct   B. 14th Precinct
        C. Mounted Unit   D. 32nd Precinct

5. On the basis of the Arrest Report and paragraph above,   5.___
   the CORRECT entry for Box Number 13 should be
        A. 523 River St.   B. 17 Water St.
        C. 275 Spring St.   D. 235 Spring St.

6. On the basis of the Arrest Report and paragraph above,   6.___
   the CORRECT entry for Box Number 14 should be
        A. 53048   B. 31724   C. 12/13   D. 82460

Questions 7-10.

DIRECTIONS: Questions 7 through 10 are to be answered SOLELY on
            the basis of the following information.

   You are required to file various documents in file drawers which
are labeled according to the following pattern:

DOCUMENTS

MEMOS		LETTERS	
File	Subject	File	Subject
84PM1 -	(A-L)	84PC1 -	(A-L)
84PM2 -	(M-Z)	84PC2 -	(M-Z)

REPORTS		INQUIRIES	
File	Subject	File	Subject
84PR1 -	(A-L)	84PQ1 -	(A-L)
84PR2 -	(M-Z)	84PQ2 -	(M-Z)

7. A letter dealing with a burglary should be filed in the   7.___
   drawer labeled
        A. 84PM1   B. 84PC1   C. 84PR1   D. 84PQ2

8. A report on *Statistics* should be found in the drawer   8.___
   labeled
      A. 84PM1   B. 84PC2   C. 84PR2   D. 84PQ2

9. An inquiry is received about parade permit procedures.   9.___
   It should be filed in the drawer labeled
      A. 84PM2   B. 84PC1   C. 84PR1   D. 84PQ2

10. A police officer has a question about a robbery report   10.___
    you filed.
    You should pull this file from the drawer labeled
      A. 84PM1   B. 84PM2   C. 84PR1   D. 84PR2

Questions 11-18.

DIRECTIONS: Questions 11 through 18 are to be answered SOLELY on
              the basis of the following information.

      Below are listed the code number, name, and area of investigation
of six detective units.

      Each question describes a crime. For each question, choose the
option (A, B, C, or D) which contains the code number for the detective unit responsible for handling that crime.

DETECTIVE UNITS

Unit Code No.	Unit Name	Unit's Area of Investigation
01	Senior Citizens Unit	All robberies of senior citizens 65 years or older
02	Major Case Unit	Any bank robbery; a commercial robbery where value of goods or money stolen is over $25,000
03	Robbery Unit	Any commercial, non-bank rob- bery where the value of the stolen goods or money is $25,000 or less; robberies of individuals under 65 years of age
04	Fraud and Larceny Unit	Confidence games and pickpockets
05	Special Investigations Unit	Burglaries of premises where the value of goods removed or monies taken is $15,000 or less
06	Burglary Unit	Burglaries of premises where the value of goods removed or monies taken is over $15,000

11. Mrs. Green calls the precinct and reports that her apart-   11.____
    ment was burglarized while she was on vacation and that
    precious jewelry and silverware, valued at $27,000, were
    taken.
    To which unit code number should her complaint be referred?
       A. 05   B. 02   C. 03   D. 06

12. Sylvia Bailey, Manager of the Building and Loan Savings   12.____
    Bank, reports that a man handed one of her tellers a note
    stating, *This is a robbery*. He had a gun and demanded
    money. The teller gave the man $500 in small bills, and
    the man then left.
    To which unit code number should the complaint be referred?
       A. 02   B. 06   C. 03   D. 05

13. Mrs. Miniver, a 67-year-old widow, states that she was   13.____
    beaten and robbed by two men in the elevator of her apart-
    ment building.
    To which unit code number should the complaint be referred?
       A. 06   B. 01   C. 03   D. 02

14. Mr. Whipple, Manager of T.V.A. Supermarket, reports that   14.____
    during the night someone entered the store and removed
    merchandise valued at $12,500.
    To which unit code number should the complaint be referred?
       A. 05   B. 03   C. 06   D. 02

15. Mr. Gold, owner of Gold's Jewelry Exchange, reports that   15.____
    two men, armed with shotguns, robbed his store and
    removed money and jewelry valued at $28,000.
    To which unit code number should the complaint be referred?
       A. 05   B. 03   C. 06   D. 02

16. Mr. Watson, a 62-year-old man, was walking in Central Park   16.____
    when he was approached by a man with a knife and was
    robbed of $72.
    To which unit code number should the complaint be referred?
       A. 01   B. 06   C. 03   D. 02

17. The Ace Jewelry Manufacturing Company was broken into over   17.____
    the weekend when the building was closed. The owner
    stated that $35,000 in gold, silver, diamonds, and jewelry
    were taken.
    To which unit code number should the complaint be referred?
       A. 02   B. 03   C. 06   D. 05

18. Mrs. Vargas, 62, reports that she gave Mr. Greene of the   18.____
    Starlite Realty Corporation $1,000 to locate a new apart-
    ment for her family. A week went by, and she never heard
    from Mr. Greene. She called the Starlite Realty Corpora-
    tion, and they informed her that Mr. Greene never worked
    for Starlite Realty Corporation and that they have no
    record of the $1,000 deposit of Mrs. Vargas.
    To which unit code number should the complaint be referred?
       A. 04   B. 03   C. 01   D. 05

Questions 19-24.

DIRECTIONS: Questions 19 through 24 consist of sentences which contain examples of correct or incorrect English usage. Examine each sentence with reference to grammar, spelling, punctuation, and capitalization. Choose one of the following options that would be BEST for correct English usage:

A. The sentence is correct.
B. There is one mistake.
C. There are two mistakes.
D. There are three mistakes.

19. Mrs. Fitzgerald came to the 59th Precinct to retreive her property which were stolen earlier in the week.

19.___

20. The two officer's responded to the call, only to find that the perpatrator and the victim have left the scene.

20.___

21. Mr. Coleman called the 61st Precinct to report that, upon arriving at his store, he discovered that there was a large hole in the wall and that three boxes of radios were missing.

21.___

22. The Administrative Leiutenant of the 62nd Precinct held a meeting which was attended by all the civilians, assigned to the Precinct.

22.___

23. Three days after the robbery occured the detective apprahended two suspects and recovered the stolen items.

23.___

24. The Community Affairs Officer of the 64th Precinct is the liaison between the Precinct and the community; he works closely with various community organizations, and elected officials.

24.___

Questions 25-32.

DIRECTIONS: Questions 25 through 32 are to be answered on the basis of the following paragraph, which contains some deliberate errors in spelling and/or grammar and/or punctuation. Each line of the paragraph is preceded by a number. There are 9 lines and 9 numbers.

Line No.	Paragraph Line
1	The protection of life and proporty are, one of
2	the oldest and most important functions of a city.
3	New York city has it's own full-time police Agency.
4	The police Department has the power an it shall
5	be there duty to preserve the Public piece,
6	prevent crime detect and arrest offenders, supress
7	riots, protect the rites of persons and property, etc.
8	The maintainance of sound relations with the community they
9	serve is an important function of law enforcement officers.

25. How many errors are contained in line one?   25.___
    A. One   B. Two   C. Three   D. None

26. How many errors are contained in line two?   26.___
    A. One   B. Two   C. Three   D. None

27. How many errors are contained in line three?   27.___
    A. One   B. Two   C. Three   D. None

28. How many errors are contained in line four?   28.___
    A. One   B. Two   C. Three   D. None

29. How many errors are contained in line five?   29.___
    A. One   B. Two   C. Three   D. None

30. How many errors are contained in line six?   30.___
    A. One   B. Two   C. Three   D. None

31. How many errors are contained in line seven?   31.___
    A. One   B. Two   C. Three   D. None

32. How many errors are contained in line eight?   32.___
    A. One   B. Two   C. Three   D. None

Questions 33-40.

DIRECTIONS: Questions 33 through 40 are to be answered on the basis
of the material contained in the INDEX OF CRIME IN
CENTRAL CITY, U.S.A. 1974-1983 appearing on the following
page. Certain information in various columns is
deliberately left blank.

The correct answer (A, B, C, or D) to these questions
requires you to make computations that will enable you
to fill in the blanks correctly.

INDEX OF CRIME IN CENTRAL CITY, 1974-1983

	Crime Index Total	Violent Crime[1]	Property Crime[2]	Murder	Forcible Rape	Robbery	Aggra- vated Assault	Burglary	Larceny Theft	Motor Vehicle Theft
1974	8,717	875		19	51	385	420	2,565	4,347	930
1975	10,252	974	9,278	20	55	443	456		5,262	977
1976	11,256	1,026	10,230	20		465	485	3,253	5,977	1,000
1977	11,304	986		18	58	420	490	3,089	6,270	959
1978	10,935	1,009	9,926	19	63	405	522	3,053	5,905	968
1979	11,140	1,061	10,079	19	67	417	558	3,104	5,983	992
1980	12,152	1,178	10,974	23	75	466	614	3,299	6,578	1,097
1981	13,294	1,308	11,986	23	83		654	3,759	7,113	1,114
1982	13,289	1,321	11,968	22	82	574	643	3,740	7,154	1,074
1983	12,856	1,285	11,571	22	77	536	650	3,415	7,108	1,048

[1]Violent crimes are offenses of Murder, Forcible Rape, Robbery, and Aggravated Assault.
[2]Property crimes are offenses of Burglary, Larceny Theft, and Motor Vehicle Theft.

33. What was the TOTAL number of Property Crimes for 1974?   33.___
    A. 9,740   B. 10,252   C. 16,559   D. 7,842

34. What was the TOTAL number of Burglaries for 1975?   34.___
    A. 2,062   B. 3,039   C. 3,259   D. 4,001

35. In 1983, the total number of Aggravated Assaults was MOST   35.___
NEARLY what percent of the total number of violent crimes
for that year?
    A. 49.1   B. 46.3   C. 50.6   D. 41.7

36. In 1978, Property Crime was MOST NEARLY what percent of   36.___
the Crime Index Total?
    A. 90.8   B. 9.3   C. 10.1   D. 89.9

37. What was the TOTAL number of Property Crimes for 1977?   37.___
    A. 10,318   B. 11,304   C. 986   D. 10,808

38. What was the TOTAL number of Robberies for 1981?   38.___
    A. 654   B. 571   C. 548   D. 1,202

39. Robbery made up what percent of the TOTAL number of Violent Crimes for 1983?

    A. 68.8%   B. 4.1%   C. 21.9%   D. 41.7%

39.___

40. What was the TOTAL number of Forcible Rapes for 1976?

    A. 47   B. 56   C. 55   D. 101

40.___

KEY (CORRECT ANSWERS)

1. D	11. D	21. A	31. A
2. B	12. A	22. C	32. A
3. B	13. B	23. C	33. D
4. A	14. A/B	24. C	34. B
5. D	15. D/C	25. C	35. C
6. D	16. C	26. D	36. A
7. B	17. C/A	27. C	37. A
8. C	18. A	28. B	38. C
9. D	19. C	29. C	39. D
10. D	20. D	30. B	40. B

TEST 2

DIRECTIONS: Each question or incomplete statement is followed by several suggested answers or completions. Select the one that BEST answers the question or completes the statement. *PRINT THE LETTER OF THE CORRECT ANSWER IN THE SPACE AT THE RIGHT.*

Questions 1-8.

DIRECTIONS: Each of Questions 1 through 8 consists of three lines of code letters and numbers. The numbers on each line should correspond to the code letters on the same line in accordance with the table below.

Code Letter	X	B	L	T	V	M	P	F	J	S
Corresponding Number	0	1	2	3	4	5	6	7	8	9

On some of the lines, an error exists in the coding. Compare the letters and numbers in each question carefully. If you find an error or errors on:

> Only <u>one</u> of the lines in the question, mark your answer A;
> any <u>two</u> lines in the question, mark your answer B;
> all <u>three</u> lines in the question, mark your answer C;
> <u>none</u> of the lines in the question, mark your answer D.

<u>SAMPLE QUESTION</u>

    MSXVLPT---5904263
    SBFJLTP---9178246
    XVMBTPF---8451367

In the above sample, the first line is correct since each code letter listed has the correct corresponding number. On the second line, an error exists because code letter T should have number 3 instead of number 4. On the third line, an error exists because the code letter X should have the number 0 instead of the number 8. Since there are errors on two of the three lines, the correct answer is B.

1. VFSTPLM---4793625
    SBXFLTP---9017236
    BTPJFSV---1358794   1._____

2. TSLFVPJ---3927468
    JLFTVXS---8273409
    MVSXBFL---5490172   2._____

3. XFTJSVT---0739843
    VFMTFLB---4753721
    LTFJSFM---2378985   3._____

4.   SJMSJVL---9859742   4.___
       VFBXMPF---3710568
       PFPXLBS---7670219

5.   MFPXVFP---5764076   5.___
       PTFJBLX---6378120
       VXSVSTB---4094931

6.   BXFPVJT---1076483   6.___
       STFMVLT---9375423
       TXPBTTM---3061335

7.   VLSBLVP---4290246   7.___
       FPSFBMV---7679154
       XTMXMLL---0730522

8.   JFVPMTJ---8746538   8.___
       TFPMXBL---3765012
       TJSFMFX---4987570

Questions 9-18.

DIRECTIONS: Questions 9 through 18 each consists of two columns, each containing four lines of names, numbers and/or addresses. For each question, compare the lines in Column I with the lines in Column II to see if they match exactly, and mark your answer (A, B, C, or D) according to the following instructions:
           A - all four lines match exactly
           B - only three lines match exactly
           C - only two lines match exactly
           D - only one line matches exactly

     COLUMN I   COLUMN II

9.   (1) Earl Hodgson   Earl Hodgson   9.___
     (2) 1409870   1408970
     (3) Shore Ave.   Schore Ave.
     (4) Macon Rd.   Macon Rd.

10. (1) 9671485   9671485   10.___
     (2) 470 Astor Court   470 Astor Court
     (3) Halprin, Phillip   Halperin, Phillip
     (4) Frank D. Poliseo   Frank D. Poliseo

11. (1) Tandem Associates   Tandom Associates   11.___
     (2) 144-17 Northern Blvd. 144-17 Northern Blvd.
     (3) Alberta Forchi   Albert Forchi
     (4) Kings Park, NY 10751 Kings Point, NY 10751

COLUMN I	COLUMN II	
12. (1) Bertha C. McCormack (2) Clayton, MO. (3) 976-4242 (4) New City, NY 10951	Bertha C. McCormack Clayton, MO. 976-4242 New City, NY 10951	12.___
13. (1) George C. Morill (2) Columbia, SC 29201 (3) Louis Ingham (4) 3406 Forest Ave.	George C. Morrill Columbia, SD 29201 Louis Ingham 3406 Forest Ave.	13.___
14. (1) 506 S. Elliott Pl. (2) Herbert Hall (3) 4712 Rockaway Pkway (4) 169 E. 7 St.	506 S. Elliott Pl. Hurbert Hall 4712 Rockaway Pkway 169 E. 7 St.	14.___
15. (1) 345 Park Ave. (2) Colman Oven Corp. (3) Robert Conte (4) 6179846	345 Park Pl. Coleman Oven Corp. Robert Conti 6179846	15.___
16. (1) Grigori Schierber (2) Des Moines, Iowa (3) Gouverneur Hospital (4) 91-35 Cresskill Pl.	Grigori Schierber Des Moines, Iowa Gouverneur Hospital 91-35 Cresskill Pl.	16.___
17. (1) Jeffery Janssen (2) 8041071 (3) 40 Rockefeller Plaza (4) 407 6 St.	Jeffrey Janssen 8041071 40 Rockafeller Plaza 406 7 St.	17.___
18. (1) 5971996 (2) 3113 Knickerbocker Ave. (3) 8434 Boston Post Rd. (4) Penn Station	5871996 3113 Knickerbocker Ave. 8424 Boston Post Rd. Penn Station	18.___

Questions 19-22.

DIRECTIONS: Questions 19 through 22 are to be answered by looking at the 4 groups of names and addresses listed below (I, II, III, and IV) and then finding out the number of groups that have their corresponding numbered lines exactly the same.

	Group I	Group II
Line 1.	Ingersoll Public Library	Ingersoil Public Library
Line 2.	Reference and Research Dept.	Reference and Research Dept.
Line 3.	95-12 238 St.	95-12 238 St.
Line 4.	East Elmhurst, N.Y. 11357	East Elmhurst, N.Y. 11357

	Group III	Group IV
Line 1.	Ingersoll Public Library	Ingersoll Poblic Library
Line 2.	Reference and Research Dept.	Referance and Research Dept.
Line 3.	92-15 283 St.	95-12 283 St.
Line 4.	East Elmhurst, N.Y. 11357	East Elmhurst, N.Y. 11357

19. In how many groups is line one exactly the same?   19.____
    A. Two   B. Three   C. Four   D. None

20. In how many groups is line two exactly the same?   20.____
    A. Two   B. Three   C. Four   D. None

21. In how many groups is line three exactly the same?   21.____
    A. Two   B. Three   C. Four   D. None

22. In how many groups is line four exactly the same?   22.____
    A. Two   B. Three   C. Four   D. None

Questions 23-26.

DIRECTIONS: Questions 23 through 26 are to be answered by looking at the 4 groups of names and addresses listed below (I, II, III, and IV) and then finding out the number of groups that have their corresponding numbered lines exactly the same.

	Group I	Group II
Line 1.	Richmond General Hospital	Richman General Hospital
Line 2.	Geriatric Clinic	Geriatric Clinic
Line 3.	3975 Paerdegat St.	3975 Peardegat St.
Line 4.	Loudonville, New York 11538	Londonville, New York 11538

	Group III	Group IV
Line 1.	Richmond General Hospital	Richmend General Hospital
Line 2.	Geriatric Clinic	Geriatric Clinic
Line 3.	3795 Paerdegat St.	3975 Paerdegat St.
Line 4.	Loudonville, New York 11358	Loudonville, New York 11538

23. In how many groups is line one exactly the same?   23.____
    A. Two   B. Three   C. Four   D. None

24. In how many groups is line two exactly the same?   24.____
    A. Two   B. Three   C. Four   D. None

25. In how many groups is line three exactly the same?   25.____
    A. Two   B. Three   C. Four   D. None

26. In how many groups is line four exactly the same?   26.____
    A. Two   B. Three   C. Four   D. None

Questions 27-34.

DIRECTIONS: Each of Questions 27 through 34 consists of four or six
               numbered names. For each question, choose the option
               (A, B, C, or D) which indicates the order in which the
               names should be filed in accordance with the following
               filing instructions:

               - File alphabetically according to last name, then first
                 name, then middle initial.
               - File according to each successive letter within a name.
               - When comparing two names where the letters in the longer
                 name are identical with the corresponding letters in the
                 shorter name, the shorter name is filed first.
               - When the last names are the same, initials are always
                 filed before names beginning with the same letter.

27.   I. Ralph Robinson   II. Alfred Ross   27.___
      III. Luis Robles   IV. James Roberts

      The CORRECT filing sequence for the above names should be
          A. IV, II, I, III   B. I, IV, III, II
          C. III, IV, I, II   D. IV, I, III, II

28.   I. Irwin Goodwin   II. Inez Gonzalez   28.___
      III. Irene Goodman   IV. Ira S. Goodwin
        V. Ruth I. Goldstein   VI. M.B. Goodman

      The CORRECT filing sequence for the above names should be
          A. V, II, I, IV, III, VI   B. V, II, VI, III, IV, I
          C. V, II, III, VI, IV, I   D. V, II, III, VI, I, IV

29.   I. George Allan   II. Gregory Allen   29.___
      III. Gary Allen   IV. George Allen

      The CORRECT filing sequence for the above names should be
          A. IV, III, I, II   B. I, IV, II, III
          C. III, IV, I, II   D. I, III, IV, II

30.   I. Simon Kauffman   II. Leo Kaufman   30.___
      III. Robert Kaufmann   IV. Paul Kauffmann

      The CORRECT filing sequence for the above names should be
          A. I, IV, II, III   B. II, IV, III, I
          C. III, II, IV, I   D. I, II, III, IV

31.   I. Roberta Williams   II. Robin Wilson   31.___
      III. Roberta Wilson   IV. Robin Williams

      The CORRECT filing sequence for the above names should be
          A. III, II, IV, I   B. I, IV, III, II
          C. I, II, III, IV   D. III, I, II, IV

32.   I. Lawrence Shultz   II. Albert Schultz   32.____
     III. Theodore Schwartz   IV. Thomas Schwarz
       V. Alvin Schultz   VI. Leonard Shultz

The CORRECT filing sequence for the above names should be
      A. II, V, III, IV, I, VI   B. IV, III, V, I, II, VI
      C. II, V, I, VI, III, IV   D. I, VI, II, V, III, IV

33.   I. McArdle   II. Mayer   III. Maletz   33.____
      IV. McNiff   V. Meyer   VI. MacMahon

The CORRECT filing sequence for the above names should be
      A. I, IV, VI, III, II, V   B. II, I, IV, VI, III, V
      C. VI, III, II, I, IV, V   D. VI, III, II, V, I, IV

34.   I. Jack E. Johnson   II. R. H. Jackson   34.____
     III. Bertha Jackson   IV. J. T. Johnson
       V. Ann Johns   VI. John Jacobs

The CORRECT filing sequence for the above names should be
      A. II, III, VI, V, IV, I   B. III, II, VI, V, IV, I
      C. VI, II, III, I, V, IV   D. III, II, VI, IV, V, I

Questions 35-40.

DIRECTIONS: Questions 35 through 40 are to be answered SOLELY on
             the basis of the following passage.

An aide assigned to the Complaint Room must be familiar with the
various forms used by that office. Some of these forms and their
uses are:

Complaint Report   Used to record information on or information
                          about crimes reported to the Police Department.

Complaint Report   Used to record additional information after the
Follow-Up   initial complaint report has been filed.

Aided Card   Used to record information pertaining to sick and
                          injured persons aided by the police.

Accident Report   Used to record information on or information about
                          injuries and/or property damage involving motorized
                          vehicles.

Property Voucher   Used to record information on or information about
                          property which comes into possession of the Police
                          Department. (Motorized vehicles are not included.)

Auto Voucher   Used to record information on or information about
                          a motorized vehicle which comes into possession of
                          the Police Department.

35. Mr. Brown walks into the police precinct and informs the
    Administrative Aide that, while he was at work, someone
    broke into his apartment and removed property belonging
    to him. He does not know everything that was taken, but
    he wants to make a report now and will make a list of
    what was taken and bring it in later.
    According to the above passage, the CORRECT form to use
    in this situation should be the
     A. Property Voucher
     B. Complaint Report
     C. Complaint Report Follow-Up
     D. Aided Card

  35.____

36. Mrs. Wilson telephones the precinct and informs the
    Administrative Aide she wishes to report additional pro-
    perty which was taken from her apartment. The Administra-
    tive Aide finds a Complaint Report had been previously
    filed for Mrs. Wilson.
    According to the above passage, the CORRECT form to use in
    this situation should be the
     A. Property Voucher
     B. Complaint Report
     C. Complaint Report Follow-Up
     D. Aided Card

  36.____

37. Police Officer Jones walks into the Complaint Room and
    informs the Administrative Aide that, while he was on
    patrol, he observed a woman fall to the sidewalk and
    remain there, apparently hurt. He comforted the injured
    woman and called for an ambulance, which came and brought
    the woman to the hospital.
    According to the above passage, the CORRECT form on which
    to record this information should be the
     A. Accident Report
     B. Complaint Report
     C. Complaint Report Follow-Up
     D. Aided Card

  37.____

38. Police Officer Smith informed the Administrative Aide
    assigned to the Complaint Room that Mr. Green, while
    crossing the street, was struck by a motorcycle and had
    to be taken to the hospital.
    According to the above passage, the facts regarding this
    incident should be recorded on which one of the following
    forms?
     A. Accident Report
     B. Complaint Report
     C. Complaint Report Follow-Up
     D. Aided Card

  38.____

39. Police Officer Williams reports to the Administrative   39.____
    Aide assigned to the Complaint Room that he and his
    partner, Police Office Murphy, found an auto which was
    reported stolen and had the auto towed into the police
    garage.
    Of the following forms listed in the above passage,
    which is the CORRECT one to use to record this informa-
    tion?
       A. Property Voucher
       B. Auto Voucher
       C. Complaint Report Follow-Up
       D. Complaint Report

40. Administrative Aide Lopez has been assigned to the   40.____
    Complaint Room. During her tour of duty, a person who
    does not identify herself hands Ms. Lopez a purse. The
    person states that she found the purse on the street.
    She then leaves the station house.
    According to the information in the above passage, which
    is the CORRECT form to fill out to record the incident?
       A. Property Voucher
       B. Auto Voucher
       C. Complaint Report Follow-Up
       D. Complaint Report

KEY (CORRECT ANSWERS)

1. B	11. D	21. A	31. B
2. D	12. A	22. C	32. A
3. B	13. C	23. A	33. C
4. C	14. B	24. C	34. B
5. A	15. D	25. A	35. B
6. D	16. A	26. A	36. C
7. C	17. D	27. D	37. D
8. A	18. C	28. C	38. A
9. C	19. D	29. D	39. B
10. B	20. B	30. A	40. A

INTERPRETING STATISTICAL DATA
GRAPHS, CHARTS AND TABLES

DIRECTIONS: Each question or incomplete statement is followed by several suggested answers or completions. Select the one that BEST answers the question or completes the statement. *PRINT THE LETTER OF THE CORRECT ANSWER IN THE SPACE AT THE RIGHT.*

TEST 1

Questions 1-6.

DIRECTIONS: Questions 1 through 6 are to be answered SOLELY on the basis of the following notes and tables.

1. Assume that a certain imaginary jurisdiction, Perryville, contains five correctional facilities. These facilities are named Howe, Jackson, Grant, Pershing, and Marshall.

2. Assume that there are 365 days in each year.

3. Assume that the number of inmates at each institution listed above does not change during 1965 or 1970.

TABLE A
SOME CHARACTERISTICS OF PERRYVILLE'S CORRECTIONAL FACILITIES
1965

Facility	Inmate Population (No. of inmates)	Yearly Budget	Daily Cost Per Inmate	Total Personnel (Staff)	Ratio of Staff to Inmate Population
Howe	75	$191,625	$7.00	25	1:3
Jackson	100	$182,500		25	1:4
Grant	125	$200,750	$4.40	25	1:5
Pershing		$242,725	$3.50		1:5
Marshall	375		$5.25	125	1:3

TABLE B
SOME CHARACTERISTICS OF PERRYVILLE'S CORRECTIONAL FACILITIES
1970

Facility	Inmate Population (No. of inmates)	Yearly Budget	Daily Cost Per Inmate	Total Personnel (Staff)	Ratio of Staff to Inmate Population
Howe	90	$229,950	$7.00	30	1:3
Jackson	140	$281,050	$5.50	20	1:7
Grant	150	$273,750	$5.00	25	1:6
Pershing	200	$292,000	$4.00	50	1:4
Marshall	300	$602,250	$5.50	60	1:5

1. In 1965, the daily cost per inmate at the Jackson
   Correctional Facility was

   A. $4.10   B. $5.00   C. $6.25   D. $6.50

   1.___

2. If the total number of inmates at all five of Perryville's
   correctional institutions was 865 in 1965, the TOTAL number
   of personnel at the Pershing Correctional Facility during
   the same year was

   A. 28   B. 32   C. 36   D. 38

   2.___

3. In 1970, the percentage of the total inmate population of
   Perryville's correctional facilities held at the Grant
   Facility was MOST NEARLY

   A. 14%   B. 17%   C. 23%   D. 32%

   3.___

4. The average number of personnel at Perryville's correctional facilities in 1970 was MOST NEARLY

   A. 28   B. 38   C. 47   D. 168

   4.___

5. Of the following, the facility which showed the GREATEST
   percent increase in number of inmates in 1970 as compared
   to 1965 was

   A. Marshall   B. Grant   C. Jackson   D. Howe

   5.___

6. If, for 1971, the total inmate population of Perryville's
   five correctional facilities increased by 200 inmates, the
   percentage increase over the total 1970 population was
   MOST NEARLY

   A. 18%   B. 23%   C. 31%   D. 33%

   6.___

TEST 2

Questions 1-6.

DIRECTIONS: Questions 1 through 6 are to be answered SOLELY on the
             basis of the information contained in the following
             charts and notes.

NOTES: Inmates can enter a section of the program at any point.
        Inmates can complete a section of the program at any point
        by passing an examination.
        Enrollment at the end of a section does not necessarily
        indicate successful completion of that section.

CHART I

Number of Inmates Enrolled in Libertyville's Basic Office Skills Program

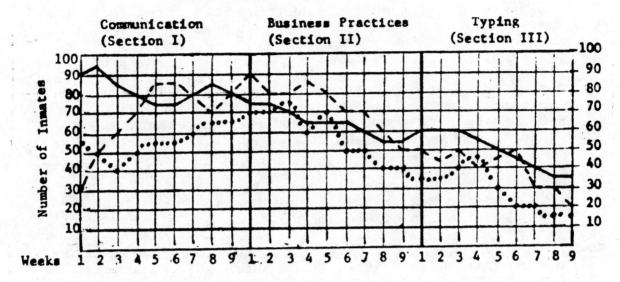

Symbol	Crime Category
———	Victimless Crimes
- - - - - -	Crimes Against Property
· · · · · ·	Violent Crimes

CHART II

Number of Inmates Who Successfully Completed Each Section of Libertyville's Office Skills Program

Crime Category	Completed Section I	Completed Section II	Completed Section III
Victimless Crimes	78	55	37
Crimes Against Property	43	57	28
Violent Crimes	80	50	18

CHART III

Percentage of Recidivism Within First Year of Parole Among Inmates Who Successfully Completed Various Stages of Libertyville's Office Skills Program

Crime Category	Completed Section I	Completed Section II	Completed Section III
Victimless Crimes	40%	30%	15%
Crimes Against Property	30%	15%	5%
Violent Crimes	35%	25%	10%

1. The percentage of inmates who successfully completed
   Section I and were recidivists is MOST NEARLY
      A. 21%   B. 35%   C. 38%   D. 47%

2. The ratio of the number of inmates who started Section III
   the first week to the number who successfully completed
   Section III is MOST NEARLY
      A. 1.5:1   B. 1.7:1   C. 2.1:1   D. 2.5:1

3. During which of the following weeks of the program was
   the enrollment by those who committed victimless crimes
   EXCEEDED by both those who committed crimes against
   property and by those who committed violent crimes?
   Week
      A. 1 of the Communication Section
      B. 3 of the Business Practices Section
      C. 9 of the Business Practices Section
      D. 6 of the Typing Section

4. If the average number of inmates enrolled in any stage of
   the program is considered to be the number of inmates
   enrolled during Week 5 of that Section, what is the
   difference between the average number of inmates enrolled
   in Section I and in Section III?
      A. 90   B. 125   C. 190   D. 215

5. Assume that 60 percent of the inmates who completed Section
   III of the Office Skills Program enrolled the first week
   of the program and completed all three sections of the
   program.
   The percent of the initial enrollees who completed the
   entire Office Skills Program was MOST NEARLY
      A. 21%   B. 28%   C. 36%   D. 49%

6. The one of the following periods which exhibits the
   GREATEST percentage change in enrollment of inmates in
   the crimes against property category is Weeks
      A. 1 to 2 in the Communication Section
      B. 2 to 4 in the Communication Section
      C. 4 to 6 in the Business Practices Section
      D. 3 to 4 in the Typing Section

1._____
2._____
3._____
4._____
5._____
6._____

4

TEST 3

Questions 1-3.

DIRECTIONS: Questions 1 through 3 are to be answered SOLELY on the basis of the information and the list below.

The following list gives dates on which 8 children were admitted to a juvenile detention center:

Name	Admission Date
Abner, E.	November 6, 1984
Alvarez, L.	October 24, 1984
Blake, G.	October 31, 1984
Charlton, M.	November 7, 1984
Davis, A.	November 8, 1984
Green, M.	November 1, 1984
Figua, J.	October 31, 1984
Smith, O.	October 25, 1984

1. The children who have been at the center for less than one week as of November 12, 1984 are:
   A. Alvarez, L.; Blake, G.; Figua, J.
   B. Abner, E.; Charlton, M.; Davis, A.
   C. Charlton, M.; Davis, A.; Green, M.
   D. Davis, A.; Green, M.; Figua, J.

2. The children who have been at the center for at least one week but less than two weeks as of November 12, 1984 are:
   A. Blake, G.; Green, M.; Figua, J.
   B. Charlton, M.; Davis, A.; Smith, O.
   C. Alvarez, L.; Blake, G.; Figua, J.
   D. Blake, G.; Figua, J.; Smith, O.

3. The children who have been at the center for at least two weeks but less than three weeks as of November 12, 1984 are:
   A. Alvarez, L.; Smith, O.
   B. Alvarez, L.; Blake, G.; Green, M.; Figua, J.
   C. Charlton, M.; Davis, A.
   D. Alvarez, L.; Blake, G.; Figua, J.

1.___

2.___

3.___

TEST 4

DIRECTIONS: Questions 1 through 5 are to be answered SOLELY on the basis of the following tables and information.

Forest City, an imaginary jurisdiction, classifies its offenders as juvenile delinquents, youthful offenders, or adult offenders. There are two institutions for female offenders and five institutions for male offenders. Table A shows the average daily number of inmates for the years shown. Table B shows what percentage of average daily number of male inmates for the years shown were juvenile delinquents, youthful offenders, or adult offenders.

TABLE A
FOREST CITY INMATES

	1970	1980	1981 (estimate)
Institutions for Female Offenders:			
(1) Pleasantdale	70	105	120
(2) Shady Valley	W	190	210
TOTAL	195	295	330
Institutions for Male Offenders:			
(1) Leadurney	260	320	310
(2) Sherman	110	130	Y
(3) Riveredge	1700	1800	1850
(4) Thompson	650	800	Z
(5) Maxim	1200	1625	1700
TOTAL	3920	4675	5030
TOTAL MALE & FEMALE	X	4970	5360

6

TABLE B
FOREST CITY OFFENDERS

PERCENTAGE OF AVERAGE DAILY NUMBER OF INMATES
CLASSIFIED AS JUVENILE DELINQUENTS,
YOUTHFUL OFFENDERS, OR ADULT OFFENDERS

(See Code Below)

	1970			1980		
Institutions for Female Offenders:	A	B	C	A	B	C
(1) Pleasantdale	20%	60%	20%	25%	75%	-
(2) Shady Valley	15%	30%	55%	-	35%	65%
Institutions for Male Offenders:						
(1) Leadurney	5%	95%	-	80%	20%	-
(2) Sherman	10%	35%	55%	10%	35%	55%
(3) Riveredge	90%	10%	-	85%	15%	-
(4) Thompson	-	40%	60%	-	35%	65%
(5) Maxim	-	20%	80%	-	5%	95%

CODE
A - JUVENILE DELINQUENTS
B - YOUTHFUL OFFENDERS
C - ADULT OFFENDERS

1. From 1970 to 1980, the average daily number of female youthful offenders in the Pleasantdale institution increased MOST NEARLY by
   A. 20
   B. 29
   C. 37
   D. a figure greater than 40

1.___

2. One of the following sets of figures belongs in the circled spaces marked Y and Z.
Which one of the following sets of figures LOGICALLY belongs in these spaces?
   A. 115 and 990
   B. 115 and 1050
   C. 120 and 990
   D. 120 and 1050

2.___

3. The figures which LOGICALLY belong in the circled spaces marked W and X are
   A. 125 and 4115
   B. 125 and 4215
   C. 175 and 4115
   D. 175 and 4215

3.___

4. In 1980, of the average daily number of Forest City male and female inmates, the percentage to be found in Maxim was MOST NEARLY
   A. 27%   B. 30%   C. 33%   D. 36%

4.___

5. In 1970, the average daily number of adult male offenders   5.___
    was MOST NEARLY
    A. 60 in Sherman and 390 in Thompson
    B. 110 in Sherman and 650 in Thompson
    C. 390 in Thompson and 1300 in Maxim
    D. 800 in Thompson and 1625 in Maxim

TEST 5

Questions 1-5.

DIRECTIONS: Questions 1 through 5 are to be answered SOLELY on the
              basis of the following notes and charts.

NOTES

Assume that correctional facilities in the town of Libertyville
have recorded the number of individual inmate escape attempts, both
successful and unsuccessful, for the year 1984. This information is
presented in Chart I.

Assume also that records were kept on the amount of time which
elapsed between successful escapes by inmates and their recapture.
This information is presented in Chart II.

ESCAPE ATTEMPTS BY INDIVIDUAL INMATES AT LIBERTYVILLE'S
CORRECTIONAL FACILITIES, BY INMATE AGE GROUP - 1984

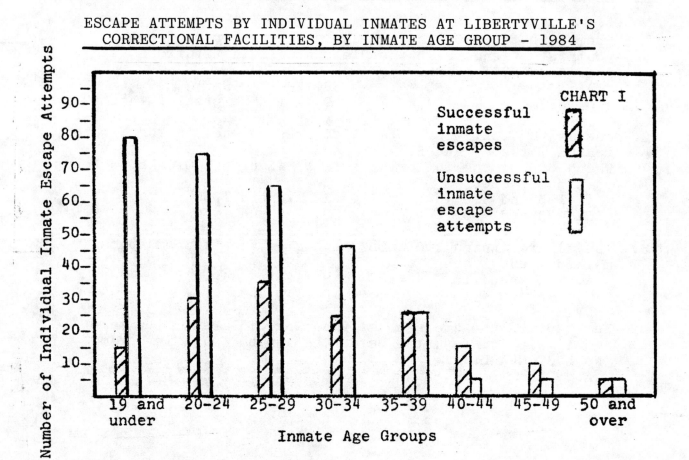

TIME PERIOD (IN MONTHS) WITHIN WHICH
ESCAPED INMATES WERE RECAPTURED

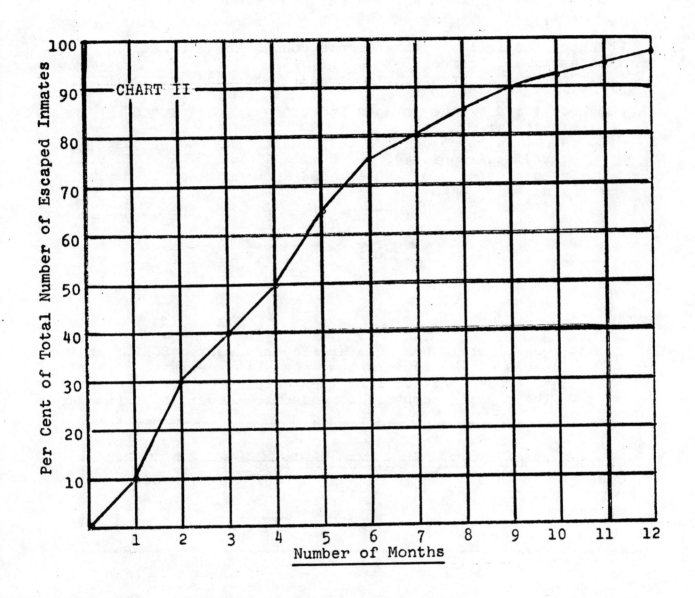

1. Which of the following age groups shows a GREATER total   1.___
    number of escape attempts than the next youngest age group?
    A. 20-24   B. 25-29   C. 30-34   D. 35-39

2. Which of the following MOST NEARLY indicates the number of   2.___
    inmates who were recaptured within nine months of their
    escape?
    A. 90   B. 130   C. 145   D. 160

3. Based on the total number of escape attempts for each of   3.___
    the following age groups, which group had the HIGHEST
    percentage of successful escapes?
    A. 19 & under   B. 25-29   C. 35-39   D. 45-49

9

4. An inmate who attempted to escape had GREATER than a 4.___
   50% chance of
   A. succeeding if he was in the 25-29 group
   B. failing if he was in the 50 and over group
   C. succeeding if he was in the 40-44 group
   D. failing if he was in the 45-49 group

5. Which of the following statements concerning escaped 5.___
   inmates is NOT correct?
   A. Most of the inmates who escaped were under 30 years
      of age.
   B. One-third of the escaped inmates were recaptured
      within three months.
   C. Less than 10 percent of the inmates who escaped were
      over 45 years of age.
   D. Seventy percent of the escaped inmates were recaptured
      within six months.

TEST 6

Questions 1-3.

DIRECTIONS: Questions 1 through 3 are to be answered SOLELY on the
              basis of the table below. Data for certain categories
              have been omitted from the table. You are to calculate
              the missing numbers if needed to answer the questions.

	1977	1978	Numerical Increase
Correction Officers	1,226	1,347	
Court Attendants		529	34
Deputy Sheriffs	38	40	
Supervisors			
	2,180	2,414	

1. The number in the *Supervisors* group in 1977 was MOST 1.___
   NEARLY
   A. 500   B. 475   C. 450   D. 425

2. The LARGEST percentage increase from 1977 to 1978 was in 2.___
   the group of
   A. Correction Officers   B. Court Attendants
   C. Deputy Sheriffs   D. Supervisors

3. In 1978, the ratio of the number of Correction Officers to 3.___
   the total of the other three categories of employees was
   MOST NEARLY
   A. 1:1   B. 2:1   C. 3:1   D. 4:1

10

TEST 7

Questions 1-4.

DIRECTIONS: Questions 1 through 4 are to be answered SOLELY on the basis of the following chart, which shows an 8-hour schedule for 4 groups of inmates. The numbers across the top of the chart stand for hours of the day: the hour beginning at 8:00, the hour beginning at 9:00, and so forth. The exact number of men in each group is given at the left-hand side of the chart. An hour when the men in a particular group are scheduled to be *OUT* of their cellblock is marked with an X.

	8	9	10	11	12	1	2	3
GROUP Q 44 men	X		X			X		
GROUP R 60 men	X		X			X	X	
GROUP S 24 men	X				X			
GROUP T 28 men	X		X		X			

1. How many of the men were in their cellblock from 11:00 to 12:00?
    A. 60   B. 96   C. 104   D. 156   1.___

2. At 10:45, how many of the men were NOT in their cellblock?   2.___
    A. 24   B. 60   C. 96   D. 132

3. At 12:30, what proportion of the men were NOT in their cellblock?   3.___
    A. 1/4   B. 1/3   C. 1/2   D. 2/3

4. During the period covered in the chart, what percentage of the time did the men in Group S spend in their cellblock?   4.___
    A. 60%   B. 65%   C. 70%   D. 75%

KEY (CORRECT ANSWERS)

TEST 1	TEST 2	TEST 3	TEST 4	TEST 5	TEST 6	TEST 7
1. B	1. B	1. B	1. C	1. A	1. D	1. B
2. D	2. B	2. A	2. D	2. C	2. D	2. D
3. B	3. B	3. A	3. A	3. D	3. A	3. B
4. B	4. A		4. C	4. C		4. D
5. C	5. B		5. A	5. A		
6. B	6. A					

CODING
EXAMINATION SECTION
COMMENTARY

An ingenious question-type called coding, involving elements of alphabetizing, filing, name and number comparison, and evaluative judgement and application, has currently won wide acceptance in testing circles for measuring clerical aptitude and general ability, particularly on the senior (middle) grades (levels).

While the directions for this question usually vary in detail, the candidate is generally asked to consider groups of names, codes, and numbers, and then, according to a given plan, to arrange codes in alphabetic order; to arrange these in numerical sequence; to re-arrange columns of names and numbers in correct order; to espy errors in coding; to choose the correct coding arrangement in consonance with the given directions and examples, etc.

This question-type appears to have few parameters in respect to form, substance, or degree of difficulty.

Accordingly acquaintance with, and practice in, the coding question is recommended for the serious candidate.

TEST 1

DIRECTIONS FOR THIS SECTION: Answer questions 1 through 8 on the basis of the code table and the instructions given below.

Code Letter for Traffic Problem	B	H	Q	J	F	L	M	I
Code Number for Action Taken	1	2	3	4	5	6	7	8

Assume that each of the capital letters on the above chart is a radio code for a particular traffic problem and that the number immediately below each capital letter is the radio code for the correct action to be taken to deal with the problem. For instance, "1" is the action to be taken to deal with problem "B", "2" is the action to be taken to deal with problem "H", and so forth.

In each question, a series of code letters is given in Column 1. Column 2 gives four different arrangements of code numbers. You are to pick the answer (A, B, C, or D) in Column 2 that gives the code numbers that match the code letters in the same order

SAMPLE QUESTION

Column 1	Column 2
BHLFMQ	A. 125678
	B. 216573
	C. 127653
	D. 126573

According to the chart, the code numbers that correspond to these code letters are as follows: B - 1, M - 2, L - 6, F - 5, M - 7, Q - 3. Therefore, the right answer is 126573. This answer is D in Column 2.

	Column 1		Column 2	
1.	BHQLMI	A.	123456	1.___
		B.	123567	
		C.	123678	
		D.	125678	
2.	HBJQLF	A.	214365	2.___
		B.	213456	
		C.	213465	
		D.	214387	
3.	QHMLFJ	A.	321654	3.___
		B.	345678	
		C.	327645	
		D.	327654	
4.	FLQJIM	A.	543287	4.___
		B.	563487	
		C.	564378	
		D	654378	
5.	FBIHMJ	A.	518274	5.___
		B.	152874	
		C.	528164	
		D.	517842	
6.	MIHFQB	A.	872341	6.___
		B.	782531	
		C.	782341	
		D.	783214	
7.	JLFHQIM	A.	465237	7.___
		B.	456387	
		C.	4652387	
		D.	4562387	
8.	LBJQIFH	A.	6143852	8.___
		B.	6134852	
		C.	61437852	
		D.	61431852	

TEST 2

DIRECTIONS FOR THIS SECTION: Questions 1 through 5 are based on the following list showing the name and number of each of nine inmates.

1. Johnson
2. Smith
3. Edwards

4. Thompson
5. Frank
6. Murray

7. Gordon
8. Porter
9. Lopez

Each question consists of 3 sets of numbers and letters. Each set should consist of the numbers of three inmates and the first letter of each of their names. The letters should be in the same order as the numbers. In at least two of the three choices, there will be an error. On your answer sheet, mark only that choice in which the letters correspond with the numbers and are in the same order. If all three sets are wrong, mark choice D in your answer space.

SAMPLE QUESTION

A. 386 EPM
B. 542 FST
C. 474 LGT

Since 3 corresponds to E for Edwards, 8 corresponds to P for Porter, and 6 corresponds to M for Murray, choice A is correct and should be entered in your answer space. Choice B is wrong because letters T and S have been reversed. Choice C is wrong because the first number, which is 4, does *NOT* correspond with the first letter of choice C, which is L. It should have been T. If choice A were also wrong, then D would be the correct answer.

1. A. 382 EGS   B. 461 TMJ   C. 875 PLF   1._____

2. A. 549 FLT   B. 692 MJS   C. 758 GSP   2._____

3. A. 936 LEM   B. 253 FSE   C. 147 JTL   3._____

4. A. 569 PML   B. 716 GJP   C. 842 PTS   4._____

5. A. 356 FEM   B. 198 JPL   C. 637 MEG   5._____

3

Questions 6-10

DIRECTIONS: Answer questions 6 through 10 on the basis of the
following information:

In order to make sure stock is properly located, incoming
units are stored as follows:

STOCK NUMBERS	BIN NUMBERS
00100 - 39999	D30, L44
40000 - 69999	I4L, D38
70000 - 99999	41L, 80D
100000 and over	614, 83D

Using the above table, choose the answer A,B,C,or D, which
lists the correct Bin Number for the Stock Number given

6. 17243   6.__
   A. 41L   B. 83D   C. I4L   D. D30

7. 9219   7.__
   A. D38   B. L44   C. 614   D. 41L

8. 90125   8.__
   A. 41L   B. 614   C. D38   D. D30

9. 10001   9.__
   A. L44   B. D38   C. 80D   D. 83D

10. 200100   10.__
    A. 41L   B. I4L   C. 83D   D. D30

_____

TEST 3

DIRECTIONS FOR THIS SECTION: Assume that the Police Department
is planning to conduct a statistical study of individuals who
have been convicted of crimes during a certain year. For the
purpose of this study, identification numbers are being
assigned to individuals in the following manner:

4

The first two digits indicate the age of the individual:

The third digit indicates the sex of the individual:
1. male
2. female

The fourth digit indicates the type of crime involved:
1. criminal homicide
2. forcible rape
3. robbery
4. aggravated assault
5. burglary
6. larceny
7. auto theft
8. other

The fifth and sixth digits indicate the month in which the conviction occurred:
01. January
02. February, etc.

Answer questions 1 through 9 *SOLELY* on the basis of the above information and the following list of individuals and identification numbers.

Abbott, Richard	271304	Morris, Chris	212705
Collins, Terry	352111	Owens, William	231412
Elders, Edward	191207	Parker, Leonard	291807
George, Linda	182809	Robinson, Charles	311102
Hill, Leslie	251702	Sands, Jean	202610
Jones, Jackie	301106	Smith, Michael	421308
Lewis, Edith	402406	Turner, Donald	191601
Mack, Helen	332509	White, Barbara	242803

1. The number of women on the above list is   1.___
      A. 6   B. 7   C. 8   D. 9

2. The two convictions which occurred during February were   2.___
   for the crimes of
      A. aggravated assault and auto theft
      B. auto theft and criminal homicide
      C. burglary and larceny
      D. forcible rape and robbery

3. The *ONLY* man convicted of auto theft was   3.___
      A. Richard Abbott   B. Leslie Hill
      C. Chris Morris   D. Leonard Parker

4. The number of people on the list who were 25 years old   4.___
   or older is
      A. 6   B. 7   C. 8   D. 9

5. The *OLDEST* person on the list is   5.___
      A. Terry Collins   B. Edith Lewis
      C. Helen Mack   D. Michael Smith

6. The two people on the list who are the same age are   6.___
   A. Richard Abbott and Michael Smith
   B. Edward Elders and Donald Turner
   C. Linda George and Helen Mack
   D. Leslie Hill and Charles Robinson

7. A 28-year-old man who was convicted of aggravated assault   7.___
   in October would have identification number
   A. 281410   B. 281509   C. 282311   D. 282409

8. A 33-year-old woman convicted in April of criminal homi-   8.___
   cide would have identification number
   A. 331140   B. 331204   C. 332014   D. 332104

9. The number of people on the above list who were convicted   9.___
   during the first six months of the year is
   A. 6   B. 7   C. 8   D. 9

Questions 10-19.
DIRECTIONS: The following is a list of patients who were referred by various clinics to the laboratory for tests. After each name is a patient identification number. Answer questions 10 through 19 based on the information contained in this list and the explanation accompanying it.

The *first digit* refers to the clinic which made the referral:

  1. Cardiac   6. Hematology
  2. Renal   7. Gynecology
  3. Pediatrics   8. Neurology
  4. Opthalmology   9. Gastroenterology
  5. Orthopedics

The *second digit* refers to the sex of the patient:

  1. male   2. female

The *third* and *fourth digits* give the age of the patient.

The *last two digits* give the day of the month the laboratory tests were performed.

LABORATORY REFERRALS DURING JANUARY

Name	Number	Name	Number
Adams, Jacqueline	320917	Miller, Michael	511806
Black, Leslie	813406	Pratt, William	214411
Cook, Marie	511616	Rogers, Ellen	722428
Fisher, Pat	914625	Saunders, Sally	310229
Jackson, Lee	923212	Wilson, Jan	416715
James, Linda	624621	Wyatt, Mark	321326
Lane, Arthur	115702		

10. According to the list, the number of women referred to   10.____
    the laboratory during January was
    A. 4   B. 5   C. 6   D. 7

11. The clinic from which the MOST patients were referred was   11.____
    A. Cardiac   B. Gynecology
    C. Opthamology   D. Pediatrics

12. The YOUNGEST patient referred from any clinic other   12.____
    than Pediatrics was
    A. Leslie Black   B. Marie Cook
    C. Arthur Lane   D. Sally Saunders

13. The number of pateints whose laboratory tests were per-   13.____
    formed on or before January 15 was
    A. 7   B. 8   C. 9   D. 10

14. The number of patients referred for laboratory tests who   14.____
    are under age 45 is
    A. 7   B. 8   C. 9   D. 10

15. The OLDEST patient referred to the clinic during January   15.____
    was
    A. Jacqueline Adams   B. Linda James
    C. Arthur Lane   D. Jan Wilson

16. The ONLY patient treated in the Orthopedics clinic was   16.____
    A. Marie Cook   B. Pat Fisher
    C. Ellen Rogers   D. Jan Wilson

17. A woman, age 37, was referred from the Hematology clinic to 17.____
    the laboratory. Her laboratory tests were performed on
    January 9. Her identification number would be
    A. 610937   B. 623709   C. 613790   D. 623790

18. A man was referred for lab tests from the Orthopedics   18.____
    clinic. He is 30 years old and his tests were performed
    on January 6. His identification number would be
    A. 413006   B. 510360   C. 513006   D. 513060

19. A 4 year old boy was referred from Pediatrics clinic to   19.____
    have laboratory tests on January 23. His identification
    number was
    A. 310422   B. 310423   C. 310433   D. 320403

    _____

TEST 4

DIRECTIONS FOR THIS SECTION: Questions 1 through 10 are to be
answered on the basis of the information and directions given
on the following page.

Assume that you are a Senior Stenographer assigned to the personnel bureau of a city agency. Your supervisor has asked you to classify the employees in your agency into the following five groups:

A. employees who are college graduates, who are at least 35 years of age but less than 50, and who have been employed by the city for five years or more;

B. employees who have been employed by the City for less than five years, who are not college graduates, and who earn at least $22,500 a year but less than $24,500;

C. employees who have been city employees for five years or more, who are at least 21 years of age but less than 35, and who are not college graduates;

D. employees who earn at least $24,500 a year but less than $26,000 who are college graduates, and who have been employed by the city for less than five years;

E. employees who are not included in any of the foregoing groups.

NOTE: In classifying these employees you are to compute age and period of service as of January 1, 1988. In all cases, it is to be assumed that each employee has been employed continuously in City service. In each question, consider only the information which will assist you in classifying each employee. Any information which is of no assistance in classifying an employee should not be considered.

SAMPLE: Mr. Brown, a 29-year-old veteran, was appointed to his present position of Clerk on June 1, 1985. He has completed two years of college. His present salary is $23,050.

The correct answer to this sample is B, since the employee has been employed by the city for less than five years, is not a college graduate, and earns at least $22,500 a year but less than $24,500.

DIRECTIONS: Questions 1 to 10 contain excerpts from the personnel records of 10 employees in the agency. In the correspondingly numbered space on the right print the capital letter preceding the appropriate group into which you would place each employee.

1. Mr. James has been employed by the city since 1978, when he was graduated from a local college. Now 35 years of age, he earns $26,000 a year.   1.____

2. Mr. Worth began working in city service early in 1984. He was awarded his college degree in 1979, at the age of 21. As a result of a recent promotion, he now earns $24,500 a year.   2.____

8

3. Miss Thomas has been a city employee since August 1, 1983.   3.____
   Her salary is $24,500 a year. Miss Thomas, who is 25 years
   old, has had only three years of high school training.

4. Mr. Williams has had three promotions since entering city   4.____
   service on January 1, 1976. He was graduated from college
   with honors in 1959, when he was 20 years of age. His
   present salary is $27,000 a year.

5. Miss Jones left college after two years of study to take an   5.____
   appointment to a position in the city service paying $23,300 a
   year. She began work on March 1, 1982 when she was 19 years
   of age.

6. Mr. Smith was graduated from an engineering college with   6.____
   honors in January 1983 and became a city employee three months
   later. His present yearly salary is $25,810. Mr. Smith was
   born in 1961.

7. Miss Earnest was born on May 31, 1964. Her education consisted   7.____
   of four years of high school and one year of business school.
   She was appointed as a typist in a city agency on June 1,
   1982. Her annual salary is $23,500.

8. Mr. Adams, a 24-year-old clerk, began his city service on   8.____
   July 1, 1984, soon after being discharged from the U.S.
   Army. A college graduate, his present annual salary is $23,200.

9. Miss Charles attends college in the evenings, hoping to   9.____
   obtain her degree in 1989, when she will be 30 years of age.
   She has been a city employee since April 1983, and earns
   $23,350.

10. Mr. Dolan was just promoted to his present position after   10.____
    six years of city service. He was graduated from high school
    in 1967, when he was 18 years of age, but did not go on
    to college. Mr. Dolan's present salary is $23,500.

TEST 5

DIRECTIONS FOR THIS SECTION: Questions 1 through 4 each contain
five numbers that should be arranged in numerical order. The
number with the lowest numerical value should be first and
the number with the highest numerical value should be last.
Pick that option which indicates the *correct* order of the
numbers.

Examples: A. 9; 18; 14; 15; 27
            B. 9; 14; 15; 18; 27
            C. 14; 15; 18; 27; 9
            D. 9; 14; 15; 27; 18

The correct answer is B, which indicates the proper arrangement of the five numbers.

1. A. 20573; 20753; 20738; 20837; 20098
    B. 20098; 20753; 20573; 20738; 20837
    C. 20098; 20573; 20753; 20837; 20738
    D. 20098; 20573; 20738; 20753; 20837

1.___

2. A. 113492; 113429; 111314; 113114; 131413
    B. 111314; 113114; 113429; 113492; 131413
    C. 111314; 113429; 113492; 113114; 131413
    D. 111314; 113114; 131413; 113429; 113492

2.___

3. A. 1029763; 1030421; 1035681; 1036928; 1067391
    B. 1030421; 1029763; 1035681; 1067391; 1036928
    C. 1030421; 1035681; 1036928; 1067391; 1029763
    D. 1029763; 1039421; 1035681; 1067391; 1036928

3.___

4. A. 1112315; 1112326; 1112337; 1112349; 1112306
    B. 1112306; 1112315; 1112337; 1112326; 1112349
    C. 1112306; 1112315; 1112326; 1112337; 1112349
    D. 1112306; 1112326; 1112315; 1112337; 1112349

4.___

TEST 6

DIRECTIONS FOR THIS SECTION: The phonetic filing system is a
method of filing names in which the alphabet is reduced to key
code letters. The six key letters and their equivalents are
as follows:

KEY LETTERS	EQUIVALENTS
b	p, f, v
c	s, k, g, j, q, x, z
d	t
l	none
m	n
r	none

A key letter represents itself.
Vowels (a,e,i,o and u) and the letters w, h, and y are omitted.
For example, the name GILMAN would be represented as follows:
    G is represented by the key letter C.
    I is a vowel and is omitted.
    L is a key letter and represents itself.
    M is a key letter and represents itself.
    A is a vowel and is omitted.
    N is represented by the key letter M.

Therefore, the phonetic filing code for the name GILMAN is CLMM.

Answer questions 1 through 10 based on the information on the previous page.

1. The phonetic filing code for the name FITZGERALD would be   1.___
   A. BDCCRLD   B. BDCRLD   C. BDZCRLD   D. BTZCRLD

2. The phonetic filing code CLBR may represent any one of the following names EXCEPT   2.___
   A. Calprey   B. Flower   C. Glover   D. Silver

3. The phonetic filing code LDM may represent any one of the following names EXCEPT   3.___
   A. Halden   B. Hilton   C. Walton   D. Wilson

4. The phonetic filing code for the name RODRIGUEZ would be   4.___
   A. RDRC   B. RDRCC   C. RDRCZ   D. RTRCC

5. The phonetic filing code for the name MAXWELL would be   5.___
   A. MCLL   B. MCWL   C. MCWLL   D. MXLL

6. The phonetic filing code for the name ANDERSON would be   6.___
   A. AMDRCM   B. ENDRSM   C. MDRCM   D. NDERCN

7. The phonetic filing code for the name SAVITSKY would be   7.___
   A. CBDCC   B. CBDCY   C. SBDCC   D. SVDCC

8. The phonetic filing code CMC may represent any one of the following names EXCEPT   8.___
   A. James   B. Jayes   C. Johns   D. Jones

9. The *ONLY* one of the following names that could be represented by the phonetic filing code CDDDM would be   9.___
   A. Catalano   B. Chesterton   C. Cittadino   D. Cuttlerman

10. The *ONLY* one of the following names that could be represented by the phonetic filing code LLMCM would be   10.___
   A. Ellington   B. Hallerman   C. Inslerman   D. Willingham

___

KEY (CORRECT ANSWERS)

TEST 1		TEST 2		TEST 3	
1. C		1. B		1. B	11. D
2. A		2. D		2. B	12. B
3. D		3. A		3. B	13. C
4. B		4. C		4. D	14. C
5. A		5. C		5. D	15. D
6. B		6. D		6. B	16. A
7. C		7. B		7. A	17. B
8. A		8. A		8. D	18. C
		9. A		9. C	19. B
		10. C		10. B	

TEST 4	TEST 5	TEST 6
1. A	1. D	1. A
2. D	2. B	2. B
3. E	3. A	3. D
4. A	4. C	4. B
5. C		5. A
6. D		6. C
7. C		7. A
8. E		8. B
9. B		9. C
10. E		10. D

12

NAME and NUMBER COMPARISONS

COMMENTARY

This test seeks to measure your ability and disposition to do a job carefully and accurately, your attention to exactness and preciseness of detail, your alertness and versatility in discerning similarities and differences between things, and your power in systematically handling written language symbols.

It is actually a test of your ability to do academic and/or clerical work, using the basic elements of verbal (qualitative) and mathematical (quantitative) learning -- words and numbers.

EXAMINATION SECTION

DIRECTIONS FOR THIS SECTION:

In each line across the page there are three names or numbers that are much alike. Compare the three names or numbers and decide which ones are exactly alike. *PRINT IN THE SPACE AT THE RIGHT THE LETTER*

    A. if ALL THREE names or numbers are exactly ALIKE
    B. if only the FIRST and SECOND names or numbers are exactly ALIKE
    C. if only the FIRST and THIRD names or numbers are exactly ALIKE
    D. if only the SECOND and THIRD names or numbers are exactly ALIKE
    E. if ALL THREE names or numbers are DIFFERENT

TEST 1

1. Davis Hazen	David Hozen	David Hazen	1. ...
2. Lois Appel	Lois Appel	Lois Apfel	2. ...
3. June Allan	Jane Allan	Jane Allan	3. ...
4. 10235	10235	10235	4. ...
5. 32614	32164	32614	5. ...

TEST 2

1. 2395890	2395890	2395890	1. ...
2. 1926341	1926347	1926314	2. ...
3. E. Owens McVey	E. Owen McVey	E. Owen McVay	3. ...
4. Emily Neal Rouse	Emily Neal Rowse	Emily Neal Rowse	4. ...
5. H. Merritt Audubon	H. Merriott Audubon	H. Merritt Audubon	5. ...

TEST 3

1. 6219354	6219354	6219354	1. ...
2. 2312793	2312793	2312793	2. ...
3. 1065407	1065407	1065047	3. ...
4. Francis Ransdell	Frances Ramsdell	Francis Ramsdell	4. ...
5. Cornelius Detwiler	Cornelius Detwiler	Cornelius Detwiler	5. ...

TEST 4

1. 6452054	6452654	6542054	1. ...
2. 8501268	8501268	8501286	2. ...
3. Ella Burk Newham	Ella Burk Newnham	Elena Burk Newnham	3. ...
4. Jno.K.Ravencroft	Jno.H.Ravencroft	Jno.H.Ravencoft	4. ...
5. Martin Wills Pullen	Martin Wills Pulen	Martin Wills Pullen	5. ...

TEST 5

1. 3457988	3457986	3457986	1. ...
2. 4695682	4695862	4695682	2. ...
3. Stricklund Kaneydy	Sticklund Kanedy	Stricklund Kanedy	3. ...
4. Joy Harlor Witner	Joy Harloe Witner	Joy Harloe Witner	4. ...
5. R.M.O. Uberroth	R.M.O. Uberroth	R.N.O.Uberroth	5. ...

TEST 6

1. 1592514	1592574	1592574	1. ...
2. 2010202	2010202	2010220	2. ...
3. 6177396	6177936	6177396	3. ...
4. Drusilla S.Ridgeley	Drusilla S.Ridgeley	Drusilla S.Ridgeley	4. ...
5. Andrei I.Toumantzev	Andrei I.Tourmantzev	Andrei I.Toumantzov	5. ...

TEST 7

1. 5261383	5261383	5261338	1. ...
2. 8125690	8126690	8125609	2. ...
3. W.E.Johnston	W.E.Johnson	W.E.Johnson	3. ...
4. Vergil L.Muller	Vergil L.Muller	Vergil L.Muller	4. ...
5. Atherton R.Warde	Asheton R.Warde	Atherton P.Warde	5. ...

TEST 8

1. 013469.5	023469.5	02346.95	1. ...
2. 33376	333766	333766	2. ...
3. Ling-Temco-Vought	Ling-Tenco-Vought	Ling-Temco Vought	3. ...
4. Lorilard Corp.	Lorillard Corp.	Lorrilard Corp.	4. ...
5. American Agronomics Corporation	American Agronomics Corporation	American Agronomic Corporation	5. ...

TEST 9

1. 436592£ ¿	436592864	436592864	1. ...
2. 197765 ¿	197755123	197755123	2. ...
3. Dewaay ortvriendt Intern ional S.A.	Deway,Cortvriendt International S.A.	Deway,Corturiendt International S.A.	3. ...
4. Crédit vonnais	Crèdit Lyonnais	Crédit Lyonais	4. ...
5. Algemer Bank Nederland N.V.	Algamene Bank Nederland N.V.	Algemene Bank Naderland N.V.	5. ...

TEST 10

1. 00032572	0.0032572	00032522	1. ...
2. 399745	399745	398745	2. ...
3. Banca Privata Finanziaria S.p.A.	Banca Privata Finanzaria S.P.A.	Banca Privata Finanziaria S.P.A.	3. ...
4. Eastman Dillon, Union Securities & Co.	Eastman Dillon, Union Securities Co.	Eastman Dillon, Union Securities & Co.	4. ...
5. Arnhold and S.Bleichroeder,Inc.	Arnhold & S.Bleichroeder,Inc.	Arnold and S.Bleichroeder,Inc.	5. ...

Tests 11-12.
DIRECTIONS: Answer the questions below on the basis of the following instructions: For each such numbered set of names, addresses, and numbers listed in Columns I and II, select your answer from the following options:

    I. The names in Columns I and II are different.
    II. The addresses in Columns I and II are different.
   III. The numbers in Columns I and II are different.
   IV. The names, addresses, and numbers in Columns I and II are identical.

TEST 11

<u>Column I</u>   <u>Column II</u>

1.   Francis Jones   Francis Jones   1. ...
    62 Stately Avenue   62 Stately Avenue
    96-12446   96-21446
    The CORRECT answer is:
    A. I   B. II   C. III   D. IV

2.   Julio Montez   Julio Montez   2. ...
    19 Ponderosa Road   19 Ponderosa Road
    56-73161   56-71361
    The CORRECT answer is:
    A. I   B. II   C. III   D. IV

3.   Mary Mitchell   Mary Mitchell   3. ...
    2314 Melbourne Drive   2314 Melbourne Drive
    68-92172   68-92172
    The CORRECT answer is:
    A. I   B. II   C. III   D. IV

4.   Harry Patterson   Harry Patterson   4. ...
    25 Dunne Street   25 Dunne Street
    14-33430   14-34330
    The CORRECT answer is:
    A. I   B. II   C. III   D. IV

5.   Patrick Murphy   Patrick Murphy   5. ...
    171 West Hosmer Street   171 West Hosmer Street
    93-81214   93-18214
    The CORRECT answer is:
    A. I   B. II   C. III   D. IV

TEST 12

1.   August Schultz   August Schultz   1. ...
    816 St.Clair Avenue   816 St. Claire Avenue
    53-40149   53-40149
    The CORRECT answer is:
    A. I   B. II   C. III   D. IV

2. George Taft
72 Runnymede Street
47-04033
The CORRECT answer is:
A. 1   B. II   C. III   D. IV

George Taft
72 Runnymede Street
47-04023

2. ...

3. Angus Henderson
1418 Madison Street
81-76375
The CORRECT answer is:
A. I   B. II   C. III   D. IV

Angus Henderson
1418 Madison Street
81-76375

3. ...

4. Carolyn Mazur
12 Riverview Road
38-99615
The CORRECT answer is:
A. I   B. II   C. III   D. IV

Carolyn Mazur
12 Rivervane Road
38-99615

4. ...

5. Adele Russell
1725 Lansing Lane
72-91962
The CORRECT answer is:
A. I   B. II   C. III   D. IV

Adela Russell
1725 Lansing Lane
72-91962

5. ...

TEST 13

DIRECTIONS: The following questions are based on the instructions given below. In each of the following questions, the 3-line name and address in Column I is the master-list entry, and the 3-line entry in Column 2 is the information to be checked against the master list.
If there is one line that is *not* exactly alike, mark your answer I.
If there are two lines that are *not* exactly alike, mark your answer II.
If all three lines are *not* exactly alike, mark your answer III.
If the lines *all* are exactly alike, mark your answer IV.
The CORRECT answer is: A. I   B. II   C. III   D. IV

Column 1	Column 2	
1. Jerome A.Jackson 1243 14th Avenue New York, N.Y. 10023	Jerome A. Johnson 1234 14th Avenue New York, N.Y. 10023	1. ...
2. Sophie Strachtheim 33-28 Connecticut Ave. Far Rockaway, N.Y. 11697	Sophie Strachtheim 33-28 Connecticut Ave. Far Rockaway, N.Y. 11697	2. ...
3. Elisabeth N.T. Gorrell 256 Exchange St New York, N.Y. 10013	Elizabeth N.T. Gorrell 256 Exchange St. New York, N.Y. 10013	3. ...
4. Maria J. Gonzalez 7516 E Sheepshead Rd. Brooklyn, N.Y. 11240	Maria J.Gonzalez 7516 N Shepshead Rd. Brooklyn, N.Y. 11240	4. ...
5. Leslie B. Brautenweiler 21-57A Seiler Terr. Flushing, N.Y. 11367	Leslie B. Brautenwieler 21-75A Seiler Terr. Flushing,N.J.11367	5. ...

KEYS (CORRECT ANSWERS)

TEST 1		TEST 4		TEST 7		TEST 10		TEST 13	
1.	E ✓	1.	E	1.	B	1.	E	1.	B
2.	B ✓	2.	B	2.	E	2.	B	2.	D
3.	D ✓	3.	E	3.	D	3.	E	3.	A
4.	A ✓	4.	E	4.	A	4.	C	4.	A
5.	C ✓	5.	C	5.	E	5.	E	5.	C

TEST 2		TEST 5		TEST 8		TEST 11	
1.	A	1.	D	1.	E	1.	C
2.	E	2.	C	2.	D	2.	C
3.	E	3.	E	3.	E	3.	D
4.	D	4.	D	4.	E	4.	C
5.	C	5.	B	5.	B	5.	C

TEST 3		TEST 6		TEST 9		TEST 12	
1.	A	1.	D	1.	A	1.	B
2.	A	2.	B	2.	D	2.	C
3.	B	3.	C	3.	E	3.	D
4.	E	4.	A	4.	E	4.	B
5.	A	5.	E	5.	E	5.	A

NAME AND NUMBER CHECKING
EXAMINATION SECTION

DIRECTIONS FOR THIS SECTION: This test is designed to measure your speed and accuracy. You are urged to work both quickly and accurately and to do correctly as many lists as you can in the time allowed. The test consists of lists of pairs of names and numbers. Count the number of IDENTICAL pairs in each list. Then, select the correct number, 1, 2, 3, 4, or 5, and indicate your choice by circling the corresponding number on your answer paper.

Two sample questions are presented for your guidance, together with the correct solutions.

SAMPLE QUESTIONS   CIRCLE
                                                CORRECT ANSWER

SAMPLE LIST A

   Adelphi College - Adelphia College   1 2 3 4 5
   Braxton Corp.   - Braxeton Corp.
   Wassaic State School - Wassaic State School
   Central Islip State Hospital - Central Isllip State
     Hospital
   Greenwich House - Greenwich House

NOTE that there are only two correct pairs - Wassaic State School and Greenwich House. Therefore, the CORRECT answer is 2.

SAMPLE LIST B

   78453694 - 78453684   1 2 3 4 5
   784530   - 784530
   533   - 534
   67845   - 67845
   2368745 - 2368755

NOTE that there are only two correct pairs - 784530 and 67845. Therefore, the CORRECT answer is 2.

TEST 1

LIST 1

   Diagnostic Clinic - Diagnostic Clinic   1 2 3 4 5
   Yorkville Health   - Yorkville Health
   Meinhard Clinic   - Meinhart Clinic
   Corlears Clinic   - Carlears Clinic
   Tremont Diagnostic - Tremont Diagnostic

LIST 2

   73526   - 73526   1 2 3 4 5
   7283627198   - 7283627198
   627   - 637
   728352617283 - 728352617282
   6281   - 6281

LIST 3

   Jefferson Clinic   - Jeffersen Clinic   1 2 3 4 5
   Mott Haven Center   - Mott Havan Center
   Bronx Hospital   - Bronx Hospital
   Montefiore Hospital - Montifeore Hospital
   Beth Isreal Hospital - Beth Israel Hospital

1

LIST 4
     936271826   - 936371826   1   2   3   4   5
     5271   - 5291
     82637192037   - 82637192037
     527182   - 5271882
     726354256   - 72635456

LIST 5
     Trinity Hospital   - Trinity Hospital   1   2   3   4   5
     Central Harlem   - Centrel Harlem
     St. Luke's Hospital - St. Lukes' Hospital
     Mt.Sinai Hospital   - Mt.Sinia Hospital
     N.Y.Dispensery   - N.Y.Dispensary

LIST 6
     725361552637 - 725361555637   1   2   3   4   5
     7526378   - 7526377
     6975   - 6975
     82637481028   - 82637481028
     3427   - 3429

LIST 7
     Misericordia Hospital - Miseracordia Hospital   1   2   3   4   5
     Lebonan Hospital   - Lebanon Hospital
     Gouverneur Hospital   - Gouverner Hospital
     German Polyclinic   - German Policlinic
     French Hospital   - French Hospital

LIST 8
     8277364933251 - 827364933351   1   2   3   4   5
     63728   - 63728
     367281   - 367281
     62733846273   - 6273846293
     62836   - 6283

LIST 9
     King's County Hospital - Kings County Hospital   1   2   3   4   5
     St.Johns Long Island   - St.John's Long Island
     Bellevue Hospital   - Bellvue Hospital
     Beth David Hospital   - Beth David Hospital
     Samaritan Hospital   - Samariton Hospital

LIST 10
     62836454   - 62836455   1   2   3   4   5
     42738267   - 42738369
     573829   - 573829
     738291627874   - 738291627874
     725   - 735

LIST 11
     Bloomingdal Clinic   - Bloomingdale Clinic   1   2   3   4   5
     Communitty Hospital - Community Hospital
     Metroplitan Hospital - Metropoliton Hospital
     Lenox Hill Hospital - Lonex Hill Hospital
     Lincoln Hospital   - Lincoln Hospital

LIST 12
```
6283364728 - 6283648
627385     - 627383
54283902   - 54283602
63354      - 63354
7283562781 - 7283562781
```
1 2 3 4 5

LIST 13
```
Sydenham Hospital   - Sydanham Hospital
Roosevalt Hospital  - Roosevelt Hospital
Vanderbilt Clinic   - Vanderbild Clinic
Women's Hospital    - Woman's Hospital
Flushing Hospital   - Flushing Hospital
```
1 2 3 4 5

LIST 14
```
62738        - 62738
727355542321 - 72735542321
263849332    - 263849332
262837       - 263837
47382912     - 47382922
```
1 2 3 4 5

LIST 15
```
Episcopal Hospital - Episcapal Hospital
Flower Hospital    - Flouer Hospital
Stuyvesent Clinic  - Stuyvesant Clinic
Jamaica Clinic     - Jamaica Clinic
Ridgwood Clinic    - Ridgewood Clinic
```
1 2 3 4 5

LIST 16
```
628367299    - 628367399
111          - 111
118293304829 - 1182839489
4448         - 4448
333693678    - 333693678
```
1 2 3 4 5

LIST 17
```
Arietta Crane Farm - Areitta Crane Farm
Bikur Chilim Home  - Bikur Chilom Home
Burke Foundation   - Burke Foundation
Blythedale Home    - Blythdale Home
Campbell Cottages  - Cambell Cottages
```
1 2 3 4 5

LIST 18
```
32123        - 32132
273893326783 - 27389326783
473829       - 473829
7382937      - 7383937
362890122332 - 36289012332
```
1 2 3 4 5

LIST 19
```
Caraline Rest       - Caroline Rest
Loreto Rest         - Loretto Rest
Edgewater Creche    - Edgwater Creche
Holiday Farm        - Holiday Farm
House of St. Giles  - House of st. Giles
```
1 2 3 4 5

LIST 20
```
557286777  - 55728677              1  2  3  4  5
3678902    - 3678892
1567839    - 1567839
7865434712 - 7865344712
9927382    - 9927382
```

LIST 21
```
Isabella Home       - Isabela Home        1  2  3  4  5
James A. Moore Home - James A. More Home
The Robin's Nest    - The Roben's Nest
Pelham Home         - Pelam Home
St.Eleanora's Home  - St. Eleanora's Home
```

LIST 22
```
273648293048 - 273648293048            1  2  3  4  5
334          - 334
7362536478   - 7362536478
7362819273   - 7362819273
7362         - 7363
```

LIST 23
```
St.Pheobe's Mission - St.Phebe's Mission    1  2  3  4  5
Seaside Home'       - Seaside Home
Speedwell Society   - Speedwell Society
Valeria Home        - Valera Home
Wiltwyck            - Wildwyck
```

LIST 24
```
63728        - 63738                1  2  3  4  5
63728192736  - 63728192738
428          - 458
62738291527  - 62738291529
63728192     - 63728192
```

LIST 25
```
McGaffin        - McGafin              1  2  3  4  5
David Ardslee   - David Ardslee
Axton Supply    - Axeton Supply Co
Alice Russell   - Alice Russell
Dobson Mfg.Co.  - Dobsen Mfg. Co.
```

TEST 2

LIST 1
```
82637381028  - 82637281028           1  2  3  4  5
928          - 928
72937281028  - 72937281028
7362         - 7362
927382615    - 927382615
```

LIST 2
```
Albee Theatre      - Albee Theatre       1  2  3  4  5
Lapland Lumber Co. - Laplund Lumber Co.
Adelphi College    - Adelphi College
Jones & Son Inc.   - Jones & Sons Inc.
S.W.Ponds Co.      - S.W. Ponds Co.
```

LIST 3
    85345   - 85345
    895643278   - 895643277
    726352   - 726353
    632685   - 632685
    7263524   - 7236524

LIST 4
    Eagle Library   - Eagle Library
    Dodge Ltd.   - Dodge Co.
    Stromberg Carlson   - Stromberg Carlsen
    Clairice Ling   - Clairice Linng
    Mason Book Co.   - Matson Book Co.

LIST 5
    66273   - 66273
    629   - 620
    7382517283   - 7382517283
    637281   - 639281
    2738261   - 2788261

LIST 6
    Robert MacColl   - Robert McColl
    Buick Motor   - Buck Motors
    Murray Bay & Co.Ltd.   - Murray Bay Co.Ltd.
    L.T. Ltyle   - L.T. Lyttle
    A.S. Landas   - A.S. Landas

LIST 7
    627152637490   - 627152637490
    73526189   - 73526189
    5372   - 5392
    63728142   - 63728124
    4783946   - 4783046

LIST 8
    Tyndall Burke   - Tyndell Burke
    W. Briehl   - W. Briehl
    Burritt Publishing Co. - Buritt Publishing Co.
    Frederick Breyer & Co. - Frederick Breyer Co.
    Bailey Buulard   - Bailey Bullard

LIST 9
    634   - 634
    162837   - 163837
    273892223678   - 27389223678
    527182   - 527782
    3628901223   - 3629002223

LIST 10
    Ernest Boas   - Ernest Boas
    Rankin Barne   - Rankin Barnes
    Edward Appley   - Edward Appely
    Camel   - Camel
    Caiger Food Co.   - Caiger Food Co.

5

LIST 11

6273	- 6273	

LIST 11

LIST 11

```
6273          - 6273
322           - 332
15672839      - 15672839
63728192637   - 63728192639
738           - 738
```
CIRCLE CORRECT ANSWER
1 2 3 4 5

LIST 12
```
Wells Fargo Co.  - Wells Fargo Co.
W.D. Brett       - W.D. Britt
Tassco Co.       - Tassko Co.
Republic Mills   - Republic Mill
R.W. Burnham     - R.W. Burhnam
```
1 2 3 4 5

LIST 13
```
7283529152    - 7283529152
6283          - 6383
52839102738   - 5283910238
308           - 398
82637201927   - 8263720127
```
1 2 3 4 5

LIST 14
```
Schumacker Co.   - Shumacker Co.
C.H. Caiger      - C.H. Caiger
Abraham Strauss  - Abram Straus
B.F. Boettjer    - B.F. Boettijer
Cut-Rate Store   - Cut-Rate Stores
```
1 2 3 4 5

LIST 15
```
15273826      - 15273826
72537         - 73537
726391027384  - 72639107384
637389        - 627399
725382910     - 725382910
```
1 2 3 4 5

LIST 16
```
Hixby Ltd.           - Hixby Lt'd.
S. Reiner            - S. Riener
Reynard Co.          - Reynord Co.
Esso Gassoline Co.   - Esso Gasolene Co.
Belle Brock          - Belle Brock
```
1 2 3 4 5

LIST 17
```
7245          - 7245
819263728192  - 819263728172
682537289     - 682537298
789           - 789
82936542891   - 82936542891
```
1 2 3 4 5

LIST 18
```
Joseph Cartwright   - Joseph Cartwrite
Foote Food Co.      - Foot Food Co.
Weiman & Held       - Weiman & Held
Sanderson Shoe Co.  - Sandersen Shoe Co.
A.M. Byrne          - A.N. Byrne
```
1 2 3 4 5

6

LIST 19
```
4738267        - 4738277
63728          - 63729
6283628901    '- 6283628991
918264         - 918264
263728192037   - 2637728192073
```
1 2 3 4 5

LIST 20
```
Exray Laboratories  - Exray Labratories
Curley Toy Co.      - Curly Toy Co.
J. Lauer & Cross    - J. Laeur & Cross
Mireco Brands       - Mireco Brands
Sandor Lorand       - Sandor Larand
```
1 2 3 4 5

LIST 21
```
607      - 609
6405     - 6403
976      - 996
101267   - 101267
2065432  - 20965432
```
1 2 3 4 5

LIST 22
```
John Macy & Sons    - John Macy & Son
Venus Pencil Co.    - Venus Pencil Co.
Nell McGinnis       - Nell McGinnis
McCutcheon & Co.    - McCutcheon & Co.
Sun-Tan Oil         - Sun-Tan Oil
```
1 2 3 4 5

LIST 23
```
703345700 - 703345700
46754     - 466754
3367490   - 3367490
3379      - 3778
47384     - 47394
```
1 2 3 4 5

LIST 24
```
arthritis              - athritis
asthma                 - asthma
endocrene              - endocrene
gastro-enterological   - gastrol-enteralogical
orthopedic             - orthopedic
```
1 2 3 4 5

LIST 25
```
743829432    - 743828432
998          - 998
732816253902 - 732816252902
46829        - 46830
7439120249   - 7439210249
```
1 2 3 4 5

KEYS (CORRECT ANSWERS)

TEST 1				TEST 2			
1. 3		11. 1		1. 4		11. 3	
2. 3		12. 2		2. 3		12. 1	
3. 1		13. 1		3. 2		13. 1	
4. 1		14. 2		4. 1		14. 1	
5. 1		15. 1		5. 2		15. 2	
6. 2		16. 3		6. 1		16. 1	
7. 1		17. 1		7. 2		17. 3	
8. 2		18. 1		8. 1		18. 1	
9. 1		19. 1		9. 1		19. 1	
10. 2		20. 2		10. 3		20. 1	
		21. 1				21. 1	
		22. 4				22. 4	
		23. 2				23. 2	
		24. 1				24. 3	
		25. 2				25. 1	

———

NAME AND NUMBER CHECKING
EXAMINATION SECTION
TEST 1

DIRECTIONS: Questions 1 through 17 consist of sets of names and addresses. In each question, the name and address in Column II should be an exact copy of the name and address in Column I.
If there is:
a mistake only in the name, mark your answer A;
a mistake only in the address, mark your answer B;
a mistake in both name and address, mark your answer C;
NO mistake in either name or address, mark your answer D.

SAMPLE QUESTION

Column I
Christina Magnusson
288 Greene Street
New York, N.Y. 10003

Column II
Christina Magnusson
288 Greene Street
New York, N.Y. 10013

Since there is a mistake only in the address (the zip code should be 10003 instead of 10013), the answer to the sample question is B.

COLUMN I   COLUMN II

1. Ms. Joan Kelly   Ms. Joan Kielly   1.___
    313 Franklin Ave.   318 Franklin Ave.
    Brooklyn, N.Y. 11202   Brooklyn, N.Y. 11202

2. Mrs. Eileen Engel   Mrs. Ellen Engel   2.___
    47-24 86 Road   47-24 86 Road
    Queens, N.Y. 11122   Queens, N.Y. 11122

3. Marcia Michaels   Marcia Michaels   3.___
    213 E. 81 St.   213 E. 81 St.
    New York, N.Y. 10012   New York, N.Y. 10012

4. Rev. Edward J. Smyth   Rev. Edward J. Smyth   4.___
    1401 Brandeis Street   1401 Brandies Street
    San Francisco, Calif. 96201   San Francisco, Calif. 96201

5. Alicia Rodriguez   Alicia Rodriguez   5.___
    24-68 81 St.   2468 81 St.
    Elmhurst, N.Y. 11122   Elmhurst, N.Y. 11122

6. Ernest Eisemann   Ernest Eisermann   6.___
    21 Columbia St.   21 Columbia St.
    New York, N.Y. 10007   New York, N.Y. 10007

7. Mr. & Mrs. George Petersson   Mr. & Mrs. George Peterson 7.___
    87-11 91st Avenue   87-11 91st Avenue
    Woodhaven, N.Y. 11421   Woodhaven, N.Y. 11421

COLUMN I	COLUMN II	
8. Mr. Ivan Klebnikov 1848 Newkirk Avenue Brooklyn, N.Y. 11226	Mr. Ivan Klebikov 1848 Newkirk Avenue Brooklyn, N.Y. 11622	8.___
9. Samuel Rothfleisch 71 Pine Street New York, N.Y. 10005	Samuel Rothfleisch 71 Pine Street New York, N.Y. 10005	9.___
10. Mrs. Isabel Tonnessen 198 East 185th Street Bronx, N.Y. 10458	Mrs. Isabel Tonnessen 189 East 185th Street Bronx, N.Y. 10458	10.___
11. Esteban Perez 173 Eighth Street Staten Island, N.Y. 10306	Estaban Perez 173 Eighth Street Staten Island, N.Y. 10306	11.___
12. Esta Wong 141 West 68 St. New York, N.Y. 10023	Esta Wang 141 West 68 St. New York, N.Y. 10023	12.___
13. Dr. Alberto Grosso 3475 12th Avenue Brooklyn, N.Y. 11218	Dr. Alberto Grosso 3475 12th Avenue Brooklyn, N.Y. 11218	13.___
14. Mrs. Ruth Bortlas 482 Theresa Ct. Far Rockaway, N.Y. 11691	Ms. Ruth Bortlas 482 Theresa Ct. Far Rockaway, N.Y. 11169	14.___
15. Mr. & Mrs. Howard Fox 2301 Sedgwick Ave. Bronx, N.Y. 10468	Mr. & Mrs. Howard Fox 231 Sedgwick Ave. Bronx, N.Y. 10468	15.___
16. Miss Marjorie Black 223 East 23 Street New York, N.Y. 10010	Miss Margorie Black 223 East 23 Street New York, N.Y. 10010	16.___
17. Michelle Herman 806 Valley Rd. Old Tappan, N.J. 07675	Michelle Hermann 806 Valley Dr. Old Tappan, N.J. 07675	17.___

KEY (CORRECT ANSWERS)

1. C	6. A	11. A	16. A
2. A	7. A	12. A	17. C
3. D	8. C	13. D	
4. B	9. D	14. C	
5. B	10. B	15. B	

TEST 2

DIRECTIONS: Questions 1 through 15 are to be answered SOLELY on the instructions given below. *PRINT THE LETTER OF THE CORRECT ANSWER IN THE SPACE AT THE RIGHT.*

INSTRUCTIONS:

In each of the following questions, the 3-line name and address in Column I is the master-list entry, and the 3-line entry in Column 2 is the information to be checked against the master list.
If there is one line that does not match, mark your answer A;
if there are two lines that do not match, mark your answer B;
if all three lines do not match, mark your answer C;
if the lines all match exactly, mark your answer D.

SAMPLE QUESTION

Column I
Mark L. Field
11-09 Prince Park Blvd.
Bronx, N.Y. 11402

Column II
Mark L. Field
11-99 Prince Park Way
Bronx, N.Y. 11401

The first lines in each column match exactly. The second lines do not match since 11-09 does not match 11-99; and Blvd. does not match Way. The third lines do not match either since 11402 does not match 11401. Therefore, there are two lines that do not match, and the CORRECT answer is B.

	COLUMN I	COLUMN II	
1.	Jerome A. Jackson 1243 14th Avenue New York, N.Y. 10023	Jerome A. Johnson 1234 14th Avenue New York, N.Y. 10023	1.___
2.	Sophie Strachtheim 33-28 Connecticut Ave. Far Rockaway, N.Y. 11697	Sophie Strachtheim 33-28 Connecticut Ave. Far Rockaway, N.Y. 11697	2.___
3.	Elisabeth N.T. Gorrell 256 Exchange St. New York, N.Y. 10013	Elizabeth N.T. Gorrell 256 Exchange St. New York, N.Y. 10013	3.___
4.	Maria J. Gonzalez 7516 E. Sheepshead Rd. Brooklyn, N.Y. 11240	Maria J. Gonzalez 7516 N. Shepshead Rd. Brooklyn, N.Y. 11240	4.___
5.	Leslie B. Brautenweiler 21 57A Seiler Terr. Flushing, N.Y. 11367	Leslie B. Brautenwieler 21-75A Seiler Terr. Flushing, N.J. 11367	5.___
6.	Rigoberto J. Peredes 157 Twin Towers, #18F Tottenville, S.I., N.Y.	Rigoberto J. Peredes 157 Twin Towers, #18F Tottenville, S.I., N.Y.	6.___

COLUMN I	COLUMN II	
7. Pietro F. Albino P.O. Box 7548 Floral Park, N.Y. 11005	Pietro F. Albina P.O. Box 7458 Floral Park, N.Y. 11005	7.___
8. Joanne Zimmermann Bldg. SW, Room 314 532-4601	Joanne Zimmermann Bldg. SW, Room 314 532-4601	8.___
9. Carlyle Whetstone Payroll Div.-A, Room 212A 262-5000, ext. 471	Caryle Whetstone Payroll Div.-A, Room 212A 262-5000, ext. 417	9.___
10. Kenneth Chiang Legal Council, Room 9745 (201) 416-9100, ext. 17	Kenneth Chiang Legal Counsel, Room 9745 (201) 416-9100, ext. 17	10.___

11. Ethel Koenig
Personnel Services Division,
  Room 433
635-7572
	Ethel Hoenig
	Personal Services Division,
	  Room 433
	635-7527
		11.___

12. Joyce Ehrhardt
Office of the Administrator,
  Room W56
387-8706
	Joyce Ehrhart
	Office of the Administrator,
	  Room W56
	387-7806
		12.___

13. Ruth Lang EAM Bldg., Room C101 625-2000, ext. 765	Ruth Lang EAM Bldg., Room C110 625-2000, ext. 765	13.___
14. Anne Marie Ionozzi Investigations, Room 827 576-4000, ext. 832	Anna Marie Ionozzi Investigation, Room 827 566-4000, ext. 832	14.___
15. Willard Jameson Fm C Bldg., Room 687 454-3010	Willard Jamieson Fm C Bldg., Room 687 454-3010	15.___

KEY (CORRECT ANSWERS)

1. B	6. D	11. C
2. D	7. B	12. B
3. A	8. D	13. A
4. A	9. B	14. C
5. C	10. A	15. A

TEST 3

DIRECTIONS: Questions 1 through 10 are to be answered on the basis of the following instructions. *PRINT THE LETTER OF THE CORRECT ANSWER IN THE SPACE AT THE RIGHT.*

INSTRUCTIONS:
For each such set of names, addresses, and numbers listed in Columns I and II, select your answer from the following options:

A. The names in Columns I and II are different.
B. The addresses in Columns I and II are different.
C. The numbers in Columns I and II are different.
D. The names, addresses, and numbers in Columns I and II are identical.

COLUMN I	COLUMN II	
1. Francis Jones 62 Stately Avenue 96-12446	Francis Jones 62 Stately Avenue 96-21446	1.____
2. Julio Montez 19 Ponderosa Road 56-73161	Julio Montez 19 Ponderosa Road 56-71361	2.____
3. Mary Mitchell 2314 Melbourne Drive 68-92172	Mary Mitchell 2314 Melbourne Drive 68-92172	3.____
4. Harry Patterson 25 Dunne Street 14-33430	Harry Patterson 25 Dunne Street 14-34330	4.____
5. Patrick Murphy 171 West Hosmer Street 93-81214	Patrick Murphy 171 West Hosmer Street 93-18214	5.____
6. August Schultz 816 St. Clair Avenue 53-40149	August Schultz 816 St. Claire Avenue 53-40149	6.____
7. George Taft 72 Runnymede Street 47-04033	George Taft 72 Runnymede Street 47-04023	7.____
8. Angus Henderson 1418 Madison Street 81-76375	Angus Henderson 1418 Madison Street 81-76375	8.____
9. Carolyn Mazur 12 Riverview Road 38-99615	Carolyn Mazur 12 Rivervane Road 38-99615	9.____

COLUMN I   COLUMN II

10. Adele Russell   Adela Russell   10.___
     1725 Lansing Lane   1725 Lansing Lane
     72-91962   72-91962

_____

KEY (CORRECT ANSWERS)

1.	C	6.	B
2.	C	7.	C
3.	D	8.	D
4.	C	9.	B
5.	C	10.	A

_____

TEST 4

DIRECTIONS: Questions 1 through 20 test how good you are at catching
mistakes in typing or printing. In each question, the
name and address in Column II should be an exact copy
of the name and address in Column I.
Mark your answer
    A. if there is no mistake in either name or address;
    B. if there is a mistake in both name and address;
    C. if there is a mistake only in the name;
    D. if there is a mistake only in the address.
*PRINT THE LETTER OF THE CORRECT ANSWER IN THE SPACE AT
THE RIGHT.*

COLUMN I	COLUMN II	
1. Milos Yanocek 33-60 14 Street Long Island City, N.Y. 11011	Milos Yanocek 33-60 14 Street Long Island City, N.Y. 11001	1.___
2. Alphonse Sabattelo 24 Minnetta Lane New York, N.Y. 10006	Alphonse Sabbattelo 24 Minetta Lane New York, N.Y. 10006	2.___
3. Helen Stearn 5 Metropolitan Oval Bronx, N.Y. 10462	Helene Stearn 5 Metropolitan Oval Bronx, N.Y. 10462	3.___
4. Jacob Weisman 231 Francis Lewis Boulevard Forest Hills, N.Y. 11325	Jacob Weisman 231 Francis Lewis Boulevard Forest Hills, N.Y. 11325	4.___
5. Riccardo Fuente 134 West 83 Street New York, N.Y. 10024	Riccardo Fuentes 134 West 88 Street New York, N.Y. 10024	5.___
6. Dennis Lauber 52 Avenue D Brooklyn, N.Y. 11216	Dennis Lauder 52 Avenue D Brooklyn, N.Y. 11216	6.___
7. Paul Cutter 195 Galloway Avenue Staten Island, N.Y. 10356	Paul Cutter 175 Galloway Avenue Staten Island, N.Y. 10365	7.___
8. Sean Donnelly 45-58 41 Avenue Woodside, N.Y. 11168	Sean Donnelly 45-58 41 Avenue Woodside, N.Y. 11168	8.___
9. Clyde Willot 1483 Rockaway Avenue Brooklyn, N.Y. 11238	Clyde Willat 1483 Rockway Avenue Brooklyn, N.Y. 11238	9.___

	COLUMN I	COLUMN II	

10. Michael Stanakis
419 Sheriden Avenue
Staten Island, N.Y. 10363

Michael Stanakis
419 Sheraden Avenue
Staten Island, N.Y. 10363

10.___

11. Joseph DiSilva
63-84 Saunders Road
Rego Park, N.Y. 11431

Joseph Disilva
64-83 Saunders Road
Rego Park, N.Y. 11431

11.___

12. Linda Polansky
2225 Fenton Avenue
Bronx, N.Y. 10464

Linda Polansky
2255 Fenton Avenue
Bronx, N.Y. 10464

12.___

13. Alfred Klein
260 Hillside Terrace
Staten Island, N.Y. 15545

Alfred Klein
260 Hillside Terrace
Staten Island, N.Y. 15545

13.___

14. William McDonnell
504 E. 55 Street
New York, N.Y. 10103

William McConnell
504 E. 55 Street
New York, N.Y. 10108

14.___

15. Angela Cipolla
41-11 Parson Avenue
Flushing, N.Y. 11446

Angela Cipola
41-11 Parsons Avenue
Flushing, N.Y. 11446

15.___

16. Julie Sheridan
1212 Ocean Avenue
Brooklyn, N.Y. 11237

Julia Sheridan
1212 Ocean Avenue
Brooklyn, N.Y. 11237

16.___

17. Arturo Rodriguez
2156 Cruger Avenue
Bronx, N.Y. 10446

Arturo Rodrigues
2156 Cruger Avenue
Bronx, N.Y. 10446

17.___

18. Helen McCabe
2044 East 19 Street
Brooklyn, N.Y. 11204

Helen McCabe
2040 East 19 Street
Brooklyn, N.Y. 11204

18.___

19. Charles Martin
526 West 160 Street
New York, N.Y. 10022

Charles Martin
526 West 160 Street
New York, N.Y. 10022

19.___

20. Morris Rabinowitz
31 Avenue M
Brooklyn, N.Y. 11216

Morris Rabinowitz
31 Avenue N
Brooklyn, N.Y. 11216

20.___

KEY (CORRECT ANSWERS)

1. D		11. B	
2. B		12. D	
3. C		13. A	
4. A		14. B	
5. B		15. B	
6. C		16. C	
7. D		17. C	
8. A		18. D	
9. B		19. A	
10. D		20. D	

TEST 5

DIRECTIONS: In copying the addresses below from Column A to the same
line in Column B, an Agent-in-Training made some errors.
For Questions 1 through 5, if you find that the Agent
made an error in

        only one line, mark your answer A;
        only two lines, mark your answer B;
        only three lines, mark your answer C;
        all four lines, mark your answer D.

EXAMPLE

Column A	Column B
24 Third Avenue	24 Third Avenue
5 Lincoln Road	5 Lincoln Street
50 Central Park West	6 Central Park West
37-21 Queens Boulevard	21-37 Queens Boulevard

Since errors were made on only three lines, namely the second, third,
and fourth, the CORRECT answer is C.
PRINT THE LETTER OF THE CORRECT ANSWER IN THE SPACE AT THE RIGHT.

COLUMN A	COLUMN B	
1. 57-22 Springfield Boulevard	75-22 Springfield Boulevard	1.___
94 Gun Hill Road	94 Gun Hill Avenue	
8 New Dorp Lane	8 New Drop Lane	
36 Bedford Avenue	36 Bedford Avenue	
2. 538 Castle Hill Avenue	538 Castle Hill Avenue	2.___
54-15 Beach Channel Drive	54-15 Beach Channel Drive	
21 Ralph Avenue	21 Ralph Avenue	
162 Madison Avenue	162 Morrison Avenue	
3. 49 Thomas Street	49 Thomas Street	3.___
27-21 Northern Blvd.	21-27 Northern Blvd.	
86 125th Street	86 125th Street	
872 Atlantic Ave.	872 Baltic Ave.	
4. 261-17 Horace Harding Expwy.	261-17 Horace Harding Pkwy.	4.___
191 Fordham Road	191 Fordham Road	
6 Victory Blvd.	6 Victoria Blvd.	
552 Oceanic Ave.	552 Ocean Ave.	
5. 90-05 38th Avenue	90-05 36th Avenue	5.___
19 Central Park West	19 Central Park East	
9281 Avenue X	9281 Avenue X	
22 West Farms Square	22 West Farms Square	

KEY (CORRECT ANSWERS)

1. C
2. A
3. B
4. C
5. B

———

TEST 6

Questions 1-10.

DIRECTIONS: For Questions 1 through 10, choose the letter in Column II
next to the number which EXACTLY matches the number in
Column I. *PRINT THE LETTER OF THE CORRECT ANSWER IN THE
SPACE AT THE RIGHT.*

	COLUMN I	COLUMN II	
1.	14235	A. 13254	1.___
		B. 12435	
		C. 13245	
		D. 14235	
2.	70698	A. 90768	2.___
		B. 60978	
		C. 70698	
		D. 70968	
3.	11698	A. 11689	3.___
		B. 11986	
		C. 11968	
		D. 11698	
4.	50497	A. 50947	4.___
		B. 50497	
		C. 50749	
		D. 54097	
5.	69635	A. 60653	5.___
		B. 69630	
		C. 69365	
		D. 69635	
6.	1201022011	A. 1201022011	6.___
		B. 1201020211	
		C. 1202012011	
		D. 1021202011	
7.	3893981389	A. 3893891389	7.___
		B. 3983981389	
		C. 3983891389	
		D. 3893981389	
8.	4765476589	A. 4765476598	8.___
		B. 4765476588	
		C. 4765476589	
		D. 4765746589	
9.	8679678938	A. 8679687938	9.___
		B. 8679678938	
		C. 8697678938	
		D. 8678678938	

COLUMN I	COLUMN II	
10. 6834836932	A. 6834386932	10.____
	B. 6834836923	
	C. 6843836932	
	D. 6834836932	

Questions 11-15.

DIRECTIONS: For Questions 11 through 15, determine how many of the symbols in Column Z are exactly the same as the symbol in Column Y.
If none is exactly the same, answer A;
if only one symbol is exactly the same, answer B;
if two symbols are exactly the same, answer C;
if three symbols are exactly the same, answer D.

SYMBOL COLUMN Y	SYMBOL COLUMN Z	
11. A123B1266	A123B1366	11.____
	A123B1266	
	A133B1366	
	A123B1266	
12. CC28D3377	CD22D3377	12.____
	CC38D3377	
	CC28C3377	
	CC28D2277	
13. M21AB201X	M12AB201X	13.____
	M21AB201X	
	M21AB201Y	
	M21BA201X	
14. PA383Y744	AP383Y744	14.____
	PA338Y744	
	PA388Y744	
	PA383Y774	
15. PB2Y8893	PB2Y8893	15.____
	PB2Y8893	
	PB3Y8898	
	PB2Y8893	

KEY (CORRECT ANSWERS)

1. D	6. A	11. C
2. C	7. D	12. A
3. D	8. C	13. B
4. B	9. B	14. A
5. D	10. D	15. D

ABILITY TO APPLY STATED LAWS, RULES AND REGULATIONS
EXAMINATION SECTION

DIRECTIONS: For each of the questions below, select the letter that represents the BEST of the four choices. *PRINT THE LETTER OF THE CORRECT ANSWER IN THE SPACE AT THE RIGHT.*

Questions 1-2.

DIRECTIONS: Questions 1 and 2 are to be answered on the basis of the following passage.

Effective December 1, 1984, employees who are entitled to be paid at an overtime minimum wage rate according to the terms of a state minimum wage order must be paid for overtime at a rate at least time and one-half of the appropriate regular minimum wage rate for non-overtime work. For the purpose of this policy statement, the term *appropriate regular minimum wage rate* means $3.35 per hour or a lower minimum wage rate established in accordance with the provisions of a state minimum wage order. OVERTIME MINIMUM WAGES MAY NOT BE OFFSET BY PAYMENTS IN EXCESS OF THE REGULAR MINIMUM RATE FOR NON-OVERTIME WORK.

1. A worker who ordinarily works forty hours a week at an agreed wage of $4.00 an hour is required to work ten hours in excess of forty during a payroll week and is paid for the extra ten hours at his $4.00 per hour rate.
Using the information contained in the above passage, it is BEST to conclude
   A. this was a correct application of the regulation
   B. this was an incorrect application of the regulation
   C. the employee was not underpaid because he or she agreed upon the wage rate
   D. the employee did not perform his job well

1.___

2. According to the information in the above passage, the employee in Question 1 was MOST likely underpaid at least
   A. $60.00
   C. $20.00
   B. $10.25
   D. not underpaid at all

2.___

Question 3.

DIRECTIONS: Question 3 is to be answered on the basis of the following passage.

The following guidelines establish a range of monetary assessments for various types of child labor violations. They are general in nature and may not cover every specific situation. In determining the appropriate monetary amount within the range shown, consideration will be given to the criteria enumerated in the statute, namely *the size of the employer's business, the good faith of the employer, the gravity of the violation, the history of previous violations, and the failure to comply with record keeping or other requirements.* For example, the penalty for a larger firm (25 or more employees) would tend to be in the higher range since such firms should have knowledge of the laws. The gravity of the violation would depend on such factors as the age of the minor, whether required to be in school, and the degree of exposure to the hazards of prohibited occupations. Failure to keep records of the hours of work of the minors would also have a bearing on the size of the penalty.

1. a. No employment certificate - child of employer (Sec. 131 or 132)
   b. No posted hours of work (Sec. 178)

1. 1st violation - $ 0-$100
   2nd violation - $100-$250
   3rd violation - $250-$500

2. a. Invalid employment certificate, e.g., *student non-factory* rather than *general* for a 16 year old in non-factory work (Sec. 132)
   b. Maximum or prohibited hours - less than one half hour beyond limit on any day, occasional, no pattern. (Sec. 130.2e, 131.3f, 170.1, 171.1, 170.2, 172.1, 173.1; Ed.L. 3227, 3228)

2. 1st violation - $ 0-$100
   2nd violation - $150-$250
   3rd violation - $250-$500

3. a. No employment certificate. (Sec. 130.2e, 131.3f, 131, 132, 138; Ed.L. 3227, 3228; ACAL 35.01, 35.05)
   b. Maximum or prohibited hours - (1) less than one half hour beyond limit on regular basis, (2) more than one half hour beyond limit either occasional or on a regular basis (Sec. 130.2e, 131.3f, 170.1, 171.1, 170.2, 172.1, 173.1; Ed.L. 3227, 3228)

3. 1st violation - $100-$250
   2nd violation - $250-$500
   3rd violation - $400-$500

4. Prohibited Occupations - Hazardous Employment (Sec. 130.1, 131.3f, 131.2, 133)

4. 1st violation - $300-$500
   2nd violation - $400-$500
   3rd violation - $400-$500

COMPLIANCE CONFERENCE PRIOR TO ASSESSMENT OF PENALTY.

After a child labor violation is reported, a compliance conference will be scheduled affording the employer the opportunity to be heard on the reported violation. A determination regarding the assessment of a civil penalty will be made following the conference.

RIGHT TO APPEAL

If the employer is aggrieved by the determination following such conference, the employer has the right to appeal such determination within 60 days of the date of issuance to the Industrial Board of Appeals, 194 Washington Avenue, Albany, New York 12210 as prescribed by its Rules of Procedure.

3. According to the above passage, a firm with its third   3.___
   violation of child labor laws regarding no posted hours
   of work (Sec. 178) and prohibited occupations-hazardous
   employment would be fined
   A. $600-$1,000
   B. $650
   C. $1,000
   D. cannot be determined from the information given

Question 4.

DIRECTIONS: Question 4 is to be answered on the basis of the following passage.

Section 198c. Benefits or Wage Supplements.

1. In addition to any other penalty or punishment otherwise prescribed by law, any employer who is party to an agreement to pay or provide benefits or wage supplements to employees or to a third party or fund for the benefit of employees and who fails, neglects, or refuses to pay the amount or amounts necessary to provide such benefits or furnish such supplements within thirty days after such payments are required to be made, shall be guilty of a misdemeanor, and upon conviction shall be punished as provided in Section One Hundred Ninety-Eight-a of this article. Where such employer is a corporation, the president, secretary, treasurer, or officers exercising corresponding functions shall each be guilty of a misdemeanor.

2. As used in this section, the term *benefits or wage supplements* includes, but is not limited to, reimbursement for expenses; health, welfare, and retirement benefits; and vacation, separation or holiday pay.

4. According to the above passage, an employer who had agreed   4.___
   to furnish an employee with a car and then failed to
   provide a car is
   A. not guilty of a misdemeanor
   B. most likely guilty of a misdemeanor
   C. not affected by the above regulation
   D. guilty of a felony

Question 5.

DIRECTIONS: Question 5 is to be answered on the basis of the
              following passage.

Manual workers must be paid weekly and not later than seven
calendar days after the end of the week in which the wages are
earned. However, a manual worker employed by a non-profitmaking
organization must be paid in accordance with the agreed terms of
employment, but not less frequently than semi-monthly. A manual
worker means a mechanic, workingman, or laborer. Railroad workers,
other than executives, must be paid on or before Thursday of each
week the wages earned during the seven-day period ending on
Tuesday of the preceding week. Commission sales personnel must be
paid in accordance with the agreed terms of employment but not
less frequently than once in each month and not later than the
last day of the month following the month in which the money is
earned. If the monthly payment of wages, salary, drawing account
or commissions is substantial, then additional compensation such
as incentive earnings may be paid less frequently than once in each
month, but in no event later than the time provided in the employment agreement.

5.   A non-executive railroad worker has not been paid for the   5.___
     previous week's work. It is Wednesday.
     According to the above passage, which of the following is
     TRUE?
     The above regulation
        A. was not violated since the ending period is the
           following Tuesday
        B. was violated
        C. was not violated since the employee could be paid
           on Thursday
        D. does not apply in this case

Question 6.

DIRECTIONS: Question 6 is to be answered on the basis of the
              following passage.

No deductions may be made from wages except deductions
authorized by law, or which are authorized in writing by the
employee and are for the employee's benefit. Authorized deductions include payments for insurance premiums, pensions, U.S.
bonds, and union dues, as well as similar payments for the
benefit of the employee. An employer may not make any payment
by separate transaction unless such charge or payment is permitted as a deduction from wages. Examples of illegal deductions
or charges include payments by the employee for spoilage, breakage,
cash shortages or losses, and cost and maintenance of required
uniforms.

6. An employee working on a cash register is short $40 at   6.___
the end of his shift. The $40 is deducted from his wages.
According to the above passage, the deduction is
   A. legal because it is legal to deduct cash losses
   B. legal because the employee is at fault
   C. illegal because the employee was not told of the
      deduction in advance
   D. illegal

Questions 7-8.

DIRECTIONS: Questions 7 and 8 are to be answered on the basis
of the following passage.

No employee shall be paid a wage at a rate less than the rate
at which an employee of the opposite sex in the same establishment
is paid for equal work on a job, the performance of which requires
equal skill, effort, and responsibility, and which is performed
under similar working conditions, except where payment is made
pursuant to a differential based on:
   a. A system which measures earnings by quantity or quality
      of production
   b. A merit system
   c. A seniority system; or
   d. Any other factor other than sex.

Any violation of the above is illegal.

7. A woman working in a factory on a piece-rate system as a   7.___
sewing machine operator received less pay than a male
sewing machine operator who finished more items.
According to the above regulation, this is
   A. legal
   B. illegal
   C. legal, but not ethical
   D. no conclusion can be made from the information given

8. A male worker is in the same job title as a female worker.   8.___
The male worker has been employed by the firm for three
years, the female for two.
Using the regulation stated above, if the male worker is
paid more than the female worker, the action is
   A. legal
   B. illegal
   C. legal, but not ethical
   D. no conclusion can be made from the information given

Question 9.

DIRECTIONS: Question 9 is to be answered on the basis of the
following passage.

Section 162. Time Allowed for Meals.

1. Every person employed in or in connection with a factory
shall be allowed at least sixty minutes for the noon day meal.

2. Every person employed in or in connection with a mercantile or other establishment or occupation coming under the provisions of this chapter shall be allowed at least forty-five minutes
for the noon day meal, except as in this chapter otherwise provided.

3. Every person employed for a period or shift starting before
noon and continuing later than seven o'clock in the evening shall
be allowed an additional meal period of at least twenty minutes
between five and seven o'clock in the evening.

4. Every person employed for a period or shift of more than
six hours starting between the hours of one o'clock in the afternoon and six o'clock in the morning, shall be allowed at least
sixty minutes for a meal period when employed in or in connection
with a factory, and forty-five minutes for a meal period when
employed in or in connection with a mercantile or other establishment or occupation coming under the provision of this chapter, at
a time midway between the beginning and end of such employment.

5. The commissioner may permit a shorter time to be fixed for
meal periods than hereinbefore provided. The permit therefore shall
be in writing and shall be kept conspicuously posted in the main
entrance of the establishment. Such permit may be revoked at any
time.

In administering this statute, the Department applies the
following interpretations and guidelines:

Employee Coverage. Section 162 applies to every *person* in any
establishment or occupation covered by the Labor Law. Accordingly,
all categories of workers are covered, including white collar
management staff.

Shorter Meal Periods. The Department will permit a shorter meal
period of not less than 30 minutes as a matter of course, without
application by the employer, so long as there is no indication of
hardship to employees. A meal period of not less than 20 minutes
will be permitted only in special or unusual cases after investigation and issuance of a special permit.

9. An employee is given twenty minutes for lunch.   9._____
    According to the information given in the above passage,
    the employer
        A. is in violation
        B. is not in violation
        C. should be fined $250
        D. no conclusion can be made from the information given

Question 10.

DIRECTIONS: Question 10 is to be answered on the basis of the
following passage.

An employee shall not be obliged to incur expenses in the
arrangement whereby the employee's wages or salary are directly
deposited in a bank or financial institution or in the withdrawal
of such wages or salary from the bank or financial institution.
Some examples of expenses are as follows:

1. A service charge, *per check* charge, or administrative
or processing charge
2. Carfare in order to get to the bank or financial institution to withdraw wages

An employee shall not be obliged to lose a substantial amount
of uncompensated time in order to withdraw wages from a bank or
financial institution. Although the employer is not required to
provide employees with paid time in which to withdraw such monies,
the Department has held that the employer should provide for the
loss of time when the employee requires more than 15 minutes to
withdraw wages. Such time includes travel time to and from, as
well as actual time spent at the bank or financial institution in
withdrawing such monies. The loss of such time without compensation constitutes a difficulty.

The withdrawal of wages may not interfere with an employee's
meal period to the extent that it decreases the meal period to less
than 30 minutes. Thus, although the time required for withdrawal
of wages may be 15 minutes or less, the loss of even 8 or 9 minutes
from a thirty minute meal period creates a difficulty.

10. An employee is unable to withdraw wages at any time other   10.___
than her lunch break. She needs twenty minutes to with-
draw wages and has a forty-five minute lunch break.
According to the information contained in the above passage,
the employer
A. is in violation
B. is not in violation
C. should be fined $250
D. no conclusion can be made from the information given

KEY (CORRECT ANSWERS)

1.	B	6.	D
2.	B	7.	A
3.	D	8.	A
4.	B	9.	D
5.	C	10.	A

MEMORY FOR FACTS AND INFORMATION
EXAMINATION SECTION
TEST 1

DIRECTIONS: Questions 1 through 15 test your ability to remember key facts and details. You are given a rather long reading passage, which you will have approximately ten minutes to read. The reading selection should then be turned over. Then immediately answer the fifteen questions that refer to this passage. Please do NOT refer back to the reading passage at any time while you are answering the questions. Select the letter that represents the BEST of the four possible choices.

THE CASE OF THE MISSING OVERTIME WAGES

Melba Tolliber is a new Labor Standards Investigator assigned to investigate a complaint of nonpayment of some overtime wages. The complaint came in the form of a telephone call from Albert Brater, employed by the Whizzer Audio and Video Store in Dorchester. Whizzer Audio and Video, Inc. is a fast-growing and very successful chain in the Northeast. Their headquarters is in Dorchester.

Melba Tolliber drives the eight miles to Dorchester on a breezy Monday morning. She meets with Albert Brater, the employee who called. He is employed in the warehouse unit.

Hello, Mr. Brater, my name is Melba Tolliber, and I'm here to investigate whether you've been paid the proper amount of overtime wages.

Nice to meet you, Ms. Tolliber. I'm not the only one with this problem. Two salesclerks in the Dorchester store, Mary and Martin, have also gotten less for overtime than they should have.

Can I talk with them, too? Melba asks.

Well, the problem is, we're worried about getting into a lot of trouble with the company. We were hoping you could talk just to me. I'm a little worried about talking with you myself.

This is a confidential interview; don't worry. It would be very helpful, however, if I could at least get copies of their paystubs.

Albert hesitates and then says, *Gee, I hope I can find my last paystub. Anyway, we've been working forty-six hours a week the last four weeks, but only getting paid our usual rate of $3.25 an hour.*

Melba says, *But that's below the minimum wage.*

Maybe it's $3.35; I get confused; I'll have to check. I think it's $3.35. Yeah, I'm pretty sure it's $3.35. But you know what else? I was promised a raise of $.50 per hour after eight months of working here, and that's up next week. We'll see if I get it or not.

Have the other employees here gotten the raises they were promised?

Yeah, I think they have. But I know of at least one person, a truckdriver, who hasn't gotten his raise yet.

Do you know his name?

Just his first name. But the next time I see him, I'll ask him if he's gotten the raise yet. I'll let you know if he hasn't.

What day would be good for you to drop off the paystubs and have a second interview?

Well, you have to give me some time to get them from Mary and Martin, too. How about this Thursday afternoon at one?

Fine, here's my card. I'll see you this Thursday at one.

At the beginning of their next meeting, Albert gives Melba the paystubs for the last month's work for all three employees.

Let's do you first, Albert. What have your hours been each week for the last four weeks?

I've worked the same schedule for the past month, my usual forty hours - 8 to 5 with an hour for lunch, which I don't like, on Mondays, Tuesdays, and Thursdays. Wednesdays and Fridays I've worked from 8 A.M. to 9 P.M. because those are the days we do our most shipping. They give us from 5 to 6 P.M. as a dinner break on those days.

So that adds up to forty-six hours. Give me a few minutes to go over these figures with my calculator.

That's a great calculator; it's so small. Looks like a credit card.

Thanks, but I have to be careful how I hit the numbers; there's not much room.... Well, according to my calculations, you're owed $40.20 in overtime pay for the last four weeks. But there's something else wrong, too. It looks like they've been taking out a little too much money for Social Security. Let me recheck this.

1. In the passage, Melba Tolliber visited   1.___
    A. Midwood   B. Dorchester
    C. Midale   D. Midville

2. In the passage, Melba talked with   2.___
    A. Albert who works in the warehouse unit
    B. Albert who works in the warehouse unit and in the
       store
    C. Robert who works in the warehouse
    D. Robert, Martin, and Mary who work in the warehouse
       and the store

3. The organization whose payment of overtime wages is in   3.___
    question
    A. is struggling to succeed
    B. is the most successful of the new audio-visual store
       chains in the Northeast
    C. has its headquarters in the town that Melba travels to
    D. has successfully switched from selling just records to
       selling records, tapes, and video equipment

4. During their initial discussion, how sure of his rate of   4.___
    pay was the employee to whom Melba spoke?
    A. Not sure at all   B. Very sure
    C. Pretty sure   D. Totally unsure

5. What day of the week did Melba conduct the initial inter- 5.___
    view?
    A. Monday   B. Wednesday
    C. Tuesday   D. Thursday

6. When did Melba conduct the second interview?   6.___
    A. Monday at 1 P.M.   B. Thursday at 1 P.M.
    C. Wednesday at 1 P.M.   D. Friday at 1 P.M.

7. In order to calculate how much money the employee should 7.___
    have received, Melba used a
    A. credit card
    B. calculator
    C. credit card/calculator/watch combination
    D. desk top personal computer

8. According to the passage, what did Melba do to try to   8.___
    make the employee feel more at ease?
    She
    A. gave him time to collect his thoughts
    B. assured him that she believed what he said
    C. assured him that the interview was confidential
    D. asked if she could speak with the other two employees
       affected

9. The initial complaint from the employee
   A. resulted in his receiving back pay
   B. came in the form of a phone call
   C. was anonymous
   D. resulted in a large-scale investigation

10. The name of the establishment the employee works for
    is the
    A. Whizzer
    B. Genuine Article
    C. Electronic Era
    D. Gizmos etcetera

11. The other two employees who have questions about their
    overtime pay
    A. are truckdrivers   B. work in the warehouse
    C. are salesclerks   D. work in maintenance

12. The organization told the employee he would receive a
    A. $.60 per hour raise after eight months
    B. $.60 per hour raise after five months
    C. $.50 per hour raise after six months
    D. $.50 per hour raise after eight months

13. How many hours a week have the employees who are question-
    ing their pay been working for the last month?
    A. Forty-four   B. Forty-five
    C. Forty-six   D. Forty-eight

14. In the last month, what hours did the employee Melba
    interviewed work on Wednesdays?
    A. 8 A.M. to 5 P.M.   B. 9 A.M. to 10 P.M.
    C. 9 A.M. to 5 P.M.   D. 8 A.M. to 9 P.M.

15. At the start of the second interview,
    A. the employee gives Melba the paystubs for the last
       month for all three workers involved
    B. the employee gives Melba the paystubs for the last
       month for all three workers involved, with the
       exception of his last paystub
    C. the employee gives Melba only his paystubs from the
       last month
    D. it cannot be determined if the employee gives Melba
       any paystubs

—

KEY (CORRECT ANSWERS)

1. B	6. B	11. C
2. A	7. B	12. D
3. C	8. C	13. C
4. C	9. B	14. D
5. A	10. A	15. A

—

TEST 2

DIRECTIONS: Questions 1 through 15 test your ability to remember key facts and details. You are given a rather long reading passage, which you will have approximately ten minutes to read. The reading selection should then be turned over. Then immediately answer the fifteen questions that refer to this passage. Please do NOT refer back to the reading passage at any time while you are answering these questions. Select the letter that represents the BEST of the four possible choices.

THE CASE OF THE DELINQUENT TAXPAYER

David Owens has been a Tax Investigator for five years. His unit has received another anonymous tip about possible sales tax abuse, and David's supervisor, William, has assigned David to conduct the investigation. The organization in question is Bob's News, a 24-hour newsstand and variety store. The store is located in Hillsdell, five miles away. The anonymous caller did not provide details, but stated that she was an employee, and that there was widespread *abuse in the collection and reporting of sales tax by the store.* The agency has had a series of crank calls regarding sales tax abuse in Hillsdell.

For this investigation, David has been instructed not to work undercover, but to go in, identify himself, and discuss the situation with the owner and some employees without divulging the reason for the visit. On Wednesday, David drives to the store in a government car, a 1994 Plymouth.

David arrives at the store and buys a magazine for which he is properly not charged sales tax. He speaks to the employee whose name tag says Susan.

Hello, Susan, my name is David Owens, and I'm from the State Tax Department. Here's my identification. We're doing a routine check-up to see if things are in order with regard to sales tax collection and reporting. Is the owner around?

No, Bob is out of town today. He'll be back tomorrow. You seem surprised that his name is Bob. Some people think he must not exist, sort of like a Betty Crocker or something. Can I help you with anything? I'm the Assistant Manager.

Well, it would be helpful if you could answer a few questions for me.

As long as it doesn't get me in trouble with my boss, I'd be glad to, Susan replied.

Don't worry, I won't ask you anything that could get you in trouble.

OK, then.

Did someone tell employees how to go about collecting sales tax on items?

Bob has a list of items we're not allowed to collect tax on. It's right next to the cash register. Would you like to see it?

If you don't mind. Thanks. It says here not to collect tax on magazines, but there's no mention of newspapers.

I guess that's because he probably assumes we know better than that. I'll ask him to add it to the list.

This is a pretty good list, but what's this written on the bottom here about toilet paper? That's a taxable item.

Oh, I know. Henry who works nights put that in as a joke because he says toilet paper is a necessity, not a luxury, and shouldn't be taxed. I agree. So does Bob. But don't worry, we collect sales tax on it. Nine percent, right?

No, the rate is eight percent.

Just kidding, David. We know that. I guess I shouldn't joke about something like that; I don't want to end up in jail. What else do you need to know?

Who keeps the records and submits the sales tax money to Metro City every quarter?

Bob does that himself, but I'd rather you come back tomorrow to talk with him about that end of it....I think that would be best. I don't know much about it, except that he yells if I don't have everything - the records and stuff - ready for him when he wants it.

What time do you think Bob will be in tomorrow?

I think the morning would be best; you'll be sure to catch him then.

OK, I'll drop by tomorrow around nine. See you then. Thanks again.

The next day, David drives back to the store to meet with Bob at the time stated earlier. When he arrives, Susan immediately introduces him to Bob.

It's nice to meet you, Bob. Nice store you have here. How long have you been in business?

We've been open for five years. Time really flies, doesn't it?

It sure does. As Susan probably mentioned, I'm here on a routine type check-up about sales tax collection.

Sure thing.

Well, I just noticed you're not displaying the Sales Tax Certificate of Authority that you need to show in order to collect sales tax.

That's strange; it was there yesterday. Here it is. It fell under the counter. We're off to a great start. Let me tape this thing back up.

How many employees work here, Bob?

We have six full-time and three part-time employees, plus myself. I understand you'd like to see our books. Come on in to my office. Stay in here as long as you need. I've got it all laid out for you.

Thanks.

Several hours later, David finishes looking through the books.

Well, Bob, things look in order. The only question I have is why your receipts for 1994 were so much lower than in other years?

A chain store moved in about eight blocks away, and we initially lost a lot of business. But eventually our customers started coming back. We do the little things - save them the Boston papers, things like that. The chain moved downtown in early 1995.

Well, listen, thanks very much for all of your time. I really appreciate it.

No problem. Anytime. Well, I wouldn't go that far, but it's been nice meeting you.

1. What was the name of the Tax Investigator in the above   1.____
   passage?
   A. David Allen   B. Bob Williams
   C. Derwin Williams   D. David Owens

2. What was the name of the city the investigator visited?   2.____
   A. Hillsville   B. Hillsdale
   C. Hicksville   D. Hillsdell

3. The store under investigation is a   3.____
   A. department store
   B. 24-hour massage parlor
   C. newsstand and variety store
   D. sporting goods store

4. The phone call received by the agency was   4.____
   A. placed by an anonymous employee of the store being
      accused of sales tax fraud
   B. received by the investigator handling the case
   C. placed by an anonymous caller
   D. received by the investigator's supervisor

5. The investigator on this case   5.____
   A. did not work undercover
   B. was instructed to work undercover, but refused because
      of the nature of the case
   C. worked undercover
   D. pretended to his supervisor that he worked undercover

6. According to the above passage, it is   6.____
   A. not correct to charge sales tax for a magazine
   B. correct to charge sales tax for pet food
   C. correct to charge sales tax for a newspaper
   D. correct to charge sales tax for a magazine

7. The Assistant Manager of the store is   7.____
   A. Susan   B. David
   C. Bob   D. Betty Crocker

8. What day was the initial investigation conducted?   8.____
   A. Monday   B. Wednesday
   C. Tuesday   D. Thursday

9. The list the investigator was shown contained   9.____
   A. a list of sales taxable items
   B. a list of non-taxable items
   C. a list of products on which sales tax was mistakenly
      charged
   D. the Certificate of Authority

10. According to the above passage, sales tax was to be   10.____
    charged on
    A. pet food   B. cigarettes
    C. gasoline   D. toilet paper

11. According to the above passage, the sales tax was _____ %.   11.___
    A. seven   B. nine   C. eight   D. ten

12. According to the passage, how often was the sales tax   12.___
    submitted?
    A. Every month   B. Quarterly
    C. Twice a year   D. Once every six months

13. According to the passage, where are the sales tax monies   13.___
    sent?
    A. River City   B. Metro City
    C. Metropolis   D. Hillswood

14. According to the passage, which of the following is TRUE?   14.___
    Bob's business, called Bob's
    A. News and Variety, has been open for five years
    B. Department Store, has been open for six years
    C. Variety, has been open for six years
    D. News, has been open for five years

15. The only question the investigator had about Bob's books   15.___
    was why receipts for _____ than in other years.
    A. 1995 were so much lower
    B. 1994 were so much lower
    C. 1995 were so much higher
    D. 1994 were so much higher

KEY (CORRECT ANSWERS)

1. D	6. A	11. C
2. D	7. A	12. B
3. C	8. B	13. B
4. C	9. B	14. D
5. A	10. D	15. B

EXAMINATION SECTION

TEST 1

DIRECTIONS: Each question or incomplete statement is followed by several suggested answers or completions. Select the one that BEST answers the question or completes the statement. *PRINT THE LETTER OF THE CORRECT ANSWER IN THE SPACE AT THE RIGHT.*

Questions 1-10.

MEMORY

DIRECTIONS: Questions 1 through 10 are to be answered SOLELY on the basis of the following passage, which contains a story about an incident involving police officers. You will have ten minutes to read and study the story. You may not write or make any notes while studying it. After ten minutes, close the memory booklet and do not look at it again. Then, answer the questions that follow.

You are one of a number of police officers who have been assigned to help control a demonstration inside Baldwin Square, a major square in the city. The demonstration is to protest the U.S. involvement in Nicaragua. As expected, the demonstration has become nasty. You and nine other officers have been assigned to keep the demonstrators from going up Bell Street which enters the Square from the northwest. During the time you have been assigned to Bell Street, you have observed a number of things.

Before the demonstration began, three vans and a wagon entered the Square from the North on Howard Avenue. The first van was a 1979 blue Ford, plate number 897-JLK. The second van was a 1985 red Ford, plate number 899-LKK. The third van was a 1987 green Dodge step-van, plate number 997-KJL. The wagon was a blue 1988 Volvo with a luggage rack on the roof, plate number 989-LKK. The Dodge had a large dent in the left-hand rear door and was missing its radiator grill. The Ford that was painted red had markings under the paint which made you believe that it had once been a telephone company truck. Equipment for the speakers' platform was unloaded from the van, along with a number of demonstration signs. As soon as the vans and wagon were unloaded, a number of demonstrators picked up the signs and started marching around the square. A sign reading *U.S. Out Now* was carried by a woman wearing red jeans, a black tee shirt, and blue sneakers. A man with a beard, a blue shirt, and Army pants began carrying a poster reading *To Hell With Davis*. A tall, Black male and a Hispanic male had been carrying a large sign with *This Is How Vietnam Started* in big black letters with red dripping off the bottom of each letter.

Both the Black and the Hispanic are wearing black armbands and green tee shirts with the peace symbol on the front. A woman with very short hair who was dressed in green and yellow fatigues is carrying a triangular-shaped blue sign with white letters. The sign says *Out Of Nicaragua.*

A group of 12 demonstrators have been carrying six fake coffins back and forth across the Square between Apple Street on the West and Webb Street on the East. They are shouting *Death to Hollis and his Henchmen*. Over where Victor Avenue enters the Square from the South, a small group of demonstrators (two men and three women) just started painting slogans on the walls surrounding the construction of the First National Union Bank and Trust.

1. Which street is on the opposite side of the Square from   1.___
   Victor Avenue?
      A. Bell   B. Howard   C. Apple   D. Webb

2. How many officers are assigned with you?   2.___
      A. 8   B. 6   C. 9   D. 5

3. Howard Avenue enters the Square from which direction?   3.___
      A. Northwest B. North   C. East   D. Southwest

4. The van that had PROBABLY been a telephone truck had plate 4.___
   number
      A. 899-LKK   B. 989-LKK   C. 897-JKL   D. 997-KJL

5. What is the color of the sign carried by the woman with 5.___
   very short hair?
      A. Blue   B. White   C. Black   D. Red

6. The man wearing the army pants has a(n)   6.___
      A. Afro   B. beard
      C. triangular-shaped sign   D. black armband

7. Which vehicle had plate number 989-LKK?   7.___
   The
      A. red Ford   B. blue Ford   C. Volvo   D. Dodge

8. The bank under construction is located _____ of the Square. 8.___
      A. north   B. south   C. east   D. west

9. How many people are painting slogans on the walls 9.___
   surrounding the construction site?
      A. 4   B. 5   C. 6   D. 7

10. What is the name of the bank under construction? 10.___
       A. National Union Bank and Trust
       B. First National Bank and Trust
       C. First Union National Bank and Trust
       D. First National Union Bank and Trust

KEY (CORRECT ANSWERS)

1.	B	6.	B
2.	C	7.	C
3.	B	8.	B
4.	A	9.	B
5.	A	10.	D

TEST 2

DIRECTIONS: Each question or incomplete statement is followed by several suggested answers or completions. Select the one that BEST answers the question or completes the statement. *PRINT THE LETTER OF THE CORRECT ANSWER IN THE SPACE AT THE RIGHT.*

Questions 1-15.

DIRECTIONS: Questions 1 through 15 are to be answered SOLELY on the basis of the Memory Booklet given below.

MEMORY BOOKLET

The following passage contains a story about an incident involving police officers. You will have ten minutes to read and study the story. You may not write or make any notes while studying it. The first questions in the examination will be based on the passage. After ten minutes, close the memory booklet, and do not look at it again. Then, answer the questions that follow.

———

Police Officers Boggs and Thomas are patrolling in a radio squad car on a late Saturday afternoon in the spring. They are told by radio that a burglary is taking place on the top floor of a six-story building on the corner of 5th Street and Essex and that they should deal with the incident.

The police officers know the location and know that the Gold Jewelry Company occupies the entire sixth floor. They also know that, over the weekends, the owner has gold bricks in his office safe worth $500,000.

When the officers arrive at the location, they lock their radio car. They then find the superintendent of the building who opens the front door for them. He indicates he has neither seen nor heard anything suspicious in the building. However, he had just returned from a long lunch hour. The officers take the elevator to the sixth floor. As the door of the elevator with the officers opens on the sixth floor, the officers hear the door of the freight elevator in the rear of the building closing and the freight elevator beginning to move. They leave the elevator and proceed quickly through the open door of the office of the Gold Jewelry Company. They see that the office safe is open and empty. The officers quickly proceed to the rear staircase. They run down six flights of stairs, and they see four suspects leaving through the rear entrance of the building.

They run through the rear door and out of the building after the suspects. The four suspects are running quickly through the parking lot at the back of the building. The suspects then make a right-hand turn onto 5th Street and are clearly seen by the officers. The officers see one white male, one Hispanic male, one Black male, and one white female.

The white male has a beard and sunglasses. He is wearing blue jeans, a dark red and blue jacket, and white jogging shoes. He is carrying a large green duffel bag over his shoulder.

The Hispanic male limps slightly and has a dark moustache. He is wearing dark brown slacks, a dark green sweat shirt, and brown shoes. He is carrying a large blue duffel bag.

The Black male is clean-shaven, wearing black corduroy pants, a multi-colored shirt, a green beret, and black boots. He is carrying a tool box.

The white female has long dark hair and is wearing light-colored blue jeans, a white blouse, sneakers, and a red kerchief around her neck. She is carrying a shotgun.

The officers chase the suspects for three long blocks without getting any closer to them. At the intersection of 5th Street and Pennsylvania Avenue, the suspects separate. The white male and the Black male rapidly get into a 1972 brown Ford stationwagon. The stationwagon has a roof rack on top and a Connecticut license plate with the letters *JEAN* on it. The stationwagon departs even before the occupants close the door completely.

The Hispanic male and the white female get into an old blue Dodge van. The van has a CB antenna on top, a picture of a cougar on the back doors, a dented right rear fender, and a New Jersey license plate. The officers are not able to read the plate numbers on the van.

The officers then observe the stationwagon turn left and enter an expressway going to Connecticut. The van turns right onto Illinois Avenue and proceeds toward the tunnel to New Jersey.

The officers immediately run back to their radio car to radio in what happened.

1. Which one of the following suspects had sunglasses on?   1.___
   A. White male   B. Hispanic male
   C. Black male   D. White female

2. Which one of the following suspects was carrying a shotgun?   2.___
   A. White male   B. Hispanic male
   C. Black male   D. White female

3. Which one of the following suspects was wearing a green   3.___
   beret?
   A. White male   B. Hispanic male
   C. Black male   D. White female

4. Which one of the following suspects limped slightly?   4.___
   A. White male   B. Hispanic male
   C. Black male   D. White female

5. Which one of the following BEST describes the stationwagon   5.___
   used?
   A
   A. 1972 brown Ford   B. 1972 blue Dodge
   C. 1969 brown Ford   D. 1969 blue Dodge

6. Which one of the following BEST describes the suspect or   6.___
   suspects who used the stationwagon?
   A
   A. Black male and a Hispanic male
   B. white male and a Hispanic male
   C. Black male and a white male
   D. Black male and a white female

7. The van had a license plate from which of the following   7.___
   states?
   A. Connecticut   B. New Jersey
   C. New York   D. Pennsylvania

8. The license plate on the stationwagon read as follows: 8.___
   A. JANE   B. JOAN   C. JEAN   D. JUNE

9. The van used had a dented ____ fender.   9.___
   A. left rear   B. right rear
   C. right front   D. left front

10. When last seen by the officers, the van was headed toward   10.___
    A. Connecticut   B. New Jersey
    C. Pennsylvania   D. Long Island

11. The female suspect's hair can BEST be described as   11.___
    A. long and dark-colored   B. short and dark-colored
    C. long and light-colored D. short and light-colored

12. Which one of the following suspects was wearing a multi-   12.___
    colored shirt?
    A. White male   B. Hispanic male
    C. Black male   D. White female

13. Blue jeans were worn by the ____ male suspect and the ____   13.____
    suspect.
    A. Hispanic; white female   B. Black; Hispanic male
    C. white; white female   D. Black; white male

14. The color of the duffel bag carried by the Hispanic male   14.____
    suspect was
    A. blue   B. green   C. brown   D. red

15. The Hispanic male suspect was wearing   15.____
    A. brown shoes   B. black shoes
    C. black boots   D. jogging shoes

_____

KEY (CORRECT ANSWERS)

1.	A	6.	C	11.	A
2.	D	7.	B	12.	C
3.	C	8.	C	13.	C
4.	B	9.	B	14.	A
5.	A	10.	B	15.	A

_____

READING COMPREHENSION
UNDERSTANDING AND INTERPRETING WRITTEN MATERIAL

STRATEGIES

Surveying Passages, Sentences as Cues

While individual readers develop unique reading styles and skills, there are some known strategies which can assist any reader in improving his or her reading comprehension and performance on the reading subtest. These strategies include understanding how single paragraphs and entire passages are structured, how the ideas in them are ordered, and how the author of the passage has connected these ideas in a logical and sequential way for the reader.

The section that follows highlights the importance of reading a passage through once for meaning, and provides instruction on careful reading for context cues within the sentences before and after the missing word.

SURVEY THE ENTIRE PASSAGE

To get a sense of the topic and the organization of ideas in a passage, it is important to survey each passage initially in its entirety and to identify the main idea. (The first sentence of a paragraph usually states the main idea.) Do not try to fill in the blanks initially. The purpose of surveying a passage is to prepare for the more careful reading which will follow. You need a sense of the big picture before you start to fill in the details; for example, a quick survey of the passage on page 12, indicates that the topic is the early history of universities. The paragraphs are organized to provide information on the origin of the first universities, the associations formed by teachers and students, the early curriculum, and graduation requirements.

READ PRECEDING SENTENCES CAREFULLY

The missing words in a passage cannot be determined by reading and understanding only the sentences in which the deletions occur. Information from the sentences which precede or follow can provide important cues to determine the correct choice. For example, if you read the first sentence from the passage about universities which contains a blank, you will notice that all the alternatives make sense if this one sentence is read in isolation:

Nobody actually _____ them.

8. A. started   B. guarded
    C. blamed   D. compared
    E. remembered

The only way that you can make the correct word choice is to read the preceding sentences. In the excerpt below, notice that the first sentence tells the reader what the passage will be about: how universities developed. A key word in the first sentence is *emerged*, which is closely related in meaning to one of the five choices for the first blank. The second sentence explains the key word, *emerged*, by pointing out that we have no historical record of a decree or a date indicating when the first university was established. Understanding the ideas in the first two sentences makes it possible to select the correct word for the blank. Look at the sentence with the deleted word in the context of the preceding sentences and think about why you are now able to make the correct choice.

The first universities emerged at the end of the 11th century and beginning of the 12th. These institutions were not founded on any particular date or created by any formal action. Nobody actually _____ them.

8. A. started   B. guarded
    C. blamed   D. compared
    E. remembered

Started is the best choice because it fits the main idea of the passage and is closely related to the key word *emerged*.

READ THE SENTENCE WHICH FOLLOWS TO VERIFY YOUR CHOICE

The sentences which follow the one from which a word has been deleted may also provide cues to the correct choice. For example, look at an excerpt from the passage about universities again, and consider how the sentence which follows the one with the blank helps to reinforce the choice of the word, *started*.

The first universities emerged at the end of the 11th century and the beginning of the 12th. These institutions were not founded on any particular date or created by any formal action. Nobody actually _____ them. Instead, they developed gradually in places like Paris, Oxford, and Bologna, where scholars had long been teaching students.

1. A. started   B. guarded
    C. blamed   D. compared
    E. remembered

The words, *developed gradually*, mean the same as the key word, *emerged*. The signal word, *instead*, helps to distinguish the difference between starting on a specific date as a result of some particular act or event and emerging over a period of time as a result of various factors.

Here is another example of how the sentence which follows the one from which a word is deleted might help you decide which of two good alternatives is the correct choice. This excerpt is from the practice passage about bridges (page 11).

Bridges are built to allow a continuous flow of highway and railway traffic across water lying in their paths. But engineers cannot forget that river traffic, too, is essential to our economy. The role of _____ is important. To keep these vessels moving freely, bridges are built big enough, when possible, to let them pass underneath.

1. A. wind   B. boats
    C. weight   D. wires
    E. experiences

After the first two sentences, the reader may be uncertain about the direction the writer intended to take in the rest of the paragraph. If the writer intended to continue the paragraph with information concerning how engineers make choices about the relative importance and requirements of land traffic and river traffic, *experience* might be the appropriate choice for the missing word. However, the sentence following the one in which the deletion occurs makes it clear that *boats* is the correct choice. It provides the synonym *vessels*, which in the noun phrase *these vessels* must refer back to the previous sentence or sentences. The phrase *to let them pass underneath* also helps make it clear that *boats* is the appropriate choice. *Them* refers back to *these vessels* which, in turn, refers back to *boats* when the word *boats* is placed in the previous sentence. Thus, the reader may use these cohesive ties (the pronoun referents) to verify the final choice.

Even when the text following a sentence with a deletion is not necessary to choose the best alternative, it may be helpful in other ways. Specifically, complete sentences provide important transitions into a related topic which is developed in the rest of the paragraph or in the next paragraph of the same passage. For example, the first paragraph in the passage about universities ends with a sentence which introduces the term *guilds*: *But, over time, they joined together to form guilds.* Prior to this sentence, information about the slow emergence of universities and about how independently scholars had acted was introduced. The next paragraph begins with two sentences about guilds in general. Someone who had not read the last sentence in the first paragraph might have missed the link between guilds and scholars and universities and, thus, might have been unnecessarily confused.

Cohesive Ties As Cues

Sentences in a paragraph may be linked together by several devices called cohesive ties. Attention to these ties may provide further cues about missing words. This section will describe the different types of cohesive ties and show how attention to them can help you to select the correct word.

PERSONAL PRONOUNS

Personal pronouns (e.g., he, she, they, it, its) are often used in adjoining sentences to refer back to an already mentioned person, place, thing, or idea. The word to which the pronoun refers is called the antecedent.

Tools used in farm work changed very slowly from ancient times to the eighteenth century, and the changes were minor. Since the eighteenth century *they* have changed quickly and dramatically.

The word *they* refers back to *tools* in the example above.

In the examination reading subtest, a deleted word sometimes occurs in a sentence in which the sentence subject is a pronoun that refers back to a previously mentioned noun. You must correctly identify the referent for the particular pronoun in order to interpret the sentence and select the correct answer. Here is an example from the passage about bridges.

An ingenious engineer designed the bridge so that it did not have to be raised above traffic. Instead it was _____.

7. A. burned   B. emptied
    C. secured   D. shared
    E. lowered

Q. What is the antecedent of *it* in both cases in the example?

A. The antecedent, of course, is *bridge*.

DEMONSTRATIVE PRONOUNS

Demonstrative pronouns (e.g., this, that, these) are also used to refer to a specific, previously mentioned noun. They may occur alone as noun replacements, or they may accompany and modify nouns.

I like jogging, swimming, and tennis. *These* are the only sports I enjoy.

In the sentence above, the word *these* is a replacement noun. However, demonstrative pronouns may also occur as adjectives modifying nouns.

I like jogging, swimming, and tennis. *These* sports are the only ones I enjoy.

The word *these* in the example above is an adjective modifier. The word *these* in each of the two previous examples refers to *jogging*, *swimming*, and *tennis*.

Here is an example from the passage about universities on page 12.

Undergraduates took classes in Greek philosophy, Latin grammar, arithmetic, music, and astronomy. These were the only _____ available.

12.　A. rooms　　　　B. subjects
　　　C. clothes　　　D. pens
　　　E. company

Q.　Which word is a noun replacement?
A.　The word *these* is the replacement noun for *Greek philosophy, Latin grammar, arithmetic, music,* and *astronomy.*

Here is another example from the same passage.

The concept of a fixed program of study leading to a degree first evolved in Medieval Europe. This _____ had not appeared before.

14.　A. idea　　　　B. desk
　　　C. library　　 D. capital

Q.　What is the antecedent of *this*?
A.　The antecedent is *the concept of a fixed program of study leading to a degree.*

COMPARATIVE ADJECTIVES AND ADVERBS

When comparative adjectives or adverbs (e.g., so, such, better, more) occur, they refer to something else in the passage, otherwise a comparison could not be made.

The hotels in the city were all full; so were the motels and boarding houses.

Q.　To what in the first sentence does the word *so* refer?
A.　*So* tells us to compare the *motels* and *boarding houses* to the *hotels in the city.*

Q.　In what way are the *hotels, motels,* and *boarding houses* similar to each other?
A.　The *hotels, motels,* and *boarding houses* are similar in that they were all *full.*

Look at an example from the passage about universities.

Guilds were groups of tradespeople, somewhat akin to modern trade unions. In the Middle Ages, all the crafts had such _____.

3.　A. taxes　　　　B. secrets
　　　C. products　　D. problems
　　　E. organizations

Q. To what in the first sentence does the word *such* refer?
A. *Such* refers to *groups of tradespeople*.

SUBSTITUTIONS

Substitution is another form of cohesive tie. A substitution occurs when one linguistic item (e.g., a noun) is replaced by another. Sometimes the substitution provides new or contrasting information. The substitution is not identical to the original, or antecedent, idea. A frequently occurring substitution involves the use of *one*. A noun substitution may involve another member of the same class as the original one.

My car is falling apart. I need a new one.

Q. What in the first sentence is replaced in the second sentence with *one*?
A. *One* is a substitute for the specific car mentioned in the first sentence. The contrast comes from the fact that the *new one* isn't the writer's current car.

The substitution may also pinpoint a specific member of a general class.

1. There are many unusual courses available at the university this summer. The *one* I am taking is called *Death and Dying*.

2. There are many unusual courses available at the university this summer. *Some* have never been offered before.

Q. In these examples, what is the general class in the first sentence that is replaced by *one* and by *some*?
A. In both cases the words *one* and *some* replace *many unusual courses*.

SYNONYMS

Synonyms are words that have similar meaning. In the examination reading subtest, a synonym of a deleted word is sometimes found in one of the sentences before and/or after the sentence with the deletion. Examine the following excerpt from the passage about bridges again.

But engineers cannot forget that river traffic, too, is essential to our economy. The role of _____ is important. To keep these vessels moving freely, bridges are built high enough, when possible, to let them pass underneath.

8. A. wind   B. boats
    C. weight   D. wires
    E. experience

Q. Can you identify synonyms in the sentences, before and after
    the sentence containing the deletion, which are cues to the
    correct deleted word?
A. If you identified the correct words, you probably noticed that
    river traffic is not exactly a synonym, since it is a slightly
    more general term than the word *boats* (the correct choice).
    But the word *vessels* is a direct synonym. Demonstrative pronouns
    (this, that, these, those) are sometimes used as modifiers for
    synonymous nouns in sentences which follow those containing
    deletions. The word *these* in *these vessels* is the demonstrative
    pronoun (modifier) for the synonymous noun *vessels*.

ANTONYMS

Antonyms are words of opposite meaning. In the examination
reading subtest passages, antonyms may be cues for missing words.
A contrasting relationship, which calls for the use of an antonym,
is often signaled by the connective words *instead, however, but*, etc.
Look at an excerpt from the passage about bridges.

An ingenious engineer designed the bridge so that it did not
have to be raised above traffic. Instead it was _____.

7. A. burned   B. emptied
    C. secured   D. shared
    E. lowered

Q. Can you identify an antonym in the first sentence for one of the
    five alternatives?
A. The word *raised* is an antonym for the word *lowered*.

SUPERORDINATE-SUBORDINATE WORDS

In the examination reading subtest, a passage sometimes contains
a general term which provides a cue that a more specific term is the
appropriate alternative. At other times, the passage may contain a
specific term which provides cues that a general term is the appropriate alternative for a particular deletion. The general and more
specific words are said to have superordinate-subordinate relationships.

Look at example 1 below. The more specific word *boy* in the
first sentence serves as the antecedent for the more general word
child in the second sentence. In example 2, the relationship is
reversed. In both examples, the words *child* and *boy* reflect a
superordinate-subordinate relationship.

1. The *boy* climbed the tree. Then the *child* fell.
2. The *child* climbed the tree. Then the *boy* fell.

In the practice passage about bridges on page 11, the phrase
river traffic is a general term that is superordinate to the
alternative *boats* (item 1). Later in the passage about bridges the
following sentences also contain superordinate-subordinate words:

A lift bridge was desired, but there were wartime shortages of steel and machinery needed for the towers. It was hard to find enough _____.

6. A. work   B. material
   C. time   D. power
   E. space

Q. Can you identify two words in the first sentence that are specific examples for the correct response in the second sentence?

A. Of course, the words *steel* and *machinery* are the specific examples for the more general term *material*.

WORDS ASSOCIATED BY ENTAILMENT

Sometimes the concept described by one word within the context of the passage entails, or implies, the concept described by another word. For example, consider again item 7 in the practice passage about bridges. Notice how the follow-up sentence to item 7 provides a cue to the correct response.

An ingenious engineer designed the bridge so that it did not have to be raised above traffic. Instead it was _____. It could be submerged seven meters below the surface of the river.

7. A. burned   B. emptied
   C. secured   D. shared
   E. lowered

Q. What word in the sentence after the blank implies the concept of an alternative?

A. *Submerged* implies *lowered*. The concept of submerging something implies the idea of lowering the object beneath the surface of the water.

WORDS ASSOCIATED BY PART-WHOLE RELATIONSHIPS

Words may be related because they involve part of a whole and the whole itself; for example, *nose* and *face*. Words may also be related because they involve two parts of the same whole; for example, *radiator* and *muffler* both refer to parts of a car.

The captain of the ship was nervous. The storm was becoming worse and worse. The hardened man paced the _____.

A. floor   B. hall
C. deck   D. court

Q. Which choice has a part-whole relationship with a word in the sentences above?

A. A *deck* is a part of a *ship*. Therefore, *deck* has a part-whole relationship with *ship*.

CONJUNCTIVE AND CONNECTIVE WORDS AND PHRASES

Conjunctions or connectives are words or phrases that connect parts of sentences or parts of a passage to each other. Their purpose is to help the reader understand the logical and conceptual relationships between ideas and events within a passage. Examples of these words and phrases include coordinate conjunctions (e.g., and, but, yet), subordinate conjunctions (e.g., because, although, since, after), and other connective words and phrases (e.g, too, also, on the other hand, as a result).

Listed below are types of logical relationships expressed by conjunctive, or connective words. Also listed are examples of words used to cue relationships to the reader.

Additive and comparative words and phrases: and, in addition to, too, also, furthermore, similarly

Adversative and contrastive words and phrases: yet, though, only, but, however, instead, rather, on the other hand, in contrast, conversely

Causal words or phrases: so, therefore, because, as a result, if...then, unless, except, in that case, under the circumstances

Temporal words and phrases: before, after, when, while, initially, lastly, finally, until.

Examples

1. I enjoy fast-paced sports like tennis and volleyball, but my brother prefers _____ sports.

    A. running   B. slower
    C. team   D. active

Q. What is the connective word that tells you to look for a contrast relationship between the two clauses?
A. The connective word *but* signals that a contrast relationship exists between the two parts of the sentence.

Q. Of the four options, what is the best choice for the blank?
A. The word *slower* is the best response here.

2. The child stepped too close to the edge of the brook. As a result, he _____ in.
    A. fell   B. waded
    C. ran   D. jumped

Q. What is the connective phrase that links the two sentences?
A. The connective phrase *as a result* links the two sentences.

Q. Of the four relationships of words and phrases listed previously, what kind of relationship between the two sentences does the connective phrase in the example signal to the reader?

A. The phrase *as a result* signals that a cause and effect relationship exists between the two sentences.

Q. Identify the correct response which makes the second sentence reflect the cause and effect relationship.

A. The correct response is *fell*.

Understanding connectives is very important to success on the examination reading subtest. Sentences with deletions are often very closely related to adjacent sentences in meaning, and the relationship is often signaled by connective words or phrases. Here is an example from the practice passage about universities.

At first, these tutors had not been associated with one another. Rather, they had been _____. But, over time, they joined together to form guilds.

A. curious   B. poor
C. religious   D. ready
E. independent

Q. Identify the connective and contrastive words and phrases in the example.

A. *At first* and *over time* are connective phrases that set up temporal progression. *Rather* and *but* are contrastive items. The use of *rather* in the sentence with the deletion tells the reader that the missing word has to convey a meaning in contrast to *associated with one another*. (Notice also that *rather* occurs after a negative statement.) The use of *but* in the sentence after the one with the deletion indicates that the deleted word in the previous sentence has to reflect a meaning that contrasts with *joined together*. Thus, the reader is given two substantial cues to the meaning of the missing word. *Independent* is the only choice that meets the requirement for contrastive meaning.

SAMPLE QUESTIONS

DIRECTIONS: There are two passages on the following pages. In each
passage some words are missing. Wherever a word is
missing, there is a blank line with a number on it.
Below the passage you will find the same number and five
words. Choose the word that makes the best sense in the
blank.
You may not be sure of the answer to a question until
you read the sentences that come after the blank, so
be sure to read enough to answer the questions. As you
work on these passages, you will find that the second
passage is harder to read than the first. Answer as
many questions as you can.

Bridges are built to allow a continuous flow of highway and
railway traffic across water lying in their paths. But engineers
cannot forget that river traffic, too, is essential to our economy.
The role of _____1_____ is important. To keep these vessels moving
freely, bridges are built high enough, when possible, to let them
pass underneath. Sometimes, however, channels must accommodate very
tall ships. It may be uneconomical to build a tall enough bridge.
The _____2_____ would be too high. To save money, engineers build
movable bridges.

In the swing bridge, the middle part pivots or swings open.
When the bridge is closed, this section joins the two ends of the
bridge, blocking tall vessels. But this section _____3_____. When
swung open, it is perpendicular to the ends of the bridge, creating
two free channels for river traffic. With swing bridges, channel
width is limited by the bridge's piers. The largest swing bridge
provides only a 75-meter channel. Such channels are sometimes too
_____4_____. In such cases, a bascule bridge may be built.

Bascule bridges are drawbridges with two arms that swing upward.
They provide an opening as wide as the span. They are also versatile.
These bridges are not limited to being fully opened or fully closed.
They can be _____5_____ in many ways. They can be fixed at different
angles to accommodate different vessels.

In vertical lift bridges, the center remains horizontal. Towers
at both ends allow the center to be lifted like an elevator. One
interesting variation of this kind of bridge was built during World
War II. A lift bridge was desired, but there were wartime shortages
of the steel and machinery needed for the towers. It was hard to
find enough _____6_____. An ingenious engineer designed the bridge
so that it did not have to be raised above traffic. Instead it was
_____7_____. It could be submerged seven meters below the surface
of the river. Ships sailed over it.

1. A. wind   B. boats   C. weight
    D. wires   E. experience

2. A. levels   B. cost   C. standards
    D. waves   E. deck

3. A. stands   B. floods   C. wears
    D. turns   E. supports

4. A. narrow   B. rough   C. long
    D. deep   E. straight

5. A. crossed   B. approached   C. lighted
    D. planned   E. positioned

6. A. work   B. material   C. time
    D. power   E. space

7. A. burned   B. emptied   C. secured
    D. shared   E. lowered

The first universities emerged at the end of the 11th century and beginning of the 12th. These institutions were not founded on any particular date or created by any formal action. Nobody actually ____8____ them. Instead, they developed gradually in places like Paris, Oxford, and Bologna, where scholars had long been teaching students. At first, these tutors had not been associated with one another. Rather, they had been ____9____. But, over time, they joined together to form guilds.

Guilds were groups of tradespeople, somewhat akin to modern unions. In the Middle Ages, all the crafts had such ____10____. The scholars' guilds built school buildings and evolved an administration which charged fees and set standards for the curriculum. It set prices for members' services and fixed requirements for entering the profession.

Professors were not the only schoolpeople forming associations. In Italy, students joined guilds to which teachers had to swear obedience. The students set strict rules, fining professors for beginning class a minute late. Teachers had to seek their students' permission to marry, and such permission was not always granted. Sometimes the students ____11____. Even if they said yes, the teacher got only one day's honeymoon.

Undergraduates took classes in Greek philosophy, Latin grammar, arithmetic, music, and astronomy. These were the only ____12____ available. More advanced study was possible in law, medicine, and theology, but one could not earn such postgraduate degrees quickly. It took a long time to ____13____. Completing the requirements in theology, for example, took at least 13 years.

The concept of a fixed program of study leading to a degree first evolved in medieval Europe. This ____14____ had not appeared before. In earlier academic settings, notions about *meeting requirements* and *graduating* had been absent. Since the Middle Ages, though, we have continued to view education as a set curriculum culminating in a degree.

8. A. started   B. guarded   C. blamed
    D. compared   E. remembered

9. A. curious   B. poor   C. religious
    D. ready   E. independent

10. A. taxes   B. secrets   C. products
    D. problems   E. organizations

11. A. left   B. copied   C. refused
    D. paid   E. prepared

12. A. rooms   B. subjects   C. clothes
    D. pens   E. markets

13. A. add   B. answer   C. forget
    D. finish   E. travel

14. A. idea   B. desk   C. library
    D. capital   E. company

KEY (CORRECT ANSWERS)

1. B	8. A
2. B	9. E
3. D	10. E
4. A	11. C
5. E	12. B
6. B	13. D
7. E	14. A

READING COMPREHENSION
UNDERSTANDING AND INTERPRETING WRITTEN MATERIAL

EXAMINATION SECTION

Questions 1-40.
DIRECTIONS: Read the following passages, and select the most appropriate word from the five alternatives provided for each deleted word. Print the letter of the correct answer in the space at the right.

PASSAGE I

Bridges are built to allow a continuous flow of highway and railway traffic across water lying in their paths. But engineers cannot forget the fact that river traffic, too, is essential to our economy. The role of __1__ is important. To keep these vessels moving freely, bridges are built high enough, when possible, to let them pass underneath. Sometimes, however, channels must accommodate very tall ships. It may be uneconomical to build a tall enough bridge. The __2__ would be too high. To save money, engineers build movable bridges.

1.	A. wind	B. boats	C. weight	1. ...
	D. wires	E. experience		
2.	A. levels	B. cost	C. standards	2. ...
	D. waves	E. deck		

In the swing bridge, the middle part pivots or swings open. When the bridge is closed, this section joins the two ends of the bridge, blocking tall vessels. But this section __3__. When swung open, it is perpendicular to the ends of the bridge, creating two free channels for river traffic. With swing bridges, channel width is limited by the bridge's piers. The largest swing bridge provides only a 75-meter channel. Such channels are sometimes too __4__. In such cases, a bascule bridge may be built.

3.	A. stands	B. floods	C. wears	3. ...
	D. turns	E. supports		
4.	A. narrow	B. rough	C. long	4. ...
	D. deep	E. straight		

Bascule bridges are drawbridges with two arms that swing upward. They provide an opening as wide as the span. They are also versatile. These bridges are not limited to being fully opened or fully closed. They can be __5__ in many ways. They can be fixed at different angles to accommodate different vessels.

| 5. | A. approached | B. crossed | C. lighted | 5. ... |
| | D. planned | E. positioned | | |

In vertical lift bridges, the center remains horizontal. Towers at both ends allow the center to be lifted like an elevator. One interesting variation of this kind of bridge was built during World War II. A lift bridge was desired, but there were wartime shortages of the steel and machinery needed for the towers. It was hard to find enough __6__. An ingenious engineer designed the bridge so that it did not have to be raised above traffic. Instead it was __7__. It could be submerged seven meters below the river surface. Ships sailed over it.

6.	A. work	B. material	C. time	6. ...
	D. power	E. space		
7.	A. burned	B. emptied	C. secured	7. ...
	D. shared	E. lowered		

1

PASSAGE II

Before anesthetics were discovered, surgery was carried out under very severe time restrictions. Patients were awake, tossing and screaming in terrible pain. Surgeons were forced to hurry in order to constrain suffering and minimize shock. __8__ was essential. Haste, however, did not make for good outcomes in surgery. No surprise, then, that the __9__ were often poor.

8.   A. Blood   B. Silence   C. Speed   8. ...
     D. Water   E. Money
9.   A. quarters   B. teeth   C. results   9. ...
     D. materials   E. families

The discovery of anesthetics happened, in part, by accident. During the early 1800's, nitrous oxide and ether were used for entertainment. At "ether frolics" in theaters, volunteers would breathe these gases, become lightheaded, and run around the stage laughing and dancing. By chance, a Connecticut dentist saw such a __10__ . One volunteer banged his leg against a sharp edge. But he did not __11__ . He paid no attention to his wound, as though he felt nothing. This gave the dentist the idea of using gas to kill pain.

10.   A. show   B. machine   C. face   10. ...
     D. source   E. growth
11.   A. dream   B. recover   C. succeed   11. ...
     D. agree   E. notice

At first, using the "open drip method," ether and chloroform were filtered through a cotton pad placed over the mouth and nose. This direct dose was difficult to regulate and irritating to the nose and throat. Patients would hold their breath, cough, or gag. This made it impossible for them to relax, let alone sleep. Consequently, surgery was often __12__ . It couldn't begin until the patient had quieted and the anesthesia had taken hold.

12.   A. delayed   B. required   C. blamed   12. ...
     D. observed   E. repeated

Today's procedures are safer and more accurate. In the "closed method," a fixed amount of gas is released from sealed bottles into an inhalator bag when the patient exhales. He inhales this gas through tubes with his next breath. In this way, the gas is __13__ . The system carefully regulates how much gas reaches the patient.

13.   A. heated   B. controlled   C. cleaned   13. ...
     D. selected   E. wasted

For dentistry and minor operations, patients need not be asleep. Newer anesthetics can be used which deaden nerves only in the affected part of the body. These __14__ anesthetics offer several advantages. For instance, since the anesthesia is fairly light and patients remain awake, they can cooperate with their doctors.

14.   A. local   B. natural   C. ancient   14. ...
     D. heavy   E. three

PASSAGE III

An indispensable element in the development of telephony was the continual improvement of telephone station instruments, those operating units located at the client's premises. Modern units normally consist of a transmitter, receiver, and transformer. They also contain a bell or equivalent summoning device, a mechanism for controlling the unit's connection to the client's line, and various associated items, like

dials. All of these __15__ have changed over the years. The transmitter, especially, has undergone enormous refinement during the last
century.

15.   A. parts   B. costs   C. services   15. ...
      D. models   E. routes

   Bell's original electromagnetic transmitter functioned likewise
as receiver, the same instrument being held alternately to mouth and
ear. But having to __16__ the instrument this way was inconvenient.
Suggestions understandably emerged for mounting the transmitter and
receiver onto a common handle, thereby creating what are now known
as handsets. Transmitter and receiver were, in fact, later __17__ his
way. Combination handsets were produced for commercial utilization
late in the nineteenth century, but prospects for their acceptance
were uncertain as the initial quality of transmissions with the handsets was disappointing. But __18__ transmissions followed. With ade-
quately high transmission standards attained, acceptance of handsets
was virtually assured.

16.   A. store   B. use   C. test   16. ...
      D. strip   E. clean
17.   A. grounded   B. marked   C. covered   17. ...
      D. priced   E. coupled
18.   A. shorter   B. fewer   C. better   18. ...
      D. faster   E. cheaper

   Among the most significant improvements in transmitters has been
the enormous amplification (up to a thousandfold) of speech sounds.
This increased __19__ has benefited tele-communications enormously.
Nineteenth century telephone conversations frequently were only
marginally audible, whereas nowadays even murmured conversations
can be transmitted successfully, barring unusual atmospheric or
electronic disturbances.

19.   A. distance   B. speed   C. market   19. ...
      D. volume   E. number

   Vocal quality over nineteenth century instruments was distorted,
the speaker not readily identifiable. By comparison, current sound
is characterized by considerably greater naturalism. Modern telephony produces speech sounds more nearly resembling an individual's
actual voice. Thus it is easier to __20__ the speaker. A considerable
portion of this improvement is attributable to practical applications
of laboratory investigations concerning the mechanisms of human
speech and audition. These __21__ have exerted a profound influence.
Their results prompted technical innovations in modern transmitter
design which contributed appreciably to the excellent communication
available nowadays.

20.   A. time   B. help   C. bill   20. ...
      D. stop   E. recognize
21.   A. studies   B. rates   C. materials   21. ...
      D. machines   E. companies

3

The dramatic events of December 7, 1941, plunged this nation into war. The full 22 of the war we can not even now comprehend, but one of the effects stands out in sharp relief -- the coming of the air age. The airplane, which played a relatively 23 part in World War I, has already soared to heights undreamed of save by the few with mighty vision.

In wartime the airplane is the 24 on wings and the battleship that flies. To man in his need it symbolizes deadly extremes: friend or foe; deliverance or 25 .

It is a powerful instrument of war revolutionizing military strategy, but its peacetime role is just as 26 . This new master of time and space, fruit of man's inventive genius, has come to stay, smalling the earth and smoothing its surface.

To all of us, then, to youth, and to 27 alike, comes the winged challenge to get ourselves ready--to 28 ourselves for living in an age which the airplane seems destined to mold.

22. A. destruction B. character   C. history   D. import   22. ...
    E. picture

23. A. important   B. dull   C. vast   D. unknown   E. minor   23. ...

24. A. giant   B. ant   C. monster   D. artillery E. robot   24. ...

25. A. ecstasy   B. bombardment   C. death   D. denial   25. ...
    E. survival

26. A. revolting   B. revolutionary   C. residual   D. reliable   26. ...
    E. regressive

27. A. animals   B. nations   C. women   D. men   E. adult   27. ...

28. A. distract   B. engage   C. determine   D. deter   E. orient 28. ...

PASSAGE V

Let us consider how voice training may contribute to 29 development and an improved social 30 .

In the first place, it has been fairly well established that individuals tend to become what they believe 31 people think them to be.

When people react more favorably toward us because our voices 32 the impression that we are friendly, competent, and interesting, there is a strong tendency for us to develop those 33 in our personality.

If we are treated with respect by others, we soon come to have more respect for 34 .

Then, too, one's own consciousness of having a pleasant, effective voice of which he does not need to be ashamed contributes materially to a feeling of poise, self-confidence, and a just pride in himself.

A good voice, like good clothes, can do much for an 35 that otherwise might be inclined to droop.

29. A. facial   B. material   C. community   D. personality   29. ...
    E. physical

30. A. adjustment   B. upheaval   C. development   D. bias   30. ...
    E. theories

31.   A. some B. hostile C. jealous D. inferior E. other   31. ...

32.   A. betray B. imply C. destroy D. transfigure   32. ...
      E. convey

33.   A. defects B. qualities C. techniques D. idiosyncrasies 33. ...
      E. quirks

34.   A. others B. their children C. their teachers   34. ...
      D. ourselves   E. each other

35.   A. mind B. heart C. brain D. feeling E. ego   35. ...

—

PASSAGE VI

How are symphony orchestras launched, kept boing, and built up in smaller communities? Recent reports from five of them suggest that, though the __36__ changes, certain elements are fairly common. One thing shines out; __37__ is essential.

Also, aside from the indispensable, instrumentalists who play, the following personalities, either singly, or preferably in __38__, seem to be the chief needs: a conductor who wants to conduct so badly he will organize his own orchestra if it is the only way he can get one; a manager with plenty of resourcefulness in rounding up audiences and finding financial support; an energetic community leader, generally a woman, who will take up locating the orchestra as a __39__; and generous visiting soloists who will help draw those who are __40__ that anything local can be used.

36.   A. world B. pattern C. reason D. scene E. cast   36. ...

37.   A. hatred B. love C. enthusiasm D. participation   37. ...
      E. criticism

38.   A. combination B. particular C. isolation D. sympathy 38. ...
      E. solitary

39.   A. chore B. duty C. hobby D. delight E. career   39. ...

40.   A. convinced B. skeptical C. happy D. unhappy   40. ...
      E. unsure

KEY (CORRECT ANSWERS)

1.	B	11.	E	21.	A	31.	E
2.	B	12.	A	22.	D	32.	E
3.	D	13.	B	23.	E	33.	B
4.	A	14.	A	24.	D	34.	D
5.	E	15.	A	25.	C	35.	E
6.	B	16.	B	26.	B	36.	B
7.	E	17.	E	27.	E	37.	C
8.	C	18.	C	28.	E	38.	A
9.	C	19.	D	29.	D	39.	C
10.	A	20.	E	30.	A	40.	B

READING COMPREHENSION
UNDERSTANDING AND INTERPRETING WRITTEN MATERIAL

COMMENTARY

The ability to read, understand, and interpret written materials - texts, publications, newspapers, orders, directions, expositions, legal passages - is a skill basic to a functioning democracy and to an efficient business or viable government.

That is why almost all examinations - for beginning, middle, and senior levels - test reading comprehension, directly or indirectly.

The reading test measures how well you understand what you read. This is how it is done: You read a paragraph and several statements based on a question. From the statements, you choose the *one* statement, or answer, that is *BEST* supported by, or *BEST* matches, what is said in the paragraph.

———

SAMPLE QUESTIONS

DIRECTIONS: Each question has five suggested answers, lettered A, B, C, D, and E. Decide which one is the *BEST* answer. *PRINT THE LETTER OF THE CORRECT ANSWER IN THE SPACE AT THE RIGHT.*

1. The prevention of accidents makes it necessary not only that safety devices be used to guard exposed machinery but also that mechanics be instructed in safety rules which they must follow for their own protection and that the light in the plant be adequate.
   The paragraph BEST supports the statement that industrial accidents
   A. are always avoidable
   B. may be due to ignorance
   C. usually result from inadequate machinery
   D. cannot be entirely overcome
   E. result in damage to machinery

ANALYSIS

Remember what you have to do -
   First - Read the paragraph.
   Second - Decide what the paragraph means.
   Third - Read the five suggested answers.
   Fourth - Select the one answer which *BEST* matches what the paragraph says or is *BEST* supported by something in the paragraph. (Sometimes you may have to read the paragraph again in order to be sure which suggested answer is best.)
This paragraph is talking about three steps that should be taken to prevent industrial accidents -
   1. use safety devices on machines
   2. instruct mechanics in safety rules
   3. provide adequate lighting.

SELECTION

With this in mind, let's look at each suggested answer. Each one starts with "Industrial accidents ..."

SUGGESTED ANSWER A.
   Industrial accidents (A) are always avoidable.
   (The paragraph talks about how to avoid accidents but does not say that accidents are always avoidable.)

1

SUGGESTED ANSWER B.
    Industrial accidents (B) may be due to ignorance.
    (One of the steps given in the paragraph to prevent accidents is to instruct mechanics on safety rules. This suggests that lack of knowledge or ignorance of safety rules causes accidents. This suggested answer sounds like a good possibility for being the right answer.
SUGGESTED ANSWER C.
    Industrial accidents (C) usually result from inadequate machinery.
    (The paragraph does suggest that exposed machines cause accidents, but it doesn't say that it is the usual cause of accidents. The word *usually* makes this a wrong answer.)
SUGGESTED ANSWER D.
    Industrial accidents (D) cannot be entirely overcome.
    (You may know from your own experience that this is a true statement. But that is not what the paragraph is talking about. Therefore, it is NOT the correct answer.)
SUGGESTED ANSWER E.
    Industrial accidents (E) result in damage to machinery.
    (This is a statement that may or may not be true, but, in any case, it is NOT covered by the paragraph.)

    Looking back, you see that the one suggested answer of the five given that *BEST* matches what the paragraph says is –
    Industrial accidents (B) may be due to ignorance.
    The *CORRECT* answer then is B.
    Be sure you read *ALL* the possible answers before you make your choice. You may think that none of the five answers is really good, but choose the *BEST* one of the five.

---

2. Probably few people realize, as they drive on a concrete road, that steel is used to keep the surface flat in spite of the weight of the busses and trucks. Steel bars, deeply embedded in the concrete, provide sinews to take the stresses so that the stresses cannot crack the slab or make it wavy.
    The paragraph BEST supports the statement THAT a concrete road
    A. is expensive to build
    B. usually cracks under heavy weights
    C. looks like any other road
    D. is used only for heavy traffic
    E. is reinforced with other material

ANALYSIS
This paragraph is commenting on the fact that –
    1. few people realize, as they drive on a concrete road, that steel is deeply embedded
    2. steel keeps the surface flat
    3. steel bars enable the road to take the stresses without cracking or becoming wavy.

SELECTION
Now read and think about the possible answers:
    A. A concrete road is expensive to build.
       (Maybe so but that is not what the paragraph is about.)
    B. A concrete road usually cracks under heavy weights.
       (The paragraph talks about using steel bars to prevent heavy

weights from cracking concrete roads. It says nothing about how
usual it is for the roads to crack. The word *usually* makes this
suggested answer wrong.)

   C. A concrete road looks like any other road.
     (This may or may not be true. The important thing to note is
     that it has nothing to do with what the paragraph is about.)

   D. A concrete road is used only for heavy traffic.
     (This answer at least has something to do with the paragraph -
     concrete roads are used with heavy traffic but it does not say
     "used only.")

   E. A concrete road is reinforced with other material.
     (This choice seems to be the correct one on two counts: *First,*
     the paragraph does suggest that concrete roads are made stronger
     by embedding steel bars in them. This is another way of saying
     "concrete roads are reinforced with steel bars." *Second,* by the
     process of elimination, the other four choices are ruled out as
     correct answers simply because they do not apply.)

You can be sure that not all the reading questions will be so easy
as these.

SUGGESTIONS FOR ANSWERING READING QUESTIONS

1. Read the paragraph carefully. Then read each suggested answer carefully. Read every word, because often one word can make the difference between a right and a wrong answer.
2. Choose that answer which is supported in the paragraph itself. Do
   not choose an answer which is a correct statement unless it is based
   on information in the paragraph.
3. Even though a suggested answer has many of the words used in the
   paragraph, it may still be wrong.
4. Look out for words - such as *always, never, entirely, or only* -
   which tend to make a suggested answer wrong.
5. Answer first those questions which you can answer most easily. Then
   work on the other questions.
6. If you can't figure out the answer to the question, guess.

EXAMINATION SECTION

DIRECTIONS FOR THIS SECTION:
   The following questions are intended to test your ability to read
with comprehension and to understand and interpret written materials,
particularly legal passages.
   Each question has several suggested answers. *PRINT THE LETTER OF
THE CORRECT ANSWER IN THE SPACE AT THE RIGHT.*
   It will be necessary for you to read each paragraph carefully be-
cause the questions are based only on the material contained therein.

TEST 1

Questions 1-3.
DIRECTIONS: Answer Questions 1 to 3 *SOLELY* on the basis of the following statement:
   Foot patrol has some advantages over all other methods of patrol.
Maximum opportunity is provided for observation within range of the
senses and for close contact with people and things that enable the
patrolman to provide a maximum service as an information source and

counselor to the public and as the eyes and ears of the police department. A foot patrolman loses no time in alighting from a vehicle, and the performance of police tasks is not hampered by responsibility for his vehicle while afoot. Foot patrol, however, does not have many of the advantages of a patrol car. Lack of both mobility and immediate communication with headquarters lessens the officer's value in an emergency. The area that he can cover effectively is limited and, therefore, this method of patrol is costly.

1. According to this paragraph, the foot patrolman is the   1. ...
   eyes and ears of the police department because he is
   - A. in direct contact with the station house
   - B. not responsible for a patrol vehicle
   - C. able to observe closely conditions on his patrol post
   - D. a readily available information source to the public

2. The *MOST* accurate of the following statements concerning   2. ...
   the various methods of patrol, according to this paragraph,
   is that
   - A. foot patrol should sometimes be combined with motor patrol
   - B. foot patrol is better than motor patrol
   - C. helicopter patrol has the same advantages as motor patrol
   - D. motor patrol is more readily able to communicate with superior officers in an emergency

3. According to this paragraph, it is *CORRECT* to state that   3. ...
   foot patrol is
   - A. *economical* since increased mobility makes more rapid action possible
   - B. *expensive* since the area that can be patrolled is relatively small
   - C. *economical* since vehicle costs need not be considered
   - D. *expensive* since giving information to the public is time-consuming

Questions 4-6.
DIRECTIONS: Answer Questions 4 to 6 *SOLELY* on the basis of the following statement:

All applicants for an original license to operate a catering establishment shall be fingerprinted. This shall include the officers, employees, and stockholders of the company and the members of a partnership. In case of a change, by addition or substitution, occurring during the existence of a license, the person added or substituted shall be fingerprinted. However, in the case of a hotel containing more than 200 rooms, only the officer or manager filing the application is required to be fingerprinted. The police commissioner may also at his discretion exempt the employees and stockholders of any company. The fingerprints shall be taken on one copy of form C.E. 20 and on two copies of C.E. 21. One copy of form C.E. 21 shall accompany the application. Fingerprints are not required with a renewal application.

4. According to this paragraph, an employee added to the pay-   4. ...
   roll of a licensed catering establishment which is not in
   a hotel, must
   - A. always be fingerprinted
   - B. be fingerprinted unless he has been previously fingerprinted for another license

4

        C. be fingerprinted unless exempted by the police com-
           missioner
        D. be fingerprinted only if he is the manager or an of-
           ficer of the company
5. According to this paragraph, it would be *MOST* accurate   5. ...
   to state that
        A. form C.E. 20 must accompany a renewal application
        B. form C.E. 21 must accompany all applications
        C. form C.E. 21 must accompany an original application
        D. both forms C.E. 20 and C.E. 21 must accompany all
           applications
6. A hotel of 270 rooms has applied for a license to operate   6. ...
   a catering establishment on the premises. According to
   the instructions for fingerprinting given in this paragraph,
   the
        A. officers, employees, and stockholders shall be finger-
           printed
        B. officers and manager shall be fingerprinted
        C. employees shall be fingerprinted
        D. officer filing the application shall be fingerprinted
Questions 7-9.
DIRECTIONS: Answer Questions 7 to 9 *SOLELY* on the basis of the
following statement:
     It is difficult to instill in young people inner controls on ag-
gressive behavior in a world marked by aggression. The slum child's
environment, full of hostility, stimulates him to delinquency; he
does that which he sees about him. The time to act against delinquency
is before it is committed. It is clear that juvenile delinquency,
especially when it is committed in groups or gangs, leads almost in-
evitably to an adult criminal life unless it is checked at once. The
first signs of vandalism and disregard for the comfort, health, and
property of the community should be considered as storm warnings which
cannot be ignored. The delinquent's first crime has the underlying
element of testing the law and its ability to hit back.
7. A *suitable* title for this entire paragraph based on the   7. ...
   material it contains is:
        A. The Need for Early Prevention of Juvenile Delinquency
        B. Juvenile Delinquency as a Cause of Slums
        C. How Aggressive Behavior Prevents Juvenile Delinquency
        D. The Role of Gangs in Crime
8. According to this paragraph, an *INITIAL* act of juvenile   8. ...
   crime *usually* involves a(n)
        A. group or gang activity   B. theft of valuable property
        C. test of the strength of legal authority
        D. act of physical violence
9. According to this paragraph, acts of juvenile delinquency   9. ...
   are *most likely* to lead to a criminal career when they are
        A. acts of vandalism
        B. carried out by groups or gangs
        C. committed in a slum environment
        D. such as to impair the health of the neighborhood
Questions 10-12.
DIRECTIONS: Answer Questions 10 to 12 *SOLELY* on the basis of the
following statement:

5

The police laboratory performs a valuable service in crime investigation by assisting in the reconstruction of criminal action and by aiding in the identification of persons and things. When studied by a technician, physical things found at crime scenes often reveal facts useful in identifying the criminal and in determining what has occurred. The nature of substances to be examined and the character of the examinations to be made vary so widely that the services of a large variety of skilled scientific persons are needed in crime investigations. To employ such a complete staff and to provide them with equipment and standards needed for all possible analyses and comparisons is beyond the means and the needs of any but the largest police departments. The search of crime scenes for physical evidence also calls for the services of specialists supplied with essential equipment and assigned to each tour of duty so as to provide service at any hour.

10. If a police department employs a large staff of tech-   10. ...
nicians of various types in its laboratory, it will affect crime investigation to the extent that
    A. most crimes will be speedily solved
    B. identification of criminals will be aided
    C. search of crime scenes for physical evidence will become of less importance
    D. investigation by police officers will not usually be required

11. According to this paragraph, the *MOST* complete study of   11. ...
objects found at the scenes of crimes is
    A. always done in all large police departments
    B. based on assigning one technician to each tour of duty
    C. probably done only in large police departments
    D. probably done in police departments of communities with low crime rates

12. According to this paragraph, a large variety of skilled   12. ...
technicians is useful in criminal investigations because
    A. crimes cannot be solved without their assistance as a part of the police team
    B. large police departments need large staffs
    C. many different kinds of tests on various substances can be made
    D. the police cannot predict what methods may be tried by wily criminals

Questions 13-14.
DIRECTIONS: Answer Questions 13 and 14 *SOLELY* on the basis of the following statement:

The emotionally unstable person is always potentially a dangerous criminal, who causes untold misery to other persons and is a source of considerable trouble and annoyance to law enforcement officials. Like his fellow criminals he will be a menace to society as long as he is permitted to be at large. Police activities against him serve to sharpen his wits and imprisonment gives him the opportunity to learn from others how to commit more serious crimes when he is released. This criminal's mental structure makes it impossible for him to profit by his experience with the police officials, by punishment of any kind or by sympathetic understanding and treatment by well-intentioned persons, professional and otherwise.

6

13. According to the above paragraph, the *MOST* accurate of   13. ...
    the following statements concerning the relationship be-
    tween emotional instability and crime is that
      A. emotional instability is proof of criminal activities
      B. the emotionally unstable person can become a criminal
      C. all dangerous criminals are emotionally unstable
      D. sympathetic understanding will prevent the emotionally
         unstable person from becoming a criminal

14. According to the above paragraph, the effect of police   14. ...
    activities on the emotionally unstable criminal is that
      A. police activities aid this type of criminal to reform
      B. imprisonment tends to deter this type of criminal from
         committing future crimes
      C. contact with the police serves to assist sympathetic
         understanding and medical treatment
      D. police methods against this type of criminal develop
         him for further unlawful acts

Questions 15-17.

DIRECTIONS: Answer Questions 15 to 17 *SOLELY* on the basis of the
following statement:

    Proposals to license gambling operations are based on the belief
that the human desire to gamble cannot be suppressed and, therefore,
it should be licensed and legalized with the people sharing in the
profits, instead of allowing the underworld to benefit. If these pro-
posals are sincere, then it is clear that only one is worthwhile at
all. Legalized gambling should be completely controlled and operated
by the state with all the profits used for its citizens. A state
agency should be set up to operate and control the gambling business.
It should be as completely removed from politics as possible. In view
of the inherent nature of the gambling business, with its close relationship to lawlessness and crime, only a man of the highest integrity
should be eligible to become head of this agency. However, state
gambling would encourage mass gambling with its attending social and
economic evils in the same manner as other forms of legal gambling;
but there is no justification whatever for the business of gambling to
be legalized and then permitted to operate for private profit or for
the benefit of any political organization.

15. The *CENTRAL* thought of this paragraph may be *correctly*   15. ...
    expressed as the
      A. need to legalize gambling in the state
      B. state operation of gambling for the benefit of the people
      C. need to license private gambling establishments
      D. evils of gambling

16. According to this paragraph, a problem of legalized   16. ...
    gambling which will *still* occur if the state operates
    the gambling business is
      A. the diversion of profits from gambling to private use
      B. that the amount of gambling will tend to diminish
      C. the evil effects of any form of mass gambling
      D. the use of gambling revenues for illegal purposes

17. According to this paragraph, to legalize the business of   17. ...
    gambling would be
      A. *justified* because gambling would be operated only by
        a man of the highest integrity

B. *justified* because this would eliminate politics

C. *unjustified* under any conditions because the human desire to gamble cannot be suppressed

D. *unjustified* if operated for private or political profit

Questions 18-20.

DIRECTIONS: Answer Questions 18 to 20 *SOLELY* on the basis of the following statement:

Whenever, in the course of the performance of their duties in an emergency, members of the force operate the emergency power switch at any location on the transit system and thereby remove power from portions of the track, or they are on the scene where this has been done, they will bear in mind that, although power is removed, further dangers exist; namely, that a train may coast into the area even though the power is off, or that the rails may be energized by a train which may be in a position to transfer electricity from a live portion of the third rail through its shoe beams. Employees must look in each direction before stepping upon, crossing, or standing close to tracks, being particularly careful not to come into contact with the third rail.

18. According to this paragraph, whenever an emergency occurs   18. ...
which has resulted in operating the emergency power switch,
it is *MOST* accurate to state that

A. power is shut off and employees may perform their duties in complete safety

B. there may still be power in a portion of the third rail

C. the switch will not operate if a portion of the track has been broken

D. trains are not permitted to stop in the area of the emergency

19. An *important* precaution which this paragraph urges em-   19. ...
ployees to follow after operating the emergency power
switch, is to

A. look carefully in both directions before stepping near the rails

B. inspect the nearest train which has stopped to see if the power is on

C. examine the third rail to see if the power is on

D. check the emergency power switch to make sure it has operated properly

20. A trackman reports to you, a patrolman, that a dead body   20. ...
is lying on the road bed. You operate the emergency power
switch. A train which has been approaching comes to a stop
near the scene.
In order to act in accordance with the instructions in the
above paragraph, you *should*

A. climb down to the road bed and remove the body

B. direct the train motorman to back up to the point where his train will not be in position to transfer electricity through its shoe beams

C. carefully cross over the road bed to the body, avoiding the third rail and watching for train movements

D. have the train motorman check to see if power is on before crossing to the tracks

8

21. The treatment to be given the offender cannot alter the   21. ...
fact of his offense; but we can take measures to reduce the
chances of similar acts in the future. We should banish
the criminal, not in order to exact revenge nor directly to
encourage reform, but to deter him and others from further
illegal attacks on society.
According to this paragraph, the *PRINCIPAL* reason for punishing criminals is to
    A. prevent the commission of future crimes
    B. remove them from society   C. avenge society
    D. teach them that crime does not pay

22. Even the most comprehensive and best substantiated sum-   22. ...
maries of the total volume of criminal acts would not contribute greatly to an understanding of the varied social and
biological factors which are sometimes assumed to enter into
crime causation, nor would they indicate with any degree of
precision the needs of police forces in combating crime.
According to this statement,
    A. crime statistics alone do not determine the needs of
       police forces in combating crime
    B. crime statistics are essential to a proper understand-
       ing of the social factors of crime
    C. social and biological factors which enter into crime
       causation have little bearing on police needs
    D. a knowledge of the social and biological factors of
       crime is essential to a proper understanding of crime
       statistics

23. The policeman's art consists of applying and enforcing a   23. ...
multitude of laws and ordinances in such degree or proportion and in such manner that the greatest degree of social
protection will be secured. The degree of enforcement and
the method of application will vary with each neighborhood
and community.
According to the foregoing paragraph,
    A. each neighborhood or community must judge for itself to
       what extent the law is to be enforced
    B. a policeman should only enforce those laws which are
       designed to give the greatest degree of social protection
    C. the manner and intensity of law enforcement is not neces-
       sarily the same in all communities
    D. all laws and ordinances must be enforced in a community
       with the same degree of intensity

24. Police control in the sense of regulating the details of   24. ...
police operations, involves such matters as the technical means
for so organizing the available personnel that competent
police leadership, when secured, can operate effectively. It
is concerned not so much with the extent to which popular con-
trols can be trusted to guide and direct the course of police
protection as with the administrative relationships which
should exist between the component parts of the polie organism.
According to the foregoing statement, police control is
    A. solely a matter of proper personnel assignment
    B. the means employed to guide and direct the course of
       police protection
    C. principally concerned with the administrative relation-
       ships between units of a police organization
    D. the sum total of means employed in rendering police protection

25. Police Department Rule 5 states that a Deputy Commissioner   25. ...
acting as Police Commissioner shall carry out the orders of the
Police Commissioner, previously given, and such orders shall not,
except in cases of extreme emergency, be countermanded.
This means, most nearly, that, except in cases of extreme emergency,
    A. the orders given by a Deputy Commissioner acting as
       Police Commissioner may not be revoked
    B. a Deputy Commissioner acting as Police Commissioner should
       not revoke orders previously given by the Police Com-
       missioner
    C. a Deputy Commissioner acting as Police Commissioner is
       vested with the same authority to issue orders as the
       Police Commissioner himself
    D. only a Deputy Commissioner acting as Police Commissioner
       may issue orders in the absence of the Police Commission-
       er himself

TEST 2

Questions 1-2.
DIRECTIONS: Answer Questions 1 and 2 *SOLELY* on the basis of the
following statement:
    The medical examiner may contribute valuable data to the investi-
gator of fires which cause fatalities. By careful examination of the
bodies of any victims, he not only establishes cause of death, but
may also furnish, in many instances, answers to questions relating
to the identity of the victim and the source and origin of the fire.
The medical examiner is of greatest value to law enforcement agencies
because he is able to determine the exact cause of death through an
examination of tissue of apparent arson victims. Thorough study of
a burned body or even of parts of a burned body will frequently yield
information which illuminates the problems confronting the arson investigator and the police.
1. According to the above paragraph, the *MOST* important task   1. ...
   of the medical examiner in the investigation of arson is
   to obtain information concerning the
    A. identity of arsonists   B. cause of death
    C. identity of victims   D. source and origin of fires
2. The *CENTRAL* thought of the above paragraph is that the   2. ...
   medical examiner aids in the solution of crimes of arson
   when
    A. a person is burnt to death
    B. identity of the arsonist is unknown
    C. the cause of the fire is known
    D. trained investigators are not available
Questions 3-6.
DIRECTIONS: Answer Questions 3 to 6 *SOLELY* on the basis of the
following statement:
    A foundling is an abandoned child whose identity is unknown. Desk
officers shall direct the delivery, by a policewoman, if available, of
foundlings actually or apparently under two years of age, to the
Foundling Hospital, or if actually or apparently two years of age or
over, to the Children's Center. In all other cases of dependent or
neglected children, other than foundlings, requiring shelter, desk
officers shall provide for obtaining such shelter as follows: between 9 a.m. and 5 p.m., Monday through Friday, by telephone direct
to the Bureau of Child Welfare, in order to ascertain the shelter to
which the child shall be sent; at all other times, direct the delivery

of a child actually or apparently under two years of age to the Foundling Hospital, or, if the child is actually or apparently two years of age or over, to the Children's Center.

3. According to this paragraph, it would be *MOST* correct to state that   3. ...
    A. a foundling as well as a neglected child may be delivered to the Foundling Hospital
    B. a foundling but not a neglected child may be delivered to the Children's Center
    C. a neglected child requiring shelter, regardless of age, may be delivered to the Bureau of Child Welfare
    D. the Bureau of Child Welfare may determine the shelter to which a foundling may be delivered

4. According to this paragraph, the desk officer shall provide for obtaining shelter for a neglected child, apparently under two years of age, by   4. ...
    A. directing its delivery to the Children's Center if occurrence is on a Monday between 9 a.m. and 5 p.m.
    B. telephoning the Bureau of Child Welfare if occurrence is on a Sunday
    C. directing its delivery to the Foundling Hospital if occurrence is on a Wednesday at 4 p.m.
    D. telephoning the Bureau of Child Welfare if occurrence is at 10 a.m. on a Friday

5. According to this paragraph, the desk officer should direct delivery to the Foundling Hospital of any child who is   5. ...
    A. actually under 2 years of age and requires shelter
    B. apparently under two years of age and is neglected or dependent
    C. actually 2 years of age and is a foundling
    D. apparently under 2 years of age and has been abandoned

6. A 12-year-old neglected child requiring shelter is brought to a police station on Thursday at 2 p.m. Such a child should be sent to   6. ...
    A. a shelter selected by the Bureau of Child Welfare
    B. a shelter selected by the desk officer
    C. the Children's Center
    D. the Foundling Hospital when a brother or sister, under 2 years of age, also requires shelter

Questions 7-9.
DIRECTIONS: Answer Questions 7 to 9 *SOLELY* on the basis of the following statement:

    In addition to making the preliminary investigation of crimes, patrolmen should serve as eyes, ears, and legs for the detective division. The patrol division may be used for surveillance, to serve warrants and bring in suspects and witnesses, and to perform a number of routine tasks for the detectives which will increase the time available for tasks that require their special skills and facilities. It is to the advantage of individual detectives, as well as of the detective division, to have patrolmen working in this manner; more cases are cleared by arrest and a greater proportion of stolen property is recovered when, in addition to the detective regularly assigned, a number of patrolmen also work on the case. Detectives may stimulate the interest and participation of patrolmen by keeping them currently informed of the presence, identity, or description, hangouts, associates, vehicles, and method of operation of each criminal known to be in the community.

7. According to this paragraph, a patrolman should   7. ...
     A. assist the detective in certain of his routine functions
     B. be considered for assignment as a detective on the basis
        of his patrol performance
     C. leave the scene once a detective arrives
     D. perform as much of the detective's duties as time
        permits

8. According to this paragraph, patrolmen should aid detec-   8. ...
tives by

     A. accepting assignments from detectives which give
        promise of recovering stolen property
     B. making arrests of witnesses for the detective's
        interrogation
     C. performing all special investigative work for de-
        tectives
     D. producing for questioning individuals who may aid
        the detective in his investigation

9. According to this paragraph, detectives can keep patrol-   9. ...
men interested by
     A. ascertaining that patrolmen are doing investigative
        work properly
     B. having patrolmen directly under his supervision during
        an investigation
     C. informing patrolmen of the value of their efforts in
        crime prevention
     D. supplying the patrolmen with information regarding
        known criminals in the community

Questions 10-11.
DIRECTIONS: Answer Questions 10 and 11 *SOLELY* on the basis of the
following statement:

     State motor vehicle registration departments should and do play
a vital role in the prevention and detection of automobile thefts.
The combatting of theft is, in fact, one of the primary purposes of
the registration of motor vehicles. As of recent date, there were
approximately 61,309,000 motor vehicles registered in the United States.
That same year some 200,000 of them were stolen. All but 6 percent
have been or will be recovered. This is a very high recovery ratio
compared to the percentage of recovery of other stolen personal property. The reason for this is that automobiles are carefully identified by the manufacturers and carefully registered by many of the
states.

10. The *CENTRAL* thought of this paragraph is that there is a   10. ...
     close relationship between the
     A. number of automobiles registered in the United States
        and the number stolen
     B. prevention of automobile thefts *and* the effectiveness
        of police departments in the United States
     C. recovery of stolen automobiles *and* automobile registra-
        tion
     D. recovery of stolen automobiles *and* of other stolen
        property

11. According to this paragraph, the high recovery ratio for   11. ...
stolen automobiles is due to
     A. state registration and manufacturer identification of
        motor vehicles
     B. successful prevention of automobile thefts by state
        motor vehicle departments
     C. the fact that only 6% of stolen vehicles are not proper-
        ly registered

D. the high number of motor vehicles registered in the
    United States

Questions 12-15.
DIRECTIONS: Answer Questions 12 to 15 *SOLELY* on the basis of the
following statement:

It is not always understood that the term "physical evidence"
embraces any and all objects, living or inanimate. A knife, gun,
signature, or burglar tool is immediately recognized as physical
evidence. Less often is it considered that dust, microscopic frag-
ments of all types, even an odor, may equally be physical evidence
and often the most important of all. It is well established that the
most useful types of physical evidence are generally microscopic in
dimensions, that is, not noticeable by the eye and, therefore, most
likely to be overlooked by the criminal and by the investigator. For
this reason, microscopic evidence persists for months or years after
all other evidence has been removed and found inconclusive. Natural-
ly, there are limitations to the time of collecting microscopic evidence as it may be lost or decayed. The exercise of judgment as to
the possibility or profit of delayed action in collecting the evidence
is a field in which the expert investigator should judge.

12. The *one* of the following which the above paragraph does   12. ...
    NOT consider to be physical evidence is a
    A. criminal thought   B. minute speck of dust
    C. raw onion smell   D. typewritten note
13. According to the above paragraph, the re-checking of   13. ...
    the scene of a crime
    A. is *useless* when performed years after the occurrence
       of the crime
    B. is *advisable* chiefly in crimes involving physical
       violence
    C. *may turn up* microscopic evidence of value
    D. *should be delayed* if the microscopic evidence is not
       subject to decay or loss
14. According to the above paragraph, the criminal investi-   14. ...
    gator *should*
    A. give most of his attention to weapons used in the
       commission of the crime
    B. ignore microscopic evidence until a requiest is re-
       ceived from the laboratory
    C. immediately search for microscopic evidence and ignore
       the more visible objects
    D. realize that microscopic evidence can be easily over-
       looked
15. According to the above paragraph,   15. ...
    A. a delay in collecting evidence must definitely diminish
       its value to the investigator
    B. microscopic evidence exists for longer periods of time
       than other physical evidence
    C. microscopic evidence is generally the most useful type
       of physical evidence
    D. physical evidence is likely to be overlooked by the
       criminal and by the investigator

13

Questions 16-18.
DIRECTIONS: Answer Questions 16 to 18 *SOLELY* on the basis of the following statement:

Sometimes, but not always, firing a gun leaves a residue of nitrate particles on the hands. This fact is utilized in the paraffin test which consists of applying melted paraffin and gauze to the fingers, hands, and wrists of a suspect until a cast of approximately 1/8 of an inch is built up. The heat of the paraffin causes the pores of the skin to open and release any particles embedded in them. The paraffin cast is then removed and tested chemically for nitrate particles. In addition to gunpowder, fertilizers, tobacco ashes, matches, and soot are also common sources of nitrates on the hands.

16. Assume that the paraffin test has been given to a person   16. ...
    suspected of firing a gun and that nitrate particles have
    been found. It would be *CORRECT* to conclude that the
    suspect
        A. is guilty   B. is innocent
        C. may be guilty or innocent   D. is probably guilty

17. In testing for the presence of gunpowder particles on   17. ...
    human hands, the characteristic of paraffin which makes
    it *MOST* serviceable is that it
        A. causes the nitrate residue left by a fired gun to
           adhere to the gauze
        B. is waterproof   C. melts at a low temperature
        D. helps to distinguish between gunpowder nitrates and
           other types

18. According to the above paragraph, in the paraffin test,   18. ...
    the nitrate particles are removed from the pores because
    the paraffin
        A. enlarges the pores   B. contracts the pores
        C. reacts chemically with nitrates
        D. dissolves the particles

Questions 19-21.
DIRECTIONS: Answer Questions 19 to 21 *SOLELY* on the basis of the following statement:

Pickpockets operate most effectively when there are prospective victims in either heavily congested areas or in lonely places. In heavily populated areas, the large number of people about them covers the activities of these thieves. In lonely spots, they have the advantage of working unobserved. The main factor in the pickpocket's success is the selection of the "right" victim. A pickpocket's victim must, at the time of the crime, be inattentive, distracted, or unconscious. If any of these conditions exist, and if the pickpocket is skilled in his operations, the stage is set for a successful larceny. With the coming of winter, the crowds move southward - and so do most of the pickpockets. However, some pickpockets will remain in certain areas all year around. They will concentrate on theater districts, bus and railroad terminals, hotels or large shopping centers. A complete knowledge of the methods of this type of criminal and the ability to recognize them come only from long years of experience in performing patient surveillance and trailing of them. This knowledge is essential for the effective control and apprehension of this type of thief.

19. According to this paragraph, the pickpocket is *LEAST*   19. ...
    likely to operate in a
        A. baseball park with a full capacity attendance
        B. station in an outlying area late at night

14

      C. moderately crowded dance hall

      D. over-crowded department store

20. According to this paragraph, the *one* of the following   20. ...
factors which is *NOT* necessary for the successful operation of the pickpocket is that

      A. he be proficient in the operations required to pick
pockets

      B. the "right" potential victims be those who have been
the subject of such a theft previously

      C. his operations be hidden from the view of others

      D. the potential victim be unaware of the actions of the
pickpocket

21. According to this paragraph, it would be *MOST* correct   21. ...
to conclude that police officers who are successful in
apprehending pickpockets

      A. are generalling those who have had lengthy experience
in recognizing all types of criminals

      B. must, by intuition, be able to recognize potential
"right" victims

      C. must follow the pickpockets in their southward move-
ment

      D. must have acquired specific knowledge and skills in
this field

Questions 22-23.

DIRECTIONS: Answer Questions 22 and 23 *SOLELY* on the basis of the
following statement:

    For many years, slums had been recognized as breeding disease,
juvenile delinquency, and crime which not only threatened the health
and welfare of the people who lived there, but also weakened the
structure of society as a whole. As far back as 1834, a sanitary
inspection report in the city pointed out the connection between
insanitary, overcrowded housing and the spread of epidemics. Down
through the years, evidence of slum-produced evils accumulated as
the slums themselves continued to spread. This spread of slums was
nationwide. Its symptoms and its ill effects were peculiar to no
locality, but were characteristic of the country as a whole and im-
periled the national welfare.

22. According to this paragraph, people who live in slum   22. ...
dwellings

      A. cause slums to become worse

      B. are threatened by disease and crime

      C. create bad housing

      D. are the chief source of crime in the country

23. According to this paragraph, the effects of juvenile de-   23. ...
linquency and crime in slum areas were

      A. to destroy the structure of society

      B. noticeable in all parts of the country

      C. a chief cause of the spread of slums

      D. to spread insanitary conditions in the city

Questions 24-25.

DIRECTIONS: Questions 24 and 25 pertain to the following section of
the Penal Law:

    Section 1942. A person who, after having been three times convicted
within this state, of felonies or attempts to commit felonies, or under
the law of any other state, government or country, of crimes which if
committed within this state would be felonious, commits a felony, other
than murder, first or second degree, or treason, within this state,
shall be sentenced upon conviction of such fourth, or subsequent, of-

fense to imprisonment in a state prison for an indeterminate term the minimum of which shall be not less than the maximum term provided for first offenders for the crime for which the individual has been convicted, but, in any event, the minimum term upon conviction for a felony as the fourth,or subsequent, offense, shall be not less than fifteen years, and the maximum thereof shall be his natural life.

24. Under the terms of the above stated portion of Section 1942 of the Penal Law, a person must receive the increased punishment therein provided *if*   24. ...
    A. he is convicted of a felony and has been three times previously convicted of felonies
    B. he has been three times previously convicted of felonies, regardless of the nature of his present conviction
    C. his fourth conviction is for murder, first or second degree, or treason
    D. he has previously been convicted three times of murder, first or second degree, or treason

25. Under the terms of the above stated portion of Section 1942 of the Penal Law, a person convicted of a felony for which the penalty is imprisonment for a term not to exceed ten years, and who has been three times previously convicted of felonies in this state, shall be sentenced to a term the *minimum* of which shall be   25. ...
    A. ten years   B. fifteen years
    C. indeterminate   D. his natural life

KEYS (CORRECT ANSWERS)

	TEST 1				TEST 2		
1.	C	11.	C	1.	B	11.	A
2.	D	12.	C	2.	A	12.	A
3.	B	13.	B	3.	A	13.	C
4.	C	14.	D	4.	D	14.	D
5.	C	15.	B	5.	D	15.	C
6.	D	16.	C	6.	A	16.	C
7.	A	17.	D	7.	A	17.	A
8.	C	18.	B	8.	D	18.	A
9.	B	19.	A	9.	D	19.	C
10.	B	20.	C	10.	C	20.	B
		21.	A			21.	D
		22.	A			22.	B
		23.	C			23.	B
		24.	C			24.	A
		25.	B			25.	B

DIRECTIONS: Each question or incomplete statement is followed by several suggested answers or completions. Select the one that BEST answers the question or completes the statement. *PRINT THE LETTER OF THE CORRECT ANSWER IN THE SPACE AT THE RIGHT.*

Questions 1-5.

DIRECTIONS: Questions 1 through 5 are to be answered on the basis of the following passage.

The laws with which criminal courts are concerned contain threats of punishment for infraction of specified rules. Consequently, the courts are organized primarily for implementation of the punitive societal reaction of crime. While the informal organization of most courts allows the judge to use discretion as to which guilty persons actually are to be punished, the threat of punishment for all guilty persons always is present. Also, in recent years a number of formal provisions for the use of non-punitive and treatment methods by the criminal courts have been made, but the threat of punishment remains, even for the recipients of the treatment and non-punitive measures. For example, it has become possible for courts to grant probation, which can be non-punitive, to some offenders, but the probationer is constantly under the threat of punishment, for, if he does not maintain the conditions of his probation, he may be imprisoned. As the treatment reaction to crime becomes more popular, the criminal courts may have as their sole function the determination of the guilt or innocence of the accused persons, leaving the problem of correcting criminals entirely to outsiders. Under such conditions, the organization of the court system, the duties and activities of court personnel, and the nature of the trial all would be decidedly different.

1. Which one of the following is the BEST description of the subject matter of the above passage? 1.___
   The
   A. value of non-punitive measures for criminals
   B. effect of punishment on guilty individuals
   C. punitive functions of the criminal courts
   D. success of probation as a deterrent of crime

2. It may be INFERRED from the above passage that the present traditional organization of the criminal court system is a result of 2.___
   A. the nature of the laws with which these courts are concerned
   B. a shift from non-punitive to punitive measures for correctional purposes
   C. an informal arrangement between court personnel and the government
   D. a formal decision made by court personnel to increase efficiency

3. All persons guilty of breaking certain specified rules,   3.___
   according to the above passage, are subject to the threat
   of
   A. treatment   B. punishment
   C. probation   D. retrial

4. According to the above passage, the decision whether or   4.___
   not to punish a guilty person is a function USUALLY
   performed by
   A. the jury   B. the criminal code
   C. the judge   D. corrections personnel

5. According to the above passage, which one of the following   5.___
   is a possible effect of an increase in the *treatment
   reactions to crime*?
   A. A decrease in the number of court personnel
   B. An increase in the number of criminal trials
   C. Less reliance on probation as a non-punitive treatment
      measure
   D. A decrease in the functions of the court following
      determination of guilt

Questions 6-8.

DIRECTIONS: Questions 6 through 8 are to be answered on the basis
              of the following passage.

A glaring exception to the usual practice of the judicial trial
as a means of conflict resolution is the utilization of administrative
hearings. The growing tendency to create administrative bodies with
rule-making and quasi-judicial powers has shattered many standard
concepts. A comprehensive examination of the legal process cannot
neglect these newer patterns.

In the administrative process, the legislative, executive, and
judicial functions are mixed together, and many functions, such as
investigating, advocating, negotiating, testifying, rule making, and
adjudicating, are carried out by the same agency. The reason for the
breakdown of the separation-of-powers formula is not hard to find.
It was felt by Congress, and state and municipal legislatures, that
certain regulatory tasks could not be performed efficiently, rapidly,
expertly, and with due concern for the public interest by the traditional branches of government. Accordingly, regulatory agencies were
delegated powers to consider disputes from the earliest stage of
investigation to the final stages of adjudication entirely within
each agency itself, subject only to limited review in the regular
courts.

6. The above passage states that the usual means for conflict   6.___
   resolution is through the use of
   A. judicial trial   B. administrative hearing
   C. legislation   D. regulatory agencies

7. The above passage IMPLIES that the use of administrative   7.___
    hearing in resolving conflict is a(n) _____ approach.
        A. traditional   B. new
        C. dangerous   D. experimental

8. The above passage states that the reason for the breakdown   8.___
    of the separation-of-powers formula in the administrative
    process is that
        A. Congress believed that certain regulatory tasks
           could be better performed by separate agencies
        B. legislative and executive functions are incompatible
           in the same agency
        C. investigative and regulatory functions are not
           normally reviewed by the courts
        D. state and municipal legislatures are more concerned
           with efficiency than with legality

Questions 9-10.

DIRECTIONS: Questions 9 and 10 are to be answered SOLELY on the
             basis of the information given in the following para-
             graph.

    An assumption commonly made in regard to the reliability of
testimony is that when a number of persons report upon the same
matter, those details upon which there is an agreement may, in
general, be considered as substantiated. Experiments have shown,
however, that there is a tendency for the same errors to appear in
the testimony of different individuals, and that, quite apart from
any collusion, agreement of testimony is no proof of dependability.

9. According to the above paragraph, it is commonly assumed   9.___
    that details of an event are substantiated when
        A. a number of persons report upon them
        B. a reliable person testifies to them
        C. no errors are apparent in the testimony of different
           individuals
        D. several witnesses are in agreement about them

10. According to the above paragraph, agreement in the testi-   10.___
    mony of different witnesses to the same event is
        A. evaluated more reliably when considered apart from
           collusion
        B. not the result of chance
        C. not a guarantee of the accuracy of the facts
        D. the result of a mass reaction of the witnesses

Questions 11-12.

DIRECTIONS: Questions 11 and 12 are to be answered SOLELY on the basis of the information given in the following paragraph.

The accuracy of the information about past occurrence obtainable in an interview is so low that one must take the stand that the best use to be made of the interview in this connection is a means of finding clues and avenues of access to more reliable sources of information. On the other hand, feelings and attitudes have been found to be clearly and correctly revealed in a properly conducted personal interview.

11. According to the above paragraph, information obtained in a personal interview   11.___
    A. can be corroborated by other clues and more reliable sources of information revealed at the interview
    B. can be used to develop leads to other sources of information about past events
    C. is not reliable
    D. is reliable if it relates to recent occurrences

12. According to the above paragraph, the personal interview is suitable for obtaining   12.___
    A. emotional reactions to a given situation
    B. fresh information on factors which may be forgotten
    C. revived recollection of previous events for later use as testimony
    D. specific information on material already reduced to writing

Questions 13-15.

DIRECTIONS: Questions 13 through 15 are to be answered on the basis of the following paragraph.

Admissibility of handwriting standards (samples of handwriting for the purpose of comparison) as a basis for expert testimony is frequently necessary when the authenticity of disputed documents may be at issue. Under the older rules of common law, only that writing relating to the issues in the case could be used as a basis for hand-writing testimony by an expert. Today, most jurisdictions admit irrelevant writings as standards for comparison. However, their genuineness, in all instances, must be established to the satisfaction of the court. There are a number of types of documents, how-ever, not ordinarily relevant to the issues which are seldom accept-able to the court as handwriting standards, such as bail bonds, signatures on affidavits, depositions, etc. These are usually already before the court as part of the record in a case. Exhibits written in the presence of a witness or prepared voluntarily for a law enforcement officer are readily admissible in most jurisdictions. Testimony of a witness who is considered familiar with the writing is admissible in some jurisdictions. In criminal cases, it is possible that the signature on the fingerprint card obtained in connection with the arrest of the defendant for the crime currently charged may be admitted as a handwriting standard. In order to give the defendant the fairest possible treatment, most jurisdictions do not admit the signatures on fingerprint cards pertaining to prior arrests. However, they are admitted sometimes. In such instances, the court usually requires that the signature be photographed or removed from the card and no reference be made to the origin of the signature.

13. Of the following, the types of handwriting standards   13.___
    MOST likely to be admitted in evidence by most juris-
    dictions are those
    A. appearing on depositions and bail bonds
    B. which were written in the presence of a witness or
       voluntarily given to a law enforcement officer
    C. identified by witnesses who claim to be familiar
       with the handwriting
    D. which are in conformity with the rules of common
       law only

14. The PRINCIPAL factor which generally determines the   14.___
    acceptance of handwriting standards by the courts is
    A. the relevance of the submitted documents to the
       issues of the case
    B. the number of witnesses who have knowledge of the
       submitted documents
    C. testimony that the writing has been examined by a
       handwriting expert
    D. acknowledgment by the court of the authenticity of
       the submitted documents

15. The MOST logical reason for requiring the removal of the   15.___
    signature of a defendant from fingerprint cards pertaining
    to prior arrests, before admitting the signature in court
    as a handwriting standard, is that
    A. it simplifies the process of identification of the
       signature as a standard for comparison
    B. the need for identifying the fingerprints is elimina-
       ted
    C. mention of prior arrests may be prejudicial to the
       defendant
    D. a handwriting expert does not need information per-
       taining to prior arrests in order to make his
       identification

Questions 16-20.

DIRECTIONS: Questions 16 through 20 are to be answered SOLELY on the basis of the information contained in the following paragraph.

A statement which is offered in an attempt to prove the truth of the matters therein stated, but which is not made by the author as a witness before the court at the particular trial in which it is so offered, is hearsay. This is so whether the statement consists of words (oral or written), of symbols used as a substitute for words, or of signs or other conduct offered as the equivalent of a statement. Subject to some well-established exceptions, hearsay is not generally acceptable as evidence, and it does not become competent evidence just because it is received by the court without objection. One basis for this rule is simply that a fact cannot be proved by showing that somebody stated it was a fact. Another basis for the rule is the fundamental principle that in a criminal prosecution the testimony of the witness shall be taken before the court, so that at the time he gives the testimony offered in evidence he will be sworn and subject to cross-examination, the scrutiny of the court, and confrontation by the accused.

16.   Which of the following is hearsay?   16.___
       A(n)
       A. written statement by a person not present at the court hearing where the statement is submitted as proof of an occurrence
       B. oral statement in court by a witness of what he saw
       C. written statement of what he saw by a witness present in court
       D. re-enactment by a witness in court of what he saw

17.   In a criminal case, a statement by a person not present   17.___
       in court is
       A. *acceptable* evidence if not objected to by the prosecutor
       B. *acceptable* evidence if not objected to by the defense lawyer
       C. *not acceptable* evidence except in certain well-settled circumstances
       D. *not acceptable* evidence under any circumstances

18.   The rule on hearsay is founded on the belief that   18.___
       A. proving someone said an act occurred is not proof that the act did occur
       B. a person who has knowledge about a case should be willing to appear in court
       C. persons not present in court are likely to be unreliable witnesses
       D. permitting persons to testify without appearing in court will lead to a disrespect for law

19. One reason for the general rule that a witness in a
    criminal case must give his testimony in court is that
    A. a witness may be influenced by threats to make untrue
       statements
    B. the opposite side is then permitted to question him
    C. the court provides protection for a witness against
       unfair questioning
    D. the adversary system is designed to prevent a
       miscarriage of justice

19.___

20. Of the following, the MOST appropriate title for the
    above passage would be
    A. WHAT IS HEARSAY?   B. RIGHTS OF DEFENDANTS
    C. TRIAL PROCEDURES   D. TESTIMONY OF WITNESSES

20.___

21. A person's statements are independent of who he is or
    what he is. Statements made by a person are not proved
    true or false by questioning his character or his posi-
    tion. A statement should stand or fall on its merits,
    regardless of who makes the statement. Truth is deter-
    mined by evidence only. A person's character or person-
    ality should not be the determining factor in logic.
    Discussions should not become incidents of name calling.
    According to the above, whether or not a statement is
    true depends on the
    A. recipient's conception of validity
    B. maker's reliability
    C. extent of support by facts
    D. degree of merit the discussion has

21.___

Question 22-25.

DIRECTIONS: Questions 22 through 25 are to be answered on the basis
             of the following passage.

The question, whether an act, repugnant to the Constitution, can
become the law of the land, is a question deeply interesting to the
United States; but, happily, not of an intricacy proportioned to its
interest. It seems only necessary to recognize certain principles,
supposed to have been long and well-established, to decide it. That
the people have an original right to establish, for their future
government, such principles as, in their opinion, shall most conduce
to their own happiness, is the basis on which the whole American
fabric has been erected. The exercise of this original right is a
very great exertion; nor can it, nor ought it, to be frequently
repeated. The principles, therefore, so established are deemed
fundamental; and as the authority from which they proceed is supreme,
and can seldom act, they are designed to be permanent.

22. The BEST title for the above passage would be
    A. PRINCIPLES OF THE CONSTITUTION
    B. THE ROOT OF CONSTITUTIONAL CHANGE
    C. ONLY PEOPLE CAN CHANGE THE CONSTITUTION
    D. METHODS OF CONSTITUTIONAL CHANGE

22.___

23. According to the above passage, original right is   23.___
    A. fundamental to the principle that the people may choose their own form of government
    B. established by the Constitution
    C. the result of a very great exertion and should not often be repeated
    D. supreme, can seldom act, and is designed to be permanent

24. Whether an act not in keeping with Constitutional principles can become law is, according to the above passage,   24.___
    A. an intricate problem requiring great thought and concentration
    B. determined by the proportionate interests of legislators
    C. determined by certain long established principles, fundamental to Constitutional Law
    D. an intricate problem, but less intricate than it would seem from the interest shown in it

25. According to the above passage, the phrase *and can seldom act* refers to the   25.___
    A. principle early enacted into law by Americans when they chose their future form of government
    B. original rights of the people as vested in the Constitution
    C. original framers of the Constitution
    D. established, fundamental principles of government

KEY (CORRECT ANSWERS)

1. C		11. B	
2. A		12. A	
3. B		13. B	
4. C		14. D	
5. D		15. C	
6. A		16. A	
7. B		17. C	
8. A		18. A	
9. D		19. B	
10. C		20. A	

21. C
22. B
23. A
24. D
25. A

TEST 2

DIRECTIONS: Each question or incomplete statement is followed by several suggested answers or completions. Select the one that BEST answers the question or completes the statement. *PRINT THE LETTER OF THE CORRECT ANSWER IN THE SPACE AT THE RIGHT.*

Questions 1-3.

DIRECTIONS: Questions 1 through 3 are to be answered SOLELY on the basis of the following paragraph.

The police laboratory performs a valuable service in crime investigation by assisting in the reconstruction of criminal action and by aiding in the identification of persons and things. When studied by a technician, physical things found at crime scenes often reveal facts useful in identifying the criminal and in determining what has occurred. The nature of substances to be examined and the character of the examination to be made vary so widely that the services of a large variety of skilled scientific persons are needed in crime investigations. To employ such a complete staff and to provide them with equipment and standards needed for all possible analysis and comparisons is beyond the means and the needs of any but the largest police departments. The search of crime scenes for physical evidence also calls for the services of specialists supplied with essential equipment and assigned to each tour of duty so as to provide service at any hour.

1. If a police department employs a large staff of technicians of various types in its laboratory, it will affect crime investigations to the extent that
   A. most crimes will be speedily solved
   B. identification of criminals will be aided
   C. search of crime scenes for physical evidence will become of less importance
   D. investigation by police officers will not usually be required

1.___

2. According to the above paragraph, the MOST complete study of objects found at the scenes of crimes is
   A. always done in all large police departments
   B. based on assigning one technician to each tour of duty
   C. probably done only in large police departments
   D. probably done in police departments of communities with low crime rates

2.___

3. According to the above paragraph, a large variety of skilled technicians is useful in criminal investigations because
   A. crimes cannot be solved without their assistance as part of the police team

3.___

    B. large police departments need large staffs
    C. many different kinds of tests on various substances
       can be made
    D. the police cannot predict what methods may be tried
       by wily criminals

Questions 4-6.

DIRECTIONS: Questions 4 through 6 are to be answered SOLELY on the
               basis of the following passage.

Probably the most important single mechanism for bringing the
resources of science and technology to bear on the problems of crime
would be the establishment of a major prestigious science and technology research program within a research institute. The program
would create interdisciplinary teams of mathematicians, computer
scientists, electronics engineers, physicists, biologists, and other
natural scientists, psychologists, sociologists, economists, and
lawyers. The institute and the program must be significant enough
to attract the best scientists available, and, to this end, the
director of this institute must himself have a background in science
and technology and have the respect of scientists. Because it would
be difficult to attract such a staff into the Federal government, the
institute should be established by a university, a group of universities, or an independent nonprofit organization, and should be within a major metropolitan area. The institute would have to establish
close ties with neighboring criminal justice agencies that would
receive the benefit of serving as experimental laboratories for such
an institute. In fact, the proposal for the institute might be
jointly submitted with the criminal justice agencies. The research
program would require in order to bring together the necessary
critical mass of competent staff an annual budget which might reach
5 million dollars, funded with at least three years of lead time to
assure continuity. Such a major scientific and technological
research institute should be supported by the Federal government.

4. Of the following, the MOST appropriate title for the   4.___
    foregoing passage is
      A. RESEARCH - AN INTERDISCIPLINARY APPROACH TO FIGHTING
         CRIME
      B. A CURRICULUM FOR FIGHTING CRIME
      C. THE ROLE OF THE UNIVERSITY IN THE FIGHT AGAINST CRIME
      D. GOVERNMENTAL SUPPORT OF CRIMINAL RESEARCH PROGRAMS

5. According to the above passage, in order to attract the   5.___
    best scientists available, the research institute should
      A. provide psychologists and sociologists to counsel
         individual members of interdisciplinary teams
      B. encourage close ties with neighboring criminal
         justice agencies
      C. be led by a person who is respected in the scientific
         community
      D. be directly operated and funded by the Federal
         government

6. The term *critical mass*, as used in the above passage,   6.___
   refers MAINLY to
   A. a staff which would remain for three years of
      continuous service to the institute
   B. staff members necessary to carry out the research
      program of the institute successfully
   C. the staff necessary to establish relations with
      criminal justice agencies which will serve as
      experimental laboratories for the institute
   D. a staff which would be able to assist the institute
      in raising adequate funds

Questions 7-9.

DIRECTIONS: Questions 7 through 9 are to be answered SOLELY on
              the basis of the following paragraph.

The use of modern scientific methods in the examination of
physical evidence often provides information to the investigator
which he could not otherwise obtain. This applies particularly to
small objects and materials present in minute quantities or trace
evidence because the quantities here are such that they may be
overlooked without methodical searching, and often special means of
detection are needed. Whenever two objects come in contact with
one another, there is a transfer of material, however slight.
Usually, the softer object will transfer to the harder, but the
transfer may be mutual. The quantity of material transferred differs
with the type of material involved and the more violent the contact
the greater the degree of transference. Through scientific methods
of determining physical properties and chemical composition, we can
add to the facts observable by the investigator's unaided senses,
and thereby increase the chances of identification.

7. According to the above paragraph, the amount of material   7.___
   transferred whenever two objects come in contact with one
   another
   A. varies directly with the softness of the objects
      involved
   B. varies directly with the violence of the contact of
      the objects
   C. is greater when two soft, rather than hard, objects
      come into violent contact with each other
   D. is greater when coarse-grained, rather than smooth-
      grained, materials are involved

8. According to the above paragraph, the PRINCIPAL reason   8.___
   for employing scientific methods in obtaining trace
   evidence is that
   A. other methods do not involve a methodical search of
      the crime scene
   B. scientific methods of examination frequently reveal
      physical evidence which did not previously exist
   C. the amount of trace evidence may be so sparse that
      other methods are useless
   D. trace evidence cannot be properly identified unless
      special means of detection are employed

9. According to the above paragraph, the one of the follow-   9.___
   ing statements which BEST describes the manner in which
   scientific methods of analyzing physical evidence
   assists the investigator is that such methods
      A. add additional valuable information to the investi-
         gator's own knowledge of complex and rarely occurring
         materials found as evidence
      B. compensate for the lack of important evidential
         material through the use of physical and chemical
         analyses
      C. make possible an analysis of evidence which goes
         beyond the ordinary capacity of the investigator's
         senses
      D. identify precisely those physical characteristics of
         the individual which the untrained senses of the
         investigator are unable to discern

Questions 10-13.

DIRECTIONS: Questions 10 through 13 are to be answered SOLELY on
             the basis of the information contained in the following
             paragraph.

     Under the provisions of the Bank Protection Act of 1968, enacted
July 8, 1968, each Federal banking supervisory agency, as of January 7,
1969, had to issue rules establishing minimum standards with which
financial institutions under their control must comply with respect
to the installation, maintenance, and operation of security devices
and procedures, reasonable in cost, to discourage robberies, burglaries, and larcenies, and to assist in the identification and
apprehension of persons who commit such acts. The rules set the time
limits within which the affected banks and savings and loan associations must comply with the standards, and the rules require the
submission of periodic reports on the steps taken. A violator of a
rule under this Act is subject to a civil penalty not to exceed $100
for each day of the violation. The enforcement of these regulations
rests with the responsible banking supervisory agencies.

10. The Bank Protection Act of 1968 was designed to   10.___
      A. provide Federal police protection for banks covered
         by the Act
      B. have organizations covered by the Act take precau-
         tions against criminals
      C. set up a system for reporting all bank robberies to
         the FBI
      D. insure institutions covered by the Act from financial
         loss due to robberies, burglaries, and larcenies

11. Under the provisions of the Bank Protection Act of 1968,   11.___
   each Federal banking supervisory agency was required to
   set up rules for financial institutions covered by the
   Act governing the
      A. hiring of personnel
      B. punishment of burglars
      C. taking of protective measures
      D. penalties for violations

12. Financial institutions covered by the Bank Protection   12.___
    Act of 1968 were required to
        A. file reports at regular intervals on what they had
           done to prevent theft
        B. identify and apprehend persons who commit robberies,
           burglaries, and larcenies
        C. draw up a code of ethics for their employees
        D. have fingerprints of their employees filed with the
           FBI

13. Under the provisions of the Bank Protection Act of 1968,   13.___
    a bank which is subject to the rules established under
    the Act and which violates a rule is liable to a penalty
    of NOT _____ than $100 for each _____.
        A. more; violation   B. less; day of violation
        C. less; violation   D. more; day of violation

Questions 14-17.

DIRECTIONS: Questions 14 through 17 are to be answered SOLELY on
              the basis of the following passage.

    Specific measures for prevention of pilferage will be based on
careful analysis of the conditions at each agency. The most practical and effective method to control casual pilferage is the
establishment of psychological deterrents.

    One of the most common means of discouraging casual pilferage
is to search individuals leaving the agency at unannounced times
and places. These spot searches may occasionally detect attempts
at theft, but greater value is realized by bringing to the attention of individuals the fact that they may be apprehended if they
do attempt the illegal removal of property.

    An aggressive security education program is an effective means
of convincing employees that they have much more to lose than they
do to gain by engaging in acts of theft. It is important for all
employees to realize that pilferage is morally wrong no matter how
insignificant the value of the item which is taken. In establishing
any deterrent to casual pilferage, security officers must not lose
sight of the fact that most employees are honest and disapprove of
thievery. Mutual respect between security personnel and other
employees of the agency must be maintained if the facility is to be
protected from other more dangerous forms of human hazards. Any
security measure which infringes on the human rights or dignity of
others will jeopardize, rather than enhance, the overall protection
of the agency.

14. The $100,000 yearly inventory of an agency revealed that   14.___
    $50 worth of goods had been stolen; the only individuals
    with access to the stolen materials were the employees.
    Of the following measures, which would the author of the
    above passage MOST likely recommend to a security officer?

A. Conduct an intensive investigation of all employees
   to find the culprit.
B. Make a record of the theft, but take no investigative
   or disciplinary action against any employee.
C. Place a tight security check on all future movements
   of personnel.
D. Remove the remainder of the material to an area with
   much greater security.

15. What does the passage imply is the percentage of employees   15.___
    whom a security officer should expect to be honest?
    A. No employee can be expected to be honest all of the
       time
    B. Just 50%
    C. Less than 50%
    D. More than 50%

16. According to the above passage, the security officer   16.___
    would use which of the following methods to minimize
    theft in buildings with many exits when his staff is
    very small?
    A. Conduct an inventory of all material and place a
       guard near that which is most likely to be pilfered
    B. Inform employees of the consequences of legal prose-
       cution for pilfering
    C. Close off the unimportant exits and have all his men
       concentrate on a few exits
    D. Place a guard at each exit and conduct a casual
       search of individuals leaving the premises

17. Of the following, the title BEST suited for this passage   17.___
    is
    A. CONTROL MEASURES FOR CASUAL PILFERING
    B. DETECTING THE POTENTIAL PILFERER
    C. FINANCIAL LOSSES RESULTING FROM PILFERING
    D. THE USE OF MORAL PERSUASION IN PHYSICAL SECURITY

Questions 18-24.

DIRECTIONS: Questions 18 through 24 are to be answered SOLELY on
             the basis of the following passage.

    Burglar alarms are designed to detect intrusion automatically.
Robbery alarms enable a victim of a robbery or an attack to signal
for help. Such devices can be located in elevators, hallways,
homes and apartments, businesses and factories, and subways, as
well as on the street in high-crime areas. Alarms could deter some
potential criminals from attacking targets so protected. If alarms
were prevalent and not visible, then they might serve to suppress
crime generally. In addition, of course, the alarms can summon the
police when they are needed.

    All alarms must perform three functions: sensing or initiation
of the signal, transmission of the signal and annunciation of the
alarm. A burglar alarm needs a sensor to detect human presence or

activity in an unoccupied enclosed area like a building or a room.
A robbery victim would initiate the alarm by closing a foot or wall
switch, or by triggering a portable transmitter which would send the
alarm signal to a remote receiver. The signal can sound locally as
a loud noise to frighten away a criminal, or it can be sent silently
by wire to a central agency. A centralized annunciator requires
either private lines from each alarmed point, or the transmission of
some information on the location of the signal.

18. A conclusion which follows LOGICALLY from the above   18.___
    passage is that
        A. burglar alarms employ sensor devices; robbery alarms
           make use of initiation devices
        B. robbery alarms signal intrusion without the help of
           the victim; burglar alarms require the victim to
           trigger a switch
        C. robbery alarms sound locally; burglar alarms are
           transmitted to a central agency
        D. the mechanisms for a burglar alarm and a robbery
           alarm are alike

19. According to the above passage, alarms can be located   19.___
        A. in a wide variety of settings
        B. only in enclosed areas
        C. at low cost in high-crime areas
        D. only in places where potential criminals will be
           deterred

20. According to the above passage, which of the following   20.___
    is ESSENTIAL if a signal is to be received in a central
    office?
        A. A foot or wall switch
        B. A noise-producing mechanism
        C. A portable reception device
        D. Information regarding the location of the source

21. According to the above passage, an alarm system can   21.___
    function WITHOUT a
        A. centralized annunciating device
        B. device to stop the alarm
        C. sensing or initiating device
        D. transmission device

22. According to the above passage, the purpose of robbery   22.___
    alarms is to
        A. find out automatically whether a robbery has taken
           place
        B. lower the crime rate in high-crime areas
        C. make a loud noise to frighten away the criminal
        D. provide a victim with the means to signal for help

23. According to the above passage, alarms might aid in   23.___
    lessening crime if they were
        A. answered promptly by police
        B. completely automatic
        C. easily accessible to victims
        D. hidden and widespread

24. Of the following, the BEST title for the above passage is   24.___
    A. DETECTION OF CRIME BY ALARMS
    B. LOWERING THE CRIME RATE
    C. SUPPRESSION OF CRIME
    D. THE PREVENTION OF ROBBERY

25. Although the rural crime reporting area is much less   25.___
    developed than that for cities and towns, current data
    are collected in sufficient volume to justify the general-
    ization that rural crime rates are lower than those or
    urban communities.
    According to this statement,
    A. better reporting of crime occurs in rural areas than
       in cities
    B. there appears to be a lower proportion of crime in
       rural areas than in cities
    C. cities have more crime than towns
    D. crime depends on the amount of reporting

———

KEY (CORRECT ANSWERS)

1. B		11. C	
2. C		12. A	
3. C		13. D	
4. A		14. B	
5. C		15. D	
6. B		16. B	
7. B		17. A	
8. C		18. A	
9. C		19. A	
10. B		20. D	

21. A
22. D
23. D
24. A
25. B

———

GLOSSARY OF LEGAL TERMS

CONTENTS

GLOSSARY OF LEGAL TERMS

A

ACTION - "Action" includes a civil action and a criminal action.

A FORTIORI - A term meaning you can reason one thing from the existence of certain facts.

A POSTERIORI - From what goes after; from effect to cause.

A PRIORI - From what goes before; from cause to effect.

AB INITIO - From the beginning.

ABATE - To diminish or put an end to.

ABET - To encourage the commission of a crime.

ABEYANCE - Suspension, temporary suppression.

ABIDE - To accept the consequences of.

ABJURE - To renounce; give up.

ABRIDGE - To reduce; contract; diminish.

ABROGATE - To annul, repeal, or destroy.

ABSCOND - To hide or absent oneself to avoid legal action.

ABSTRACT - A summary.

ABUT - To border on, to touch.

ACCESS - Approach; in real property law it means the right of the owner of property to the use of the highway or road next to his land, without obstruction by intervening property owners.

ACCESSORY - In criminal law, it means the person who contributes or aids in the commission of a crime.

ACCOMMODATED PARTY - One to whom credit is extended on the strength of another person signing a commercial paper.

ACCOMMODATION PAPER - A commercial paper to which the accommodating party has put his name.

ACCOMPLICE - In criminal law, it means a person who together with the principal offender commits a crime.

ACCORD - An agreement to accept something different or less than that to which one is entitled, which extinguishes the entire obligation.

ACCOUNT - A statement of mutual demands in the nature of debt and credit between parties.

ACCRETION - The act of adding to a thing; in real property law, it means gradual accumulation of land by natural causes.

ACCRUE - To grow to; to be added to.

ACKNOWLEDGMENT - The act of going before an official authorized to take acknowledgments, and acknowledging an act as one's own.

ACQUIESCENCE - A silent appearance of consent.

ACQUIT - To legally determine the innocence of one charged with a crime.

AD INFINITUM - Indefinitely.

AD LITEM - For the suit.

AD VALOREM - According to value.

ADJECTIVE LAW - Rules of procedure.

ADJUDICATION - The judgment given in a case.

ADMIRALTY - Court having jurisdiction over maritime cases.

ADULT - Sixteen years old or over (in criminal law).

ADVANCE - In commercial law, it means to pay money or render other value before it is due.

ADVERSE - Opposed; contrary.

ADVOCATE - (v.) To speak in favor of;
        (n.) One who assists, defends, or pleads for another.

AFFIANT - A person who makes and signs an affidavit.

AFFIDAVIT - A written and sworn to declaration of facts, voluntarily made.

AFFINITY- The relationship between persons through marriage with the kindred of each other; distinguished from consanguinity, which is the relationship by blood.

AFFIRM - To ratify; also when an appellate court affirms a judgment, decree, or order, it means that it is valid and right and must stand as rendered in the lower court.

AFOREMENTIONED; AFORESAID - Before or already said.

AGENT - One who represents and acts for another.

AID AND COMFORT - To help; encourage.

ALIAS - A name not one's true name.

ALIBI - A claim of not being present at a certain place at a certain time.

ALLEGE - To assert.

ALLOTMENT - A share or portion.

AMBIGUITY - Uncertainty; capable of being understood in more than one way.

AMENDMENT - Any language made or proposed as a change in some principal writing.

AMICUS CURIAE - A friend of the court; one who has an interest in a case, although not a party in the case, who volunteers advice upon matters of law to the judge. For example, a brief amicus curiae.

AMORTIZATION - To provide for a gradual extinction of (a future obligation) in advance of maturity, especially, by periodical contributions to a sinking fund which will be adequate to discharge a debt or make a replacement when it becomes necessary.

ANCILLARY - Aiding, auxiliary.

ANNOTATION - A note added by way of comment or explanation.

ANSWER - A written statement made by a defendant setting forth the grounds of his defense.

ANTE - Before.

ANTE MORTEM - Before death.

APPEAL - The removal of a case from a lower court to one of superior jurisdiction for the purpose of obtaining a review.

APPEARANCE - Coming into court as a party to a suit.

APPELLANT - The party who takes an appeal from one court or jurisdiction to another (appellate) court for review.

APPELLEE - The party against whom an appeal is taken.

APPROPRIATE - To make a thing one's own.

APPROPRIATION - Prescribing the destination of a thing; the act of the legislature designating a particular fund, to be applied to some object of government expenditure.

APPURTENANT - Belonging to; accessory or incident to.

ARBITER - One who decides a dispute; a referee.

ARBITRARY - Unreasoned; not governed by any fixed rules or standard.

ARGUENDO - By way of argument.

ARRAIGN - To call the prisoner before the court to answer to a charge.

ASSENT - A declaration of willingness to do something in compliance with a request.

ASSERT - Declare.

ASSESS - To fix the rate or amount.

ASSIGN - To transfer; to appoint; to select for a particular purpose.

ASSIGNEE - One who receives an assignment.

ASSIGNOR - One who makes an assignment.

AT BAR - Before the court.
AT ISSUE - When parties in an action come to a point where one asserts something and the other denies it.
ATTACH - Seize property by court order and sometimes arrest a person.
ATTEST - To witness a will, etc.; act of attestation.
AVERMENT - A positive statement of facts.

B

BAIL - To obtain the release of a person from legal custody by giving security and promising that he shall appear in court; to deliver (goods, etc.) in trust to a person for a special purpose.
BAILEE - One to whom personal property is delivered under a contract of bailment.
BAILMENT - Delivery of personal property to another to be held for a certain purpose and to be returned when the purpose is accomplished.
BAILOR - The party who delivers goods to another, under a contract of bailment.
BANC (OR BANK) - Bench; the place where a court sits permanently or regularly; also the assembly of all the judges of a court.
BANKRUPT - An insolvent person, technically, one declared to be bankrupt after a bankruptcy proceeding.
BAR - The legal profession.
BARRATRY - Exciting groundless judicial proceedings.
BARTER - A contract by which parties exchange goods for other goods.
BATTERY - Illegal interfering with another's person.
BEARER - In commercial law, it means the person in possession of a commercial paper which is payable to the bearer.
BENCH - The court itself or the judge.
BENEFICIARY - A person benefiting under a will, trust, or agreement.
BEST EVIDENCE RULE, THE - Except as otherwise provided by statute, no evidence other than the writing itself is admissible to prove the content of a writing. This section shall be known and may be cited as the best evidence rule.
BEQUEST - A gift of personal property under a will.
BILL - A formal written statement of complaint to a court of justice; also, a draft of an act of the legislature before it becomes a law; also, accounts for goods sold, services rendered, or work done.
BONA FIDE - In or with good faith; honestly.
BOND - An instrument by which the maker promises to pay a sum of money to another, usually providing that upon performances of a certain condition the obligation shall be void.
BOYCOTT - A plan to prevent the carrying on of a business by wrongful means.
BREACH - The breaking or violating of a law, or the failure to carry out a duty.
BRIEF - A written document, prepared by a lawyer to serve as the basis of an argument upon a case in court, usually an appellate court.
BURDEN OF PRODUCING EVIDENCE - The obligation of a party to introduce evidence sufficient to avoid a ruling against him on the issue.
BURDEN OF PROOF - The obligation of a party to establish by evidence a requisite degree of belief concerning a fact in the mind of the trier of fact or the court. The burden of proof may require a party to raise a reasonable doubt concerning the existence of nonexistence of a fact or that he establish the existence or nonexistence of a fact by a preponderance of the evidence, by clear and convincing proof, or by proof beyond a reasonable doubt.
   Except as otherwise provided by law, the burden of proof requires proof by a preponderance of the evidence.

3

BUSINESS, A - Shall include every kind of business, profession, occupation, calling or operation of institutions, whether carried on for profit or not.

BY-LAWS - Regulations, ordinances, or rules enacted by a corporation, association, etc., for its own government.

C

CANON - A doctrine; also, a law or rule, of a church or association in particular.

CAPIAS - An order to arrest.

CAPTION - In a pleading, deposition or other paper connected with a case in court, it is the heading or introductory clause which shows the names of the parties, name of the court, number of the case on the docket or calendar, etc.

CARRIER - A person or corporation undertaking to transport persons or property.

CASE - A general term for an action, cause, suit, or controversy before a judicial body.

CAUSE - A suit, litigation or action before a court.

CAVEAT EMPTOR - Let the buyer beware. This term expresses the rule that the purchaser of an article must examine, judge, and test it for himself, being bound to discover any obvious defects or imperfections.

CERTIFICATE - A written representation that some legal formality has been complied with.

CERTIORARI - To be informed of; the name of a writ issued by a superior court directing the lower court to send up to the former the record and proceedings of a case.

CHANGE OF VENUE - To remove place of trial from one place to another.

CHARGE - An obligation or duty; a formal complaint; an instruction of the court to the jury upon a case.

CHARTER - (n.) The authority by virtue of which an organized body acts;
        (v.) in mercantile law, it means to hire or lease a vehicle or vessel for transportation.

CHATTEL - An article of personal property.

CHATTEL MORTGAGE - A mortgage on personal property.

CIRCUIT - A division of the country, for the administration of justice; a geographical area served by a court.

CITATION - The act of the court by which a person is summoned or cited; also, a reference to legal authority.

CIVIL (ACTIONS)- It indicates the private rights and remedies of individuals in contrast to the word "criminal" (actions) which relates to prosecution for violation of laws.

CLAIM (n.) - Any demand held or asserted as of right.

CODICIL - An addition to a will.

CODIFY - To arrange the laws of a country into a code.

COGNIZANCE - Notice or knowledge.

COLLATERAL - By the side; accompanying; an article or thing given to secure performance of a promise.

COMITY - Courtesy; the practice by which one court follows the decision of another court on the same question.

COMMIT - To perform, as an act; to perpetrate, as a crime; to send a person to prison.

COMMON LAW - As distinguished from law created by the enactment of the legislature (called statutory law), it relates to those principles and rules of action which derive their authority solely from usages and customs of immemorial antiquity, particularly with reference to the ancient unwritten law of England. The written pronouncements of the common law are found in court decisions.

COMMUTE - Change punishment to one less severe.

COMPLAINANT - One who applies to the court for legal redress.

COMPLAINT - The pleading of a plaintiff in a civil action; or a charge that a person has committed a specified offense.

COMPROMISE - An arrangement for settling a dispute by agreement.

CONCUR - To agree, consent.

CONCURRENT - Running together, at the same time.

CONDEMNATION - Taking private property for public use on payment therefor.

CONDITION - Mode or state of being; a qualification or restriction.

CONDUCT - Active and passive behavior; both verbal and nonverbal.

CONFESSION - Voluntary statement of guilt of crime.

CONFIDENTIAL COMMUNICATION BETWEEN CLIENT AND LAWYER - Information transmitted between a client and his lawyer in the course of that relationship and in confidence by a means which, so far as the client is aware, discloses the information to no third persons other than those who are present to further the interest of the client in the consultation or those to whom disclosure is reasonably necessary for the transmission of the information or the accomplishment of the purpose for which the lawyer is consulted, and includes a legal opinion formed and the advice given by the lawyer in the course of that relationship.

CONFRONTATION - Witness testifying in presence of defendant.

CONSANGUINITY - Blood relationship.

CONSIGN - To give in charge; commit; entrust; to send or transmit goods to a merchant, factor, or agent for sale.

CONSIGNEE - One to whom a consignment is made.

CONSIGNOR - One who sends or makes a consignment.

CONSPIRACY - In criminal law, it means an agreement between two or more persons to commit an unlawful act.

CONSPIRATORS - Persons involved in a conspiracy.

CONSTITUTION - The fundamental law of a nation or state.

CONSTRUCTION OF GENDERS - The masculine gender includes the feminine and neuter.

CONSTRUCTION OF SINGULAR AND PLURAL - The singular number includes the plural; and the plural, the singular.

CONSTRUCTION OF TENSES - The present tense includes the past and future tenses; and the future, the present.

CONSTRUCTIVE - An act or condition assumed from other parts or conditions.

CONSTRUE - To ascertain the meaning of language.

CONSUMMATE - To complete.

CONTIGUOUS - Adjoining; touching; bounded by.

CONTINGENT - Possible, but not assured; dependent upon some condition.

CONTINUANCE - The adjournment or postponement of an action pending in a court.

CONTRA - Against, opposed to; contrary.

CONTRACT - An agreement between two or more persons to do or not to do a particular thing.

CONTROVERT - To dispute, deny.

CONVERSION - Dealing with the personal property of another as if it were one's own, without right.

CONVEYANCE - An instrument transferring title to land.

CONVICTION - Generally, the result of a criminal trial which ends in a judgment or sentence that the defendant is guilty as charged.

COOPERATIVE - A cooperative is a voluntary organization of persons with a common interest, formed and operated along democratic lines for the purpose of supplying services at cost to its members and other patrons, who contribute both capital and business.

CORPUS DELICTI - The body of a crime; the crime itself.

CORROBORATE - To strengthen; to add weight by additional evidence.

COUNTERCLAIM - A claim presented by a defendant in opposition to or deduction from the claim of the plaintiff.

COUNTY - Political subdivision of a state.

COVENANT - Agreement.

CREDIBLE - Worthy of belief.

CREDITOR - A person to whom a debt is owing by another person, called the "debtor."

CRIMINAL ACTION - Includes criminal proceedings.

CRIMINAL INFORMATION - Same as complaint.

CRITERION (sing.)

CRITERIA (plural) - A means or tests for judging; a standard or standards.

CROSS-EXAMINATION - Examination of a witness by a party other than the direct examiner upon a matter that is within the scope of the direct examination of the witness.

CULPABLE - Blamable.

CY-PRES - As near as (possible). The rule of *cy-pres* is a rule for the construction of instruments in equity by which the intention of the party is carried out *as near as may be, when it* would be impossible or illegal to give it literal effect.

D

DAMAGES - A monetary compensation, which may be recovered in the courts by any person who has suffered loss, or injury, whether to his person, property or rights through the unlawful act or omission or negligence of another.

DECLARANT - A person who makes a statement.

DE FACTO - In fact; actually but without legal authority.

DE JURE - Of right; legitimate; lawful.

DE MINIMIS - Very small or trifling.

DE NOVO - Anew; afresh; a second time.

DEBT - A specified sum of money owing to one person from another, including not only the obligation of the debtor to pay, but the right of the creditor to receive and enforce payment.

DECEDENT - A dead person.

DECISION - A judgment or decree pronounced by a court in determination of a case.

DECREE - An order of the court, determining the rights of all parties to a suit.

DEED - A writing containing a contract sealed and delivered; particularly to convey real property.

DEFALCATION - Misappropriation of funds.

DEFAMATION - Injuring one's reputation by false statements.

DEFAULT - The failure to fulfill a duty, observe a promise, discharge an obligation, or perform an agreement.

DEFENDANT - The person defending or denying; the party against whom relief or recovery is sought in an action or suit.

DEFRAUD - To practice fraud; to cheat or trick.

DELEGATE (v.)- To entrust to the care or management of another.

DELICTUS - A crime.

DEMUR (v.) - To dispute the sufficiency in law of the pleading of the other side.

DEMURRAGE - In maritime law, it means, the sum fixed or allowed as remuneration to the owners of a ship for the detention of their vessel beyond the number of days allowed for loading and unloading or for sailing; also used in railroad terminology.

DENIAL - A form of pleading; refusing to admit the truth of a statement, charge, etc.

DEPONENT - One who gives testimony under oath reduced to writing.

DEPOSITION - Testimony given under oath outside of court for use in court or for the purpose of obtaining information in preparation for trial of a case.

DETERIORATION - A degeneration such as from decay, corrosion or disintegration.

DETRIMENT - Any loss or harm to person or property.

DEVIATION - A turning aside.

DEVISE - A gift of real property by the last will and testament of the donor.

DICTUM (sing.)

DICTA (plural) - Any statements made by the court in an opinion concerning some rule of law not necessarily involved nor essential to the determination of the case.

DIRECT EVIDENCE - Evidence that directly proves a fact, without an inference or presumption, and which in itself if true, conclusively establishes that fact.

DIRECT EXAMINATION - The first examination of a witness upon a matter that is not within the scope of a previous examination of the witness.

DISAFFIRM - To repudicate.

DISMISS - In an action or suit, it means to dispose of the case without any further consideration or hearing.

DISSENT - To denote disagreement of one or more judges of a court with the decision passed by the majority upon a case before them.

DOCKET (n.) - A formal record, entered in brief, of the proceedings in a court.

DOCTRINE - A rule, principle, theory of law.

DOMICILE - That place where a man has his true, fixed and permanent home to which whenever he is absent he has the intention of returning.

DRAFT (n.) - A commercial paper ordering payment of money drawn by one person on another.

DRAWEE - The person who is requested to pay the money.

DRAWER - The person who draws the commercial paper and addresses it to the drawee.

DUPLICATE - A counterpart produced by the same impression as the original enlargements and miniatures, or by mechanical or electronic re-recording, or by chemical reproduction, or by other equivalent technique which accurately reproduces the original.

DURESS - Use of force to compel performance or non-performance of an act.

E

EASEMENT - A liberty, privilege, or advantage without profit, in the lands of another.

EGRESS - Act or right of going out or leaving; emergence.

EIUSDEM GENERIS - Of the same kind, class or nature. A rule used in the construction of language in a legal document.

EMBEZZLEMENT - To steal; to appropriate fraudulently to one's own use property entrusted to one's care.

EMBRACERY - Unlawful attempt to influence jurors, etc., but not by offering value.

EMINENT DOMAIN - The right of a state to take private property for public use.

ENACT - To make into a law.

ENDORSEMENT - Act of writing one's name on the back of a note, bill or similar written instrument.

ENJOIN - To require a person, by writ of injunction from a court of equity, to perform or to abstain or desist from some act.

ENTIRETY - The whole; that which the law considers as one whole, and not capable of being divided into parts.

ENTRAPMENT - Inducing one to commit a crime so as to arrest him.

ENUMERATED - Mentioned specifically; designated.

ENURE - To operate or take effect.

EQUITY - In its broadest sense, this term denotes the spirit and the habit of fairness, justness, and right dealing which regulate the conduct of men.

ERROR - A mistake of law, or the false or irregular application of law as will nullify the judicial proceedings.

ESCROW - A deed, bond or other written engagement, delivered to a third person, to be delivered by him only upon the performance or fulfillment of some condition.

ESTATE - The interest which any one has in lands, or in any other subject of property.

ESTOP - To stop, bar, or impede.

ESTOPPEL - A rule of law which prevents a man from alleging or denying a fact, because of his own previous act.

ET AL. (alii) - And others.

ET SEQ. (sequential) - And the following.

ET UX. (uxor) - And wife.

EVIDENCE - Testimony, writings, material objects, or other things presented to the senses that are offered to prove the existence or non-existence of a fact.

Means from which inferences may be drawn as a basis of proof in duly constituted judicial or fact finding tribunals, and includes testimony in the form of opinion and hearsay.

EX CONTRACTU

EX DELICTO - In law, rights and causes of action are divided into two classes, those arising *ex contractu* (from a contract) and those arising *ex delicto* (from a delict or tort).

EX OFFICIO - From office; by virtue of the office.

EX PARTE - On one side only; by or for one.

EX POST FACTO - After the fact.

EX POST FACTO LAW - A law passed after an act was done which retroactively makes such act a crime.

EX REL. (relations) - Upon relation or information.

EXCEPTION - An objection upon a matter of law to a decision made, either before or after judgment by a court.

EXECUTOR (male)

EXECUTRIX (female) - A person who has been appointed by will to execute the will.

EXECUTORY - That which is yet to be executed or performed.

EXEMPT - To release from some liability to which others are subject.

EXONERATION - The removal of a burden, charge or duty.
EXTRADITION - Surrender of a fugitive from one nation to another.

F

F.A.S.-"Free alongside ship";delivery at dock for ship named.
F.O.B.-"Free on board";seller will deliver to car, truck, vessel, or other conveyance by which goods are to be transported, without expense or risk of loss to the buyer or consignee.
FABRICATE - To construct; to invent a false story.
FACSIMILE - An exact or accurate copy of an original instrument.
FACTOR - A commercial agent.
FEASANCE - The doing of an act.
FELONIOUS - Criminal, malicious.
FELONY - Generally, a criminal offense that may be punished by death or imprisonment for more than one year as differentiated from a misdemeanor.
FEME SOLE - A single woman.
FIDUCIARY - A person who is invested with rights and powers to be exercised for the benefit of another person.
FIERI FACIAS - A writ of execution commanding the sheriff to levy and collect the amount of a judgment from the goods and chattels of the judgment debtor.
FINDING OF FACT - Determination from proof or judicial notice of the existence of a fact. A ruling implies a supporting finding of fact; no separate or formal finding is required unless required by a statute of this state.
FISCAL - Relating to accounts or the management of revenue.
FORECLOSURE (sale) - A sale of mortgaged property to obtain satisfaction of the mortgage out of the sale proceeds.
FORFEITURE - A penalty, a fine.
FORGERY - Fabricating or producing falsely, counterfeited.
FORTUITOUS - Accidental.
FORUM - A court of justice; a place of jurisdiction.
FRAUD - Deception; trickery.
FREEHOLDER - One who owns real property.
FUNGIBLE - Of such kind or nature that one specimen or part may be used in the place of another.

G

GARNISHEE - Person garnished.
GARNISHMENT - A legal process to reach the money or effects of a defendant, in the possession or control of a third person.
GRAND JURY - Not less than 16,not more than 23 citizens of a county sworn to inquire into crimes committed or triable in the county.
GRANT - To agree to; convey, especially real property.
GRANTEE - The person to whom a grant is made.
GRANTOR - The person by whom a grant is made.
GRATUITOUS - Given without a return, compensation or consideration.
GRAVAMEN - The grievance complained of or the substantial cause of a criminal action.
GUARANTY (n.) - A promise to answer for the payment of some debt, or the performance of some duty, in case of the failure of another person, who, in the first instance, is liable for such payment or performance.
GUARDIAN - The person, committee, or other representative authorized by law to protect the person or estate or both of an incompetent (or of a sui juris person having a guardian) and to act for him in matters affecting his person or property or both. An incompetent is a person under disability imposed by law.

GUILTY - Establishment of the fact that one has committed a breach of conduct; especially, a violation of law.

H

HABEAS CORPUS - You have the body; the name given to a variety of writs, having for their object to bring a party before a court or judge for decision as to whether such person is being lawfully held prisoner.
HABENDUM - In conveyancing; it is the clause in a deed conveying land which defines the extent of ownership to be held by the grantee.
HEARING - A proceeding whereby the arguments of the interested parties are heared.
HEARSAY - A type of testimony given by a witness who relates, not what he knows personally, but what others have told hi , or what he has heard said by others.
HEARSAY RULE, THE - (a) "Hearsay evidence" is evidence of a statement that was made other than by a witness while testifying at the hearing and that is offered to prove the truth of the matter stated; (b) Except as provided by law, hearsay evidence is inadmissible; (c) This section shall be known and may be cited as the hearsay rule.
HEIR - Generally, one who inherits property, real or personal.
HOLDER OF THE PRIVILEGE - (a) The client when he has no guardian or conservator; (b) A guardian or conservator of the client when the client has a guardian or conservator; (c) The personal representative of the client if the client is dead; (d) A successor, assign, trustee in dissolution, or any similar representative of a firm, association, organization, partnership, business trust, corporation, or public entity that is no longer in existence.
HUNG JURY - One so divided that they can't agree on a verdict.
HUSBAND-WIFE PRIVILEGE - An accused in a criminal proceeding has a privilege to prevent his spouse from testifying against him.
HYPOTHECATE - To pledge a thing without delivering it to the pledgee.
HYPOTHESIS - A supposition, assumption, or toehry.

I

I.E. (id est) - That is.
IB., OR IBID.(ibidem) - In the same place; used to refer to a legal reference previously cited to avoid repeating the entire citation.
ILLICIT - Prohibited; unlawful.
ILLUSORY - Deceiving by false appearance.
IMMUNITY - Exemption.
IMPEACH - To accuse, to dispute.
IMPEDIMENTS - Disabilities, or hindrances.
IMPLEAD - To sue or prosecute by due course of law.
IMPUTED - Attributed or charged to.
IN LOCO PARENTIS - In place of parent, a guardian.
IN TOTO - In the whole; completely.
INCHOATE - Imperfect; unfinished.
INCOMMUNICADO - Denial of the right of a prisoner to communicate with friends or relatives.
INCOMPETENT - One who is incapable of caring for his own affairs because he is mentally deficient or undeveloped.
INCRIMINATION - A matter will incriminate a person if it constitutes, or forms an essential part of, or, taken in connection with other matters disclosed, is a basis for a reasonable inference of such a violation of the laws of this State as to subject him to liability to punishment therefor, unless he has become for any reason permanently immune from punishment for such violation.

10

INCUMBRANCE - Generally a claim, lien, charge or liability attached to and binding real property.

INDEMNIFY - To secure against loss or damage; also, to make reimbursement to one for a loss already incurred by him.

INDEMNITY - An agreement to reimburse another person in case of an anticipated loss falling upon him.

INDICIA - Signs; indications.

INDICTMENT - An accusation in writing found and presented by a grand jury charging that a person has committed a crime.

INDORSE - To write a name on the back of a legal paper or document, generally, a negotiable instrument

INDUCEMENT - Cause or reason why a thing is done or that which incites the person to do the act or commit a crime; the motive for the criminal act.

INFANT - In civil cases one under 21 years of age.

INFORMATION - A formal accusation of crime made by a prosecuting attorney.

INFRA - Below, under; this word occurring by itself in a publication refers the reader to a future part of the publication.

INGRESS - The act of going into.

INJUNCTION - A writ or order by the court requiring a person, generally, to do or to refrain from doing an act.

INSOLVENT - The condition of a person who is unable to pay his debts.

INSTRUCTION - A direction given by the judge to the jury concerning the law of the case.

INTERIM - In the meantime; time intervening.

INTERLOCUTORY - Temporary, not final; something intervening between the commencement and the end of a suit which decides some point or matter, but is not a final decision of the whole controversy.

INTERROGATORIES - A series of formal written questions used in the examination of a party or a witness usually prior to a trial.

INTESTATE - A person who dies without a will.

INURE - To result, to take effect.

IPSO FACTO - By the fact iself; by the mere fact.

ISSUE (n.) The disputed point or question in a case,

J

JEOPARDY - Danger, hazard, peril.

JOINDER - Joining; uniting with another person in some legal steps or proceeding.

JOINT - United; combined.

JUDGE - Member or members or representative or representatives of a court conducting a trial or hearing at which evidence is introduced.

JUDGMENT - The official decision of a court of justice.

JUDICIAL OR JUDICIARY - Relating to or connected with the administration of justice.

JURAT - The clause written at the foot of an affidavit, stating when, where and before whom such affidavit was sworn.

JURISDICTION - The authority to hear and determine controversies between parties.

JURISPRUDENCE - The philosophy of law.

JURY - A body of persons legally selected to inquire into any matter of fact, and to render their verdict according to the evidence.

L

LACHES - The failure to diligently assert a right, which results in a refusal to allow relief.

LANDLORD AND TENANT - A phrase used to denote the legal relation existing between the owner and occupant of real estate.

LARCENY - Stealing personal property belonging to another.

LATENT - Hidden; that which does not appear on the face of a thing.

LAW - Includes constitutional, statutory, and decisional law.

LAWYER-CLIENT PRIVILEGE - (1) A "client" is a person, public officer, or corporation, association, or other organization or entity, either public or private, who is rendered professional legal services by a lawyer, or who consults a lawyer with a view to obtaining professional legal services from him; (2) A "lawyer" is a person authorized, or reasonably believed by the client to be authorized, to practice law in any state or nation; (3) A "representative of the lawyer" is one employed to assist the lawyer in the rendition of professional legal services; (4) A communication is "confidential" if not intended to be disclosed to third persons other than those to whom disclosure is in furtherance of the rendition of professional legal services to the client or those reasonably necessary for the transmission of the communication.

General rule of privilege- A client has a privilege to refuse to disclose and to prevent any other person from disclosing confidential communications made for the purpose of facilitating the rendition of professional legal services to the client, (1) between himself or his representative and his lawyer or his lawyer's representative, or (2) between his lawyer and the lawyer's representative, or (3) by him or his lawyer to a lawyer representing another in a matter of common interest, or (4) between representatives of the client or between the client and a representative of the client, or (5) between lawyers representing the client.

LEADING QUESTION - Question that suggests to the witness the answer that the examining party desires.

LEASE - A contract by which one conveys real estate for a limited time usually for a specified rent; personal property also may be leased.

LEGISLATION - The act of enacting laws.

LEGITIMATE - Lawful.

LESSEE - One to whom a lease is given.

LESSOR - One who grants a lease

LEVY - A collecting or exacting by authority.

LIABLE - Responsible; bound or obligated in law or equity.

LIBEL (v.) - To defame or injure a person's reputation by a published writing.

　　　(n.) - The initial pleading on the part of the plaintiff in an admiralty proceeding.

LIEN - A hold or claim which one person has upon the property of another as a security for some debt or charge.

LIQUIDATED - Fixed; settled.

LIS PENDENS - A pending civil or criminal action.

LITERAL - According to the language.

LITIGANT - A party to a lawsuit.

LITATION - A judicial controversy.

LOCUS - A place.

LOCUS DELICTI - Place of the crime.

LOCUS POENITENTIAE - The abandoning or giving up of one's intention to commit some crime before it is fully completed or abandoning a conspiracy before its purpose is accomplished.

MALFEASANCE - To do a wrongful act.

MALICE - The doing of a wrongful act intentionally without just cause or excuse.

MANDAMUS - The name of a writ issued by a court to enforce the performance of some public duty.

MANDATORY (adj.) Containing a command.

MARITIME - Pertaining to the sea or to commerce thereon.

MARSHALING - Arranging or disposing of in order.

MAXIM - An established principle or proposition.

MINISTERIAL - That which involves obedience to instruction, but demands no special discretion, judgment or skill.

MISAPPROPRIATE - Dealing fraudulently with property entrusted to one.

MISDEMEANOR - A crime less than a felony and punishable by a fine or imprisonment for less than one year.

MISFEASANCE - Improper performance of a lawful act.

MISREPRESENTATION - An untrue representation of facts.

MITIGATE - To make or become less severe, harsh.

MITTIMUS - A warrant of commitment to prison.

MOOT (adj.) Unsettled, undecided, not necessary to be decided.

MORTGAGE - A conveyance of property upon condition, as security for the payment of a debt or the performance of a duty, and to become void upon payment or performance according to the stipulated terms.

MORTGAGEE - A person to whom property is mortgaged.

MORTGAGOR - One who gives a mortgage.

MOTION - In legal proceedings, a "motion" is an application, either written or oral, addressed to the court by a party to an action or a suit requesting the ruling of the court on a matter of law.

MUTUALITY - Reciprocation.

NEGLIGENCE - The failure to exercise that degree of care which an ordinarily prudent person would exercise under like circumstances.

NEGOTIABLE (instrument) - Any instrument obligating the payment of money which is transferable from one person to another by endorsement and delivery or by delivery only.

NEGOTIATE - To transact business; to transfer a negotiable instrument; to seek agreement for the amicable disposition of a controversy or case.

NOLLE PROSEQUI - A formal entry upon the record, by the plaintiff in a civil suit or the prosecuting officer in a criminal action, by which he declares that he "will no further prosecute" the case.

NOLO CONTENDERE - The name of a plea in a criminal action, having the same effect as a plea of guilty; but not constituting a direct admission of guilt.

NOMINAL - Not real or substantial.

NOMINAL DAMAGES - Award of a trifling sum where no substantial injury is proved to have been sustained.

NONFEASANCE - Neglect of duty.

NOVATION - The substitution of a new debt or obligation for an existing one.

NUNC PRO TUNC - A phrase applied to acts allowed to be done after the time when they should be done, with a retroactive effect.("Now for then.")

OATH - Oath includes affirmation or declaration under penalty of perjury.

OBITER DICTUM - Opinion expressed by a court on a matter not essentially involved in a case and hence not a decision; also called dicta, if plural.

OBJECT (v.) - To oppose as improper or illegal and referring the question of its propriety or legality to the court.

OBLIGATION - A legal duty, by which a person is bound to do or not to do a certain thing.

OBLIGEE - The person to whom an obligation is owed.

OBLIGOR - The person who is to perform the obligation.

OFFER (v.) - To present for acceptance or rejection.

(n.) - A proposal to do a thing, usually a proposal to make a contract.

OFFICIAL INFORMATION - Information within the custody or control of a department or agency of the government the disclosure of which is shown to be contrary to the public interest.

OFFSET - A deduction.

ONUS PROBANDI - Burden of proof.

OPINION - The statement by a judge of the decision reached in a case, giving the law as applied to the case and giving reasons for the judgment; also a belief or view.

OPTION - The exercise of the power of choice; also a privilege existing in one person, for which he has paid money, which gives him the right to buy or sell real or personal property at a given price within a specified time.

ORDER - A rule or regulation; every direction of a court or judge made or entered in writing but not including a judgment.

ORDINANCE - Generally, a rule established by authority; also commonly used to designate the legislative acts of a municipal corporation.

ORIGINAL - Writing or recording itself or any counterpart intended to have the same effect by a person executing or issuing it. An "original" of a photograph includes the negative or any print therefrom. If data are stored in a computer or similar device, any printout or other output readable by sight, shown to reflect the data accurately, is an "original."

OVERT - Open, manifest.

P

PANEL - A group of jurors selected to serve during a term of the court.

PARENS PATRIAE - Sovereign power of a state to protect or be a guardian over children and incompetents.

PAROL - Oral or verbal.

PAROLE - To release one in prison before the expiration of his sentence, conditionally.

PARITY - Equality in purchasing power between the farmer and other segments of the economy.

PARTITION - A legal division of real or personal property between one or more owners.

PARTNERSHIP - An association of two or more persons to carry on as co-owners a business for profit.

PATENT (adj.) - Evident.

(n.) - A grant of some privilege, property, or authority, made by the government or sovereign of a country to one or more individuals.

PECULATION - Stealing.

PECUNIARY - Monetary.

PENULTIMATE - Next to the last.

PER CURIAM - A phrase used in the report of a decision to distinguish an opinion of the whole court from an opinion written by any one judge.

PER SE - In itself; taken alone.

PERCEIVE - To acquire knowledge through one's senses.

PEREMPTORY - Imperative; absolute.

PERJURY - To lie or state falsely under oath.

PERPETUITY - Perpetual existence; also the quality or condition of an estate limited so that it will not take effect or vest within the period fixed by law.

PERSON - Includes a natural person, firm, association, organization, partnership, business trust, corporation, or public entity.

PERSONAL PROPERTY - Includes money, goods, chattels, things in action, and evidences of debt.

PERSONALTY - Short term for personal property.

PETITION - An application in writing for an order of the court, stating the circumstances upon which it is founded and requesting any order or other relief from a court.

PLAINTIFF - A person who brings a court action.

PLEA - A pleading in a suit or action.

PLEADINGS - Formal allegations made by the parties of their respective claims and defenses, for the judgment of the court.

PLEDGE - A deposit of personal property as a security for the performance of an act.

PLEDGEE - The party to whom goods are delivered in pledge.

PLEDGOR - The party delivering goods in pledge.

PLENARY - Full; complete.

POLICE POWER - Inherent power of the state or its political subdivisions to enact laws within constitutional limits to promote the general welfare of society or the community.

POLLING THE JURY - Call the names of persons on a jury and requiring each juror to declare what his verdict is before it is legally recorded.

POST MORTEM - After death.

POWER OF ATTORNEY - A writing authorizing one to act for another.

PRECEPT - An order, warrant, or writ issued to an officer or body of officers, commanding him or them to do some act within the scope of his or their powers.

PRELIMINARY FACT - Fact upon the existence or nonexistence of which depends the admissibility or inadmissibility of evidence. The phrase "the admissibility or inadmissibility of evidence" includes the qualification or disqualification of a person to be a witness and the existence or nonexistence of a privilege.

PREPONDERANCE - Outweighing.

PRESENTMENT - A report by a grand jury on something they have investigated on their own knowledge.

PRESUMPTION - An assumption of fact resulting from a rule of law which requires such fact to be assumed from another fact or group of facts found or otherwise established in the action.

PRIMA FACUE - At first sight.

PRIMA FACIE CASE - A case where the evidence is very patent against the defendant.

PRINCIPAL - The source of authority or rights; a person primarily liable as differentiated from "principle" as a primary or basic doctrine.

PRO AND CON - For and against.

PRO RATA - Proportionally.

PROBATE - Relating to proof, especially to the proof of wills.

PROBATIVE - Tending to prove.

PROCEDURE - In law, this term generally denotes rules which are established by the Federal, State, or local Governments regarding the types of pleading and courtroom practice which must be followed by the parties involved in a criminal or civil case.

PROCLAMATION - A public notice by an official of some order, intended action, or state of facts.

PROFFERED EVIDENCE - The admissibility or inadmissibility of which is dependent upon the existence or nonexistence of a preliminary fact.

PROMISSORY (NOTE) - A promise in writing to pay a specified sum at an expressed time, or on demand, or at sight, to a named person, or to his order, or bearer.

PROOF - The establishment by evidence of a requisite degree of belief concerning a fact in the mind of the trier of fact or the court.

PROPERTY - Includes both real and personal property.

PROPRIETARY (adj.) - Relating or pertaining to ownership; usually a single owner.

PROSECUTE - To carry on an action or other judicial proceeding; to proceed against a person criminally.

PROVISO - A limitation or condition in a legal instrument.

PROXIMATE - Immediate; nearest

PUBLIC EMPLOYEE - An officer, agent, or employee of a public entity.

PUBLIC ENTITY - Includes a national, state, county, city and county, city, district, public authority, public agency, or any other political subdivision or public corporation, whether foreign or domestic.

PUBLIC OFFICIAL - Includes an official of a political dubdivision of such state or territory and of a municipality.

PUNITIVE - Relating to punishment.

Q

QUASH - To make void.

QUASI - As if; as it were.

QUID PRO QUO - Something for something; the giving of one valuable thing for another.

QUITCLAIM (v.) - To release or relinquish claim or title to, especially in deeds to realty.

QUO WARRANTO - A legal procedure to test an official's right to a public office or the right to hold a franchise, or to hold an office in a domestic corporation.

R

RATIFY - To approve and sanction.

REAL PROPERTY - Includes lands, tenements, and hereditaments.

REALTY - A brief term for real property.

REBUT - To contradict; to refute, especially by evidence and arguments.

RECEIVER - A person who is appointed by the court to receive, and hold in trust property in litigation.

RECIDIVIST - Habitual criminal.

RECIPROCAL - Mutual.

RECOUPMENT - To keep back or get something which is due; also, it is the right of a defendant to have a deduction from the amount of the plaintiff's damages because the plaintiff has not fulfilled his part of the same contract.

RECROSS EXAMINATION - Examination of a witness by a cross-examiner subsequent to a redirect examination of the witness.

REDEEM - To release an estate or article from mortgage or pledge by paying the debt for which it stood as security.

REDIRECT EXAMINATION - Examination of a witness by the direct examiner subsequent to the cross-examination of the witness.

REFEREE - A person to whom a cause pending in a court is referred by the court, to take testimony, hear the parties, and report thereon to the court.

REFERENDUM - A method of submitting an important legislative or administrative matter to a direct vote of the people.

RELEVANT EVIDENCE - Evidence including evidence relevant to the credulity of a witness or hearsay declarant, having any tendency in reason to prove or disprove any disputed fact that is of consequence to the determination of the action.

REMAND - To send a case back to the lower court from which it came, for further proceedings.

REPLEVIN - An action to recover goods or chattels wrongfully taken or detained.

REPLY (REPLICATION) - Generally, a reply is what the plaintiff or other person who has instituted proceedings says in answer to the defendant's case.

RE JUDICATA - A thing judicially acted upon or decided.

RES ADJUDICATA - Doctrine that an issue or dispute litigated and determined in a case between the opposing parties is deemed permanently decided between these parties.

RESCIND (RECISSION) - To avoid or cancel a contract.

RESPONDENT - A defendant in a proceeding in chancery or admiralty; also, the person who contends against the appeal in a case.

RESTITUTION - In equity, it is the restoration of both parties to their original condition (when practicable), upon the rescission of a contract for fraud or similar cause.

RETROACTIVE (RETROSPECTIVE) - Looking back; effective as of a prior time.

REVERSED - A term used by appellate courts to indicate that the decision of the lower court in the case before it has been set aside.

REVOKE - To recall or cancel.

RIPARIAN (RIGHTS) - The rights of a person owning land containing or bordering on a water course or other body of water, such as lakes and rivers.

S

SALE - A contract whereby the ownership of property is transferred from one person to another for a sum of money or for any consideration.

SANCTION - A penalty or punishment provided as a means of enforcing obedience to a law; also, an authorization.

SATISFACTION - The discharge of an obligation by paying a party what is due to him; or what is awarded to him by the judgment of a court or otherwise.

SCIENTER - Knowingly; also, it is used in pleading to denote the defendant's guilty knowledge.

SCINTILLA - A spark; also the least particle.

SECRET OF STATE - Governmental secret relating to the national defense or the international relations of the United States.

SECURITY - Indemnification; the term is applied to an obligation, such as a mortgage or deed of trust, given by a debtor to insure the payment or performance of his debt, by furnishing the creditor with a resource to be used in case of the debtor's failure to fulfill the principal obligation.

SENTENCE - The judgment formally pronounced by the court or judge upon the defendant after his conviction in a criminal prosecution.

SET-OFF - A claim or demand which one party in an action credits against the claim of the opposing party.

17

SHALL and MAY - "Shall" is mandatory and "may" is permissive.

SITUS - Location.

SOVEREIGN - A person, body or state in which independent and supreme authority is vested.

STARE DECISIS - To follow decided cases.

STATE - "State" means this State, unless applied to the different parts of the United States. In the latter case, it includes any state, district, commonwealth, territory or insular possession of the United States, including the District of Columbia.

STATEMENT - (a) Oral or written verbal expression or (b) nonverbal conduct of a person intended by him as a substitute for oral or written verbal expression.

STATUTE - An act of the legislature. Includes a treaty.

STATUTE OF LIMITATION - A statute limiting the time to bring an action after the right of action has arisen.

STAY - To hold in abeyance an order of a court.

STIPULATION - Any agreement made by opposing attorneys regulating any matter incidental to the proceedings or trial.

SUBORDINATION (AGREEMENT) - An agreement making one's rights inferior to or of a lower rank than another's.

SUBORNATION - The crime of procuring a person to lie or to make false statements to a court.

SUBPOENA - A writ or order directed to a person, and requiring his attendance at a particular time and place to testify as a witness.

SUBPOENA DUCES TECUM - A subpoena used, not only for the purpose of compelling witnesses to attend in court, but also requiring them to bring with them books or documents which may be in their possession, and which may tend to elucidate the subject matter of the trial.

SUBROGATION - The substituting of one for another as a creditor, the new creditor succeeding to the former's rights.

SUBSIDY - A government grant to assist a private enterprise deemed advantageous to the public.

SUI GENERIS - Of the same kind.

SUIT - Any civil proceeding by a person or persons against another or others in a court of justice by which the plaintiff pursues the remedies afforded him by law.

SUMMONS - A notice to a defendant that an action against him has been commenced and requiring him to appear in court and answer the complaint.

SUPRA - Above; this word occurring by itself in a book refers the reader to a previous part of the book.

SURETY - A person who binds himself for the payment of a sum of money, or for the performance of something else, for another.

SURPLUSAGE - Extraneous or unnecessary matter.

SURVIVORSHIP - A term used when a person becomes entitled to property by reason of his having survived another person who had an interest in the property.

SUSPEND SENTENCE - Hold back a sentence pending good behavior of prisoner.

SYLLABUS - A note prefixed to a report, especially a case, giving a brief statement of the court's ruling on different issues of the case.

T

TALESMAN - Person summoned to fill a panel of jurors.

TENANT - One who holds or possesses lands by any kind of right or title; also, one who has the temporary use and occupation of real property owned by another person (landlord), the duration and terms of his tenancy being usually fixed by an instrument called "a lease."

TENDER - An offer of money; an expression of willingness to perform a contract according to its terms.

TERM - When used with reference to a court, it signifies the period of time during which the court holds a session, usually of several weeks or months duration.

TESTAMENTARY - Pertaining to a will or the administration of a will.

TESTATOR (male)

TESTATRIX(female) - One who makes or has made a testament or will.

TESTIFY (TESTIMONY) - To give evidence under oath as a witness.

TO WIT - That is to say; namely.

TORT - Wrong; injury to the person.

TRANSITORY - Passing from place to place.

TRESPASS - Entry into another's ground, illegally.

TRIAL - The examination of a cause, civil or criminal, before a judge who has jurisdiction over it, according to the laws of the land.

TRIER OF FACT - Includes (a) the jury and (b) the court when the court is trying an issue of fact other than one relating to the admissibility of evidence.

TRUST - A right of property, real or personal, held by one party for the benefit of another.

TRUSTEE - One who lawfully holds property in custody for the benefit of another.

U

UNAVAILABLE AS A WITNESS - The declarant is (1) Exempted or precluded on the ground of privilege from testifying concerning the matter to which his statement is relevant; (2) Disqualified from testifying to the matter; (3) Dead or unable to attend or to testify at the hearing because of then existing physical or mental illness or infirmity; (4) Absent from the hearing and the court is unable to compel his attendance by its process; or (5) Absent from the hearing and the proponent of his statement has exercised reasonable diligence but has been unable to procure his attendance by the court's process.

ULTRA VIRES - Acts beyond the scope and power of a corporation, association, etc.

UNILATERAL - One-sided; obligation upon, or act of one party.

USURY - Unlawful interest on a loan.

V

VACATE - To set aside; to move out.

VARIANCE - A discrepancy or disagreement between two instruments or two aspects of the same case, which by law should be consistent.

VENDEE - A purchaser or buyer.

VENDOR - The person who transfers property by sale, particularly real estate; the term "seller" is used more commonly for one who sells personal property.

VENIREMEN - Persons ordered to appear to serve on a jury or composing a panel of jurors.

VENUE - The place at which an action is tried, generally based on locality or judicial district in which an injury occurred or a material fact happened.

VERDICT - The formal decision or finding of a jury.

VERIFY - To confirm or substantiate by oath.

VEST - To accrue to.

VOID - Having no legal force or binding effect.

VOIR DIRE - Preliminary examination of a witness or a juror to test competence, interest, prejudice, etc.

W

WAIVE - To give up a right.

WAIVER - The intentional or voluntary relinquishment of a known right.

WARRANT (WARRANTY) (v.) - To promise that a certain fact or state of facts, in relation to the subject matter, is, or shall be, as it is represented to be.

WARRANT (n.) - A writ issued by a judge, or other competent authority, addressed to a sheriff, or other officer, requiring him to arrest the person therein named, and bring him before the judge or court to answer or be examined regarding the offense with which he is charged.

WRIT - An order or process issued in the name of the sovereign or in the name of a court or judicial officer, commanding the performance or nonperformance of some act.

WRITING - Handwriting, typewriting, printing, photostating, photographing and every other means of recording upon any tangible thing any form of communication or representation, including letters, words, pictures, sounds, or symbols, or combinations thereof.

WRITINGS AND RECORDINGS - Consists of letters, words, or numbers, or their equivalent, set down by handwriting, typewriting, printing, photostating, photographing, magnetic impulse, mechanical or electronic recording, or other form of data compilation.

Y

YEA AND NAY - Yes and no.

YELLOW DOG CONTRACT - A contract by which employer requires employee to sign an instrument promising as condition that he will not join a union during its continuance, and will be discharged if he does join.

Z

ZONING - The division of a city by legislative regulation into districts and the prescription and application in each district of regulations having to do with structural and architectural designs of buildings and of regulations prescribing use to which buildings within designated districts may be put.

USE THE SPECIAL PENCIL.   MAKE GLOSSY BLACK MARKS.

	A B C D E		A B C D E		A B C D E		A B C D E		A B C D E
1	‖ ‖ ‖ ‖ ‖	26	‖ ‖ ‖ ‖ ‖	51	‖ ‖ ‖ ‖ ‖	76	‖ ‖ ‖ ‖ ‖	101	‖ ‖ ‖ ‖ ‖
2	‖ ‖ ‖ ‖ ‖	27	‖ ‖ ‖ ‖ ‖	52	‖ ‖ ‖ ‖ ‖	77	‖ ‖ ‖ ‖ ‖	102	‖ ‖ ‖ ‖ ‖
3	‖ ‖ ‖ ‖ ‖	28	‖ ‖ ‖ ‖ ‖	53	‖ ‖ ‖ ‖ ‖	78	‖ ‖ ‖ ‖ ‖	103	‖ ‖ ‖ ‖ ‖
4	‖ ‖ ‖ ‖ ‖	29	‖ ‖ ‖ ‖ ‖	54	‖ ‖ ‖ ‖ ‖	79	‖ ‖ ‖ ‖ ‖	104	‖ ‖ ‖ ‖ ‖
5	‖ ‖ ‖ ‖ ‖	30	‖ ‖ ‖ ‖ ‖	55	‖ ‖ ‖ ‖ ‖	80	‖ ‖ ‖ ‖ ‖	105	‖ ‖ ‖ ‖ ‖
6	‖ ‖ ‖ ‖ ‖	31	‖ ‖ ‖ ‖ ‖	56	‖ ‖ ‖ ‖ ‖	81	‖ ‖ ‖ ‖ ‖	106	‖ ‖ ‖ ‖ ‖
7	‖ ‖ ‖ ‖ ‖	32	‖ ‖ ‖ ‖ ‖	57	‖ ‖ ‖ ‖ ‖	82	‖ ‖ ‖ ‖ ‖	107	‖ ‖ ‖ ‖ ‖
8	‖ ‖ ‖ ‖ ‖	33	‖ ‖ ‖ ‖ ‖	58	‖ ‖ ‖ ‖ ‖	83	‖ ‖ ‖ ‖ ‖	108	‖ ‖ ‖ ‖ ‖
9	‖ ‖ ‖ ‖ ‖	34	‖ ‖ ‖ ‖ ‖	59	‖ ‖ ‖ ‖ ‖	84	‖ ‖ ‖ ‖ ‖	109	‖ ‖ ‖ ‖ ‖
10	‖ ‖ ‖ ‖ ‖	35	‖ ‖ ‖ ‖ ‖	60	‖ ‖ ‖ ‖ ‖	85	‖ ‖ ‖ ‖ ‖	110	‖ ‖ ‖ ‖ ‖

Make only ONE mark for each answer.   Additional and stray marks may be
counted as mistakes.   In making corrections, erase errors COMPLETELY.

	A B C D E		A B C D E		A B C D E		A B C D E		A B C D E
11	‖ ‖ ‖ ‖ ‖	36	‖ ‖ ‖ ‖ ‖	61	‖ ‖ ‖ ‖ ‖	86	‖ ‖ ‖ ‖ ‖	111	‖ ‖ ‖ ‖ ‖
12	‖ ‖ ‖ ‖ ‖	37	‖ ‖ ‖ ‖ ‖	62	‖ ‖ ‖ ‖ ‖	87	‖ ‖ ‖ ‖ ‖	112	‖ ‖ ‖ ‖ ‖
13	‖ ‖ ‖ ‖ ‖	38	‖ ‖ ‖ ‖ ‖	63	‖ ‖ ‖ ‖ ‖	88	‖ ‖ ‖ ‖ ‖	113	‖ ‖ ‖ ‖ ‖
14	‖ ‖ ‖ ‖ ‖	39	‖ ‖ ‖ ‖ ‖	64	‖ ‖ ‖ ‖ ‖	89	‖ ‖ ‖ ‖ ‖	114	‖ ‖ ‖ ‖ ‖
15	‖ ‖ ‖ ‖ ‖	40	‖ ‖ ‖ ‖ ‖	65	‖ ‖ ‖ ‖ ‖	90	‖ ‖ ‖ ‖ ‖	115	‖ ‖ ‖ ‖ ‖
16	‖ ‖ ‖ ‖ ‖	41	‖ ‖ ‖ ‖ ‖	66	‖ ‖ ‖ ‖ ‖	91	‖ ‖ ‖ ‖ ‖	116	‖ ‖ ‖ ‖ ‖
17	‖ ‖ ‖ ‖ ‖	42	‖ ‖ ‖ ‖ ‖	67	‖ ‖ ‖ ‖ ‖	92	‖ ‖ ‖ ‖ ‖	117	‖ ‖ ‖ ‖ ‖
18	‖ ‖ ‖ ‖ ‖	43	‖ ‖ ‖ ‖ ‖	68	‖ ‖ ‖ ‖ ‖	93	‖ ‖ ‖ ‖ ‖	118	‖ ‖ ‖ ‖ ‖
19	‖ ‖ ‖ ‖ ‖	44	‖ ‖ ‖ ‖ ‖	69	‖ ‖ ‖ ‖ ‖	94	‖ ‖ ‖ ‖ ‖	119	‖ ‖ ‖ ‖ ‖
20	‖ ‖ ‖ ‖ ‖	45	‖ ‖ ‖ ‖ ‖	70	‖ ‖ ‖ ‖ ‖	95	‖ ‖ ‖ ‖ ‖	120	‖ ‖ ‖ ‖ ‖
21	‖ ‖ ‖ ‖ ‖	46	‖ ‖ ‖ ‖ ‖	71	‖ ‖ ‖ ‖ ‖	96	‖ ‖ ‖ ‖ ‖	121	‖ ‖ ‖ ‖ ‖
22	‖ ‖ ‖ ‖ ‖	47	‖ ‖ ‖ ‖ ‖	72	‖ ‖ ‖ ‖ ‖	97	‖ ‖ ‖ ‖ ‖	122	‖ ‖ ‖ ‖ ‖
23	‖ ‖ ‖ ‖ ‖	48	‖ ‖ ‖ ‖ ‖	73	‖ ‖ ‖ ‖ ‖	98	‖ ‖ ‖ ‖ ‖	123	‖ ‖ ‖ ‖ ‖
24	‖ ‖ ‖ ‖ ‖	49	‖ ‖ ‖ ‖ ‖	74	‖ ‖ ‖ ‖ ‖	99	‖ ‖ ‖ ‖ ‖	124	‖ ‖ ‖ ‖ ‖
25	‖ ‖ ‖ ‖ ‖	50	‖ ‖ ‖ ‖ ‖	75	‖ ‖ ‖ ‖ ‖	100	‖ ‖ ‖ ‖ ‖	125	‖ ‖ ‖

USE THE SPECIAL PENCIL.   MAKE GLOSSY BLACK MARKS.

	A B C D E		A B C D E		A B C D E		A B C D E		A B C D E
1		26		51		76		101	
2		27		52		77		102	
3		28		53		78		103	
4		29		54		79		104	
5		30		55		80		105	
6		31		56		81		106	
7		32		57		82		107	
8		33		58		83		108	
9		34		59		84		109	
10		35		60		85		110	

Make only ONE mark for each answer.   Additional and stray marks may be counted as mistakes.   In making corrections, erase errors COMPLETELY.

	A B C D E		A B C D E		A B C D E		A B C D E		A B C D E
11		36		61		86		111	
12		37		62		87		112	
13		38		63		88		113	
14		39		64		89		114	
15		40		65		90		115	
16		41		66		91		116	
17		42		67		92		117	
18		43		68		93		118	
19		44		69		94		119	
20		45		70		95		120	
21		46		71		96		121	
22		47		72		97		122	
23		48		73		98		123	
24		49		74		99		124	
25		50		75		100		125	